Ancient Astronauts Cosmic Collisions

Ancient Astronauts Cosmic Collisions

and Other Popular Theories About Man's Past

William H. Stiebing, Jr.

Prometheus Books

700 East Amherst St. Buffalo, New York 14215

Library of Congress Card Catalog No. 84-42792
ISBN: 0-87975-260-2 cloth
0-87975-285-8 paper

For Ann

Contents

Preface

"What's the latest on Noah's Ark? Weren't its remains found on Mt. Ararat a few years ago?" . . . "Do you know anything about those markings in Peru that seem to be an ancient airfield?" . . . "I recently read a book that claimed that the Great Pyramid of Giza in Egypt could not have been built within a single human lifetime or with the primitive technology of the ancient Egyptians. Is that true?"

Archaeologists, anthropologists, and historians are frequently asked such questions. Queries about ancient astronauts, Atlantis, Noah's Ark, and pre-Columbian trans-Atlantic voyages are continual reminders of the widespread influence and popularity of some very unconventional theories about man's past.

The mystery of times long past has always fascinated the general public. Archaeological exhibits of materials from early civilizations are usually well attended. And each year publishers release new books on the Egyptians, Greeks, Mayans, and other ancient cultures. But it is the startling, revolutionary hypotheses of writers like Immanuel Velikovsky, Erich von Däniken, and Barry Fell that sell the most books and attract the greatest number of adherents. Evidence and arguments supporting the occurrence of a universal Flood, the lost continent of Atlantis, near-collisions between planets of our solar system in historical times, historical visits by spacemen, mysterious pyramid powers, and a variety of early voyages to the New World have been presented not only in books but also in movies and television programs. It is no wonder that many people are persuaded that these ideas are valid.

Unfortunately, experts on various aspects of antiquity usually ignore these popular theories. Scholars seldom mention them in their books or lectures, nor do they bother to indicate what is wrong with the methodology, evidence, or arguments that are used to support such hypotheses. The silence of leading scholars tends to make the claims of the theorists seem more believable.

This book has been written for those who want answers to questions like

1

the ones just cited. It is for anyone who has wondered whether Atlantis really existed or whether Egyptians or Phoenicians might have visited America long before Columbus. Each chapter will assess the most important evidence for and against a particular popular theory about man's early history, and do it (I hope) with a minimum of technical jargon. Some individuals may wish to delve more deeply into one or more of the subjects treated here. So, for them, reference notes and an extensive bibliography have been included.

I would like to thank all those who helped in the preparation of this book. Special thanks are due to my colleagues in the anthropology and history departments at the University of New Orleans for reading sections of the manuscript and making many valuable criticisms and suggestions. My wife was one of my most helpful readers, continually taking me to task when my writing became too technical or difficult to understand. Several of my former students also gave me the benefit of their knowledge of the needs and interests of the general reader. Finally, the contribution of my editor, Doris Doyle, and the staff at Prometheus Books should not be overlooked. These people have helped make this book much better than it otherwise might have been. Undoubtedly, some errors or shortcomings still remain. Those are totally my own fault, and I suspect that at least a few of them are due to my perverse refusal to accept all of the advice offered me.

I
CHAPTER

The Deluge

Noah's Ark possibly has been photographed by an orbiting United States weather satellite! Senator Frank E. Moss (D., Utah) announced this startling news early in 1974, and soon afterward it appeared in many newspapers and magazine articles.[1] If the Ark could be found it would surely be one of the most important archaeological discoveries of all time. Many religious groups feel that proof of the Ark's existence would substantiate their faith in the Bible and convert the world to belief in the Judeo-Christian God. So expeditions have been launched to find the object in the satellite photograph. Even Jim Irwin, a former U.S. astronaut, is participating in the ongoing search.[2]

But belief in a great flood which long ago destroyed almost all of mankind is even more ancient than the Bible. It is probably the oldest and most continuously popular theory concerning man's early history. As long ago as 3000 B.C., the Sumerians, authors of the earliest civilization known, believed in a universal flood, and many people still accept this idea today. The flood story's continued popularity is undoubtedly due to the fact that it was present in both of the basic sources for Western civilization, the Judeo-Christian religious tradition and the culture of ancient Greece.

The Flood and the Origins of Geology

It is almost impossible to overstate the importance of the Judeo-Christian Scriptures in the development of Western thought. For centuries the Bible was not only a religious guide but the main source of historical and "scientific" truth as well. One of the best-known stories from the Bible is the narrative about Noah and the Deluge (Genesis 6:5-8:22). Until the eighteenth and nineteenth centuries, few Jews or Christians questioned the literal accuracy of this account.

The mythology of ancient Greece also had a flood story. It told how Zeus decided to destroy mankind with a deluge, but Prometheus forewarned his won, Deucalion. With his wife, Deucalion took refuge in a chest, or an ark, which eventually came to rest on Mount Parnassos (or on other Greek mountains in variants of the tradition). Some versions of the story tell how Deucalion sent out a dove to learn if the flood waters had receded.[3] It is likely that the myth of Deucalion and the flood was a Greek adaptation of a much older Near Eastern flood story that originated in Mesopotamia. In the eighth and seventh centuries B.C. Greek ideas and art were strongly influenced by Near Eastern civilization. It was probably during this period that their contact with the cultures of Asia Minor and trade with the Phoenicians led the Greeks to borrow the flood story as well as other Near Eastern myths.[4] But regardless of its ultimate source, the Deucalion story was accepted as history by most ancient Greeks, and it was frequently alluded to in Greek literature.

Greek tradition also told of other floods, and Plato developed these stories into a theory that deluges and other catastrophes periodically devastated the earth, destroying civilization and forcing the few survivors to develop cutlure anew.[5] When Europe was Christianized these Greek ideas were combined with the biblical flood story. Some theologians equated Deucalion's flood with that of Noah, believing that the Greek story was a less accurate account of the biblical Deluge. Others, including St. Augustine,[6] accepted the Greek floods as separate historical events, more limited in scope than the worldwide Deluge of Noah's time.

By early modern times, ancient history was still known from only two sources, classical authors and the Bible, and chronologies based on these works allowed the earth only a short span of existence. Jewish rabbinical calculations indicated that the creation of the world took place 3,740 years before the beginning of the Christian Era, while Roman Catholic tradition, based on the Vulgate, placed it in 5199 B.C. [7] But the date most commonly accepted by English-speaking scholars was that worked out in the early seventeenth century by the scholarly Archbishop of Armagh, James Ussher. Using Old Testament dates and genealogies, Ussher calculated that the creation had occurred in 4004 B.C. The Deluge was supposed to have taken place in 2349 B.C. A short time later, Ussher's chronology was refined by Dr. John Lightfoot, vice-chancellor of the University of Cambridge. Lightfoot confidently asserted that God created man on October 23, 4004 B.C. at nine o'clock in the morning! Such calculations met with widespread acceptance, and when Ussher's dates were printed in the margins of a 1701 edition of the Authorized (King James) Version of the Bible they assumed for many an authority and sanctity only slightly less than that of the Holy Scripture itself.[8]

The conflict between supporters of science and those who believed in the complete accuracy of all parts of the Bible had not yet begun. Most seventeenth- and eighteenth-century scientists saw nothing in their work that contradicted the Bible, and many would have agreed with the great chemist Robert Boyle that their discoveries in the "Book of Nature" caused them to "discern the admirable Traces of such immense Power, such unsearchable Wisdom, and such exuberant Goodness, as may justly ravish us to an Amazement at them, rather than a bare admiration of them."[9] It was generally believed that science, in uncovering the Truths of Nature, could not help but lead men to deeper reverence for Nature's God. Any interpretation of evidence that contradicted religious doctrine or the historical reliability of the Bible had to fight an uphill battle for acceptance, not only among the general public, but also within the scientific community.

However, the development of the fields of geology and archaeology eventually forced scholars to recognize that Genesis was not pure history. Fossil remains of plants and animals were frequently found in Europe in early modern times, but their true nature was seldom realized. Many educated individuals in the seventeenth century believed that fossils were natural geological formations. Following the teachings of the medieval Arab philosopher Avicenna, these people argued that a "plastic force" was at work in nature shaping stones in imitation of living things. A few supporters of this *vis plastica* theory combined it with the concept of spontaneous generation, which had been popular since the days of Aristotle and held that fossils were nature's "false starts," so to speak. The creative force within nature was thought to model creatures in stone and, when the formations were complete, to generate life within them. If the process was interrupted or faulty in some way, fossils rather than living beings resulted.[10].

Other individuals interpreted fossils of large prehistoric creatures as the remains of unicorns, giants, or dragons.[11] The fossil ivory from the skeletons of such fabled beasts fetched good prices from apothecaries, who ground up the material to produce potions supposed to have miraculous healing properties or who mounted fragments in gold or silver to make amulets believed to possess exceptional powers.

But the most popular explanation of fossils was that they were the remains of living organisms that had been destroyed as a result of the biblical Flood. Skeletons of fish and other marine creatures found on high mountain-slopes were thought to provide evidence of the absolute veracity of the Genesis account.[12]

However, study of the earth by eighteenth-century naturalists began to produce problems for those who sought to interpret geological remains as results of the Deluge. Most fossils proved to belong to species that were extinct. Since Genesis made no mention of the disappearance of numerous forms of life as a result of the Flood, this evidence was puzzling. In fact, Genesis 6:19-20 states that Noah was ordered to take two of every living creature into the ark so that no species would be totally destroyed by the

Deluge. It was becoming more difficult to reconcile Genesis with the "Book of Nature" than it once had been.

It was also discovered in the first half of the eighteenth century that the earth was hot at its center. This fact suggested that the earth had once been in a molten state and that its surface gradually had cooled and hardened. However, experiments showed that the amount of time needed for a body the size of the earth to cool to its present state was much longer than the six or seven thousand years allowed by biblical chronology.[13]

In 1778 such considerations led French naturalist Georges Buffon to postulate a series of "epochs" in the earth's history, each lasting a considerable period of time. He reconciled this view with Genesis by arguing that the "days" of creation were actually six time periods of unknown duration, not ordinary twenty-four hour days. He said that fossils and coal deposits had been formed in earlier "epochs," thousands of years before the appearance of man. Buffon insisted that the six or seven thousand years of Mosaic chronology was valid for the history of man, the end of the creative process, but not for the earth itself.[14]

Other naturalists proposed similar ideas. One group, the Neptunists, agreed that there had been stages in the creation of the earth but held that all geological formations were precipitated from a primeval briny sea.[15] Another school of thought, known as catastrophism, argued that there had been cataclysms separating the various epochs in the earth's history. The Great Flood of Genesis was the last of these catastrophes, but it was not as devastating as previous ones. The lack of overlap of fossil species from one rock layer to another seemed to prove that the geological periods these strata represented had been separated by total destructions. After each great catastrophe, these theorists argued, God recreated living beings similar to (but not identical with) those from the previous era. Present-day species, including man, belonged to the last of these creations, the one described in the Bible; fossils belonged to earlier ones. Thus, according to catastrophists, man could not have been associated with any of the extinct fossil species.[16] While they disagreed about the way the earth's features had been formed, both Neptunists and catastrophists upheld the basic accuracy of Genesis, including the historicity of the Flood.

Opposing the ideas of Buffon, the Neptunists, and the catastrophists were a few scholars who accepted the principle of uniformitarianism. This doctrine stated, in the words of its founder, James Hutton (1785): "No processes are to be employed that are not natural to the globe; no action to be admitted except those of which we know the principle."[17] Uniformitarians explained the earth's physical features as the results of natural, noncatastrophic processes that can be observed in action at the present time: the weathering of stone, erosion, deposition of sediments in river beds or on ocean floors, volcanic activity, etc. Since such processes operate very slowly, they reasoned, the earth must be extremely old. Genesis was rejected as an accurate account of the creation of the world.[18]

The turning point in the battle against catastrophist and Neptunist geology came with the publication of Charles Lyell's three-volume work, *Principles of Geology, Being an Attempt to Explain the Former Changes of the Earth's Surface by Reference to Causes Now in Action* (1830-33). This work supported the principle of uniformitarianism and provided such a wealth of geological data to illustrate that principle that even its most unyielding opponents were impressed. Lyell pointed out that what seemed to be evidence for global convulsions and violent revolutions was actually misinterpreted by geologists who failed to note gaps in the succession of strata and to appreciate the duration of past time. If the events of thousands of years of human history were compressed into the span of a few centuries, the appearance would also be one of constant and unnatural change and revolution rather than of slow and gradual development. Once the immensity of geological time is accepted, Lyell argued, there is no need to postulate supernatural cataclysms to explain the shaping of the earth's features. Given millions of years in which to operate, the agencies of wind, water, ice, and vulcanism were sufficient to produce even the most dramatic alterations of the earth's surface.[19] Naturally, Lyell's arguments did not convince everyone. But they did force most geologists to reevaluate their positions, and they had a strong influence on a whole generation of young scientists (among whom was Charles Darwin) who in 1830 were completing their education or just beginning their careers.

One aspect of the geology of Europe that seemed to support the views of the catastrophists was the occurrence of huge boulders and piles of smaller stones on the plains, miles away from the nearest mountains. How had such stones gotten there if not by the agency of some tremendous upheaval, such as a catalysmic volcanic eruption or a universal Deluge? Soon after the appearance of *Principles of Geology* the question was answered by Swiss professor Louis Agassiz, who led a team of men into the Alps to study glaciers. Through his investigations, Agassiz was able to show not only that the erratic boulders found on European plains had been carried there by ice but also that many other features of the European landscape had been produced by the advance and retreat of one or more great glaciers.[20] Geological features formerly attributed to the Flood were now seen to be products of an Ice Age that must have had an extremely long duration.

Evidence proving that man had existed more than six or seven thousand years also began to be recognized. During the late eighteenth and early nineteenth centuries, scholars in Germany, Belgium, France, and England had found deposits of human bones and artifacts associated with the remains of extinct species of animals.[21] But these discoveries had been ignored or explained away by Neptunists and catastrophists who remained convinced that all fossils belonged to periods earlier than the creation of man. However, a similar discovery in 1837 by Jacques Boucher de Perthes, a French customs official, could not be ignored, and attempts to explain it away failed. Boucher de Perthes uncovered flint weapons and tools side by side with the remains of extinct Ice Age creatures like mammoths, cave bears, woolly rhinoceroses, and bison in gravel deposits of the Somme valley near Abbeville.[22] Opponents of his claims came to examine the evidence for themselves or undertook their own excavations to prove him wrong. One by one, they were converted to the view that man had been coeval with extinct animals of the Ice Age. In 1859, after visiting the site of Boucher de Perthes's discoveries and satisfying themselves of the validity of his finds, the eminent British scholars Joseph Prestwich and John Evans presented papers at meetings of the Royal Society and the Society of Antiquaries stating their conviction of the antiquity of man.[23]

The year 1859 was decisive in the long conflict over the validity of Mosaic chronology and the biblical view of the early history of mankind. It was not only the year in which the finds of Boucher de Perthes were publicly accepted, but also the year in which William Pengelly's discoveries dispelled virtually all doubt about man's association with vanished species. Pengelly, a noted British scholar, had been excavating for a year in Windmill Hill Cave overlooking Brixham Harbour, a coastal site about one hundred and sixty-five miles southwest of London. The cave, which could not have been used by human occupants since the Ice Age, had been accidentally uncovered by quarrying operations. From the beginning of the investigation, a committee of prestigious members of the Royal and Geological societies oversaw the work and could vouch for its accuracy. Pengelly found the cave floor covered with a sheet of stalagmite from 3 to 8 inches thick, sealing within it and below it remains of lions, hyenas, bears, mammoths, rhinoceroses, and reindeer. In the layer of earth beneath the stalagmite floor, flint tools were lying with the bones of Ice Age fauna. The existence of fossil men had finally been established beyond reasonable doubt.[24]

Charles Darwin's *Origin of Species by Means of Natural Selection, or the Preservation of Favored Races in the Struggle for Life* also appeared in 1859. Lyell's theories had strongly influenced Darwin and had removed one stumbling block encountered by earlier proponents of evolution, the short history of life on earth. If one accepted uniformitarian geological principles, then fossil remains in rock strata would indicate that life had existed on earth for an extremely long time—long enough to allow the slow development and modification of species to take place as assumed in evolutionary theories. Darwin cited a wealth of evidence from comparative anatomy studies and the fossil record to support the evolutionary hypothesis, but his major contribution to the theory was his presentation of a likely method by which evolution might occur. His description of the way "natural selection" and the "struggle for existence" determined which species or which individuals within a species would survive was extremely persuasive.[25] And while many people, particularly some clergymen and theologians, objected to the theory of evolution because it eliminated the biblical concept of the special creation of living things, in a relatively short time the Darwinian hypothesis became the accepted doctrine of most scientists and educated laymen. The era of Mosaic chronology and the Deluge as dominant features in both geological and historical study had come to an end.

The Mesopotamian Flood Story and the Bible

The battle over the scientific and historical accuracy of Genesis came to an end within the scientific community, but it continued to rage in public forums into the early twentieth century. This conflict was responsible for much of the public interest in and financial support for nineteenth- and early twentieth-century archaeological excavations in the Near East. Discoveries there, especially in Mesopotamia, tended to confirm the accuracy of biblical accounts.

In the 1840s and 1850s French and British excavators in Mesopotamia uncovered sites dating from the time of the ancient Assyrian Empire, an enemy of Israel frequently mentioned in the Bible. By 1857 scholars were able to decipher the ancient Mesopotamian script, called "cuneiform," and Assyrian and Babylonian texts could be read. For the first time, biblical references to historical events and individuals were confirmed. An obelisk from Nimrud (ancient Calah) showed King Jehu of Israel (1 Kings 19:16, 2 Kings 9–10) paying homage to Shalmaneser III of Assyria. Reliefs found at Kuyunjik, the site of ancient Nineveh, depicted the Assyrian king Sennacherib capturing the Judean city of Lachish, and a portion of his annals recorded his siege of Jerusalem. These records agreed remarkably well with the biblical account in 2 Kings 18 and 19. None of this directly related to the Flood, of course, but it was argued that if the biblical history in the books of *Kings* was accurate, the accounts of Genesis could be trusted as well.

Then, in 1872, George Smith, an assistant in the Assyrian section of the British Museum, made a sensational discovery when sorting and classifying cuneiform tablets from the Assyrian library that had been found at Kuyunjik. While working through a pile of tablets that were thought to contain legends and myths, Smith came across "half of a curious tablet which had evidently contained originally six columns . . . On looking down the third column, my eye cought the statement that the ship rested on the mountains of Nizir."[26] Excitedly he read on:

> When the seventh day arrived, I sent out a dove; I released it.
> The dove went away, but came back;
> Since no resting-place appeared, she returned.
> Then I sent out a swallow; I released it.
> The swallow went away, but came back;
> Since no resting-place appeared, she returned.
> Then I sent out a raven; I released it.
> The raven went away, and seeing that the waters had diminished,
> It ate, circled, cawed and did not return.

Smith immediately recognized that he had found a Mesopotamian version of the Deluge.

A search through the tablets produced additional parts of the story, and on December 3, 1872, George Smith reported his discovery in a paper read before the Society of Biblical Archaeology. The audience listened in rapt attention to a narrative that in many ways was similar to the biblical story of Noah. It told how the gods decided to destroy mankind by a great flood. But Ea, the god of wisdom, warned one man of the coming catastrophe. He and his family took refuge on an ark along with many craftsmen and representatives of the various animal species. Then a fearsome storm came. For six days and nights it raged, and floodwaters rose until the mountains were covered. But on the seventh day the storm abated, and the ship was grounded on Mount Nizir (a peak northeast of Mesopotamia). After determining that the waters had receded by sending forth three birds, the passengers of the ark descended. They built an altar and offered a sacrifice to the gods.[27]

There was a gap of some seventeen lines near the beginning of the narrative which Smith had been unable to restore from the tablets and fragments in the museum. But so great was the public interest in news reports of Smith's discovery that the London *Daily Telegraph* offered a thousand pounds to equip an expedition to Nineveh to search for the missing portions of the account. In May 1873 Smith arrived at Kuyunjik and began digging through the debris left by previous British excavations at the site. In five days he found over three hundred fragments of tablets that had been overlooked or discarded by earlier excavators. He related that on the evening of the fifth day of excavation:[28]

> I sat down to examine the store of fragments of cuneiform inscriptions from the day's digging, taking out and brushing off the earth from the fragments to read their contents. On cleaning one of them I found to my surprise and gratification that it contained the greater portion of the seventeen lines of inscription belonging to the first column of the Chaldean account of the

Deluge, and fitting into the only place where there was a serious blank in the story.

The flood account discovered by Smith was part of a seventh century B.C. Assyrian copy of *The Epic of Gilgamesh,* which had been in the library of King Asshurbanipal at Nineveh. But this version clearly rested on more ancient Mesopotamian traditions concerning the Flood. For example, a similar flood story was soon noted in fragments of the *Atrahasis Epic,* another composition found among the tablets of Asshurbanipal's library. Later discoveries confirmed the belief of Smith and other scholars that the Mesopotamian (or Chaldean) flood traditions were indeed very ancient. They have been traced back to the Sumerians, the non-Semitic inhabitants of southern Mesopotamia who first invented writing and created the earliest known civilization. The Sumerian flood story, probably created somewhere between c. 3000 and 2400 B.C., provided the inspiration for Old Babylonian versions that seem to have been composed c. 2000-1800 B.C. The Babylonian narratives, in turn, served as models for the Assyrian accounts.[29]

The similarity between the Mesopotamian Deluge tradition and the Hebrew account in Genesis was remarkable. Clearly the two must be related in some way. But how? Believers in biblical inerrancy argued that the Mesopotamian stories proved that the Flood had really occurred. They claimed that the similarities were the result of two independent accounts recording the same historical event; both traditions must derive from stories told by Noah and his family. But while the Hebrews had faithfully passed on the original tale, the Mesopotamian accounts had become debased by polytheism and were riddled with factual errors.

But many scholars, including professors of the Old Testament at leading universities, rejected this theory. Instead, they claimed that the ancient Israelites had borrowed the flood myth from Mesopotamia. Furthermore, leading biblical scholars pointed out that there was not one but *two* Deluge traditions in the Bible, and these accounts differed in many details.

Such views resulted from application of the historical-critical method (or "higher criticism") to the study of the Bible. Biblical criticism had its roots in the seventeenth and eighteenth centuries, but it didn't blossom until the latter half of the nineteenth century, partially as a result of the conflict between geology and Mosaic chronology. Biblical scholars began to apply to the Bible the same methods of study and the same standards of reliability utilized in evaluating other ancient writings. When the biblical text was studied in this way, many contradictions, duplications, and differences in style and vocabulary became evident. For example, Moses had been traditionally accepted as the author of Genesis, but when Genesis 1 and 2 were compared, it was recognized that they were written in different styles and disagreed on the order of creation. In Genesis 1:26-27 man is the last of God's creations. However, in Genesis 2:7-22, God creates the Garden of Eden and animals *after* man. Furthermore, He creates a woman only after it is determined that the animals are not suitable companions for the man. In the poetical account of Genesis 1:1-2:4a, God creates by command alone: "And God said, 'Let there be . . .,' and it was so." On the other hand, the prose story of Genesis 2:4b-3:24 depicts God much more anthropomorphically. He molds man and the animals out of clay; He walks in the garden; He speaks directly with Adam and Eve.

Similar difficulties were noted in other narratives. According to Exodus 6:2-3 God told Moses, "I am Yahweh ["Jehovah" or "the LORD"]. As God the Almighty I appeared to Abraham, Isaac, and Jacob, but my name, Yahweh, I did not make known to them." Yet Genesis 28:13 describes a dream in which God reveals to Jacob that His name is Yahweh! Furthermore, Abraham, Isaac, and Jacob refer to God as Yahweh a number of times.[30] Moses' father-in-law is named Jethro in Exodus 3:1 and 18:1, but in Numbers 10:29 and Judges 4:11 Hobab is Moses' father-in-law. Some passages state that Aaron, Moses' brother, died and was buried at Mount Hor on the border of Edom (Numbers 20:22-29; 33:38; Deuteronomy 32:50). However, Deuternomy 10:6 states that Aaron died and was buried at Moserah (or Moseroth), a place somewhere between Sinai and Mount Hor (Numbers 33:30-37). The route that the Israelites followed from Mount Hor into Canaan, according to Numbers 33, is different from the one described in Numbers 21.

By the last quarter of the nineteenth century, these and other discrepancies led biblical scholars to recognize that the Pentateuch was not written entirely by Moses, but rather was the product of a number of authors.[31] Analysis showed the Deluge narrative to be a composite account formed by weaving together two separate sources, usually designated *J* and *P*. *J* was so called because its author normally referred to God by His personal name, Yahweh (or Jehovah); *P*, for "Priestly source," got its name because its author put particular emphasis on genealogy (a guarantee of purity of line) and on matters of a ritual or cultic nature.

The two strands of the Genesis Flood story were disentangled by noting numerous duplications and contradictions. For instance, the reason for the Flood is stated in 6:5-7 (*J*) as well as in 6:11-13 (*P*), and two separate commands to enter the Ark are given (6:18-20 [*P*] and 7:1-3 [*J*]). In 6:19 (*P*) Noah is told to take two of each animal into the Ark, but 7:2 (*J*) states that he is to take seven pairs of each of the clean animals and one pair of each of the unclean ones. *J* attributes the Flood to rainfall alone (7:4), and states that it lasted forty days (7:4, 12, 17; 8:6). But *P* claims that the Deluge resulted from rainfall and a bursting forth of underground waters (7:11; 8:2), and that the Flood lasted for an entire year (7:24; 8:1, 2a, 3b-5, 13a). Today biblical scholars generally agree that the two sources should be divided as follows (words within square brackets are an editorial gloss by the person who wove the accounts together):[32]

The Yahwistic Account (*J*)

(6:5) Yahweh saw how great was man's wickedness on earth, and how every plan devised by his mind was nothing but evil all the time. (6) And Yahweh regretted that he had made man on earth, and his heart was saddened. (7) So Yahweh said, "I will wipe out from the earth the men whom I have created—the men together with the beasts, creeping things, and birds of the sky, for I am sorry that I made them." (8) But Noah found favor with Yahweh.

(7:1) Then Yahweh said to Noah, "Go into the ark, you and all your household, for you alone have I found to be truly righteous in this

The Priestly Account (*P*)

(6:9) These are the descendants of Noah. Noah was a righteous man, blameless in his age, for Noah walked with God. (10) Noah had three sons: Shem, Ham, and Japheth. (11) The earth was corrupt in God's sight, and it was filled with injustice. (12) When God saw how corrupt the earth was, for all flesh had corrupted its ways on earth, (13) God said to Noah, "I have decided to put an end to all flesh, for the earth is filled with lawlessness because of them. Therefore, I am going to destroy them with the earth. (14) Make yourself an ark of gopherwood; make compartments in the ark, and cover it inside and out with bitumen. (15) This is how you shall make it: the length of the ark shall be three hundred cubits, its width fifty cubits, and its height thirty cubits. (16) Make an opening for daylight in the ark, and terminate it within a cubit of the top. Put the entrance to the ark in its side, and construct it with bottom, second, and third decks. (17) For my part, I am about to bring the Flood — waters upon the earth — to destroy everywhere all creatures in which there is the breath of life. Everything on earth shall perish.

(18) But I will establish my covenant with you, and you shall enter the ark—you, your sons, your wife, and your sons' wives. (19) And of all else

age. (2) Take with you seven pairs of every clean animal, males and their mates, and of every unclean animal, one pair, a male and its mate; (3) likewise, of the birds of the sky, seven pairs, male and female, to keep their issue alive over all the earth. (4) For seven days from now I will make it rain upon the earth for forty days and forty nights, and I will wipe out from the surface of the earth all existence that I created." (5) And Noah did just as Yahweh commanded him.

(7) Noah, with his sons, his wife, and his sons' wives, went into the ark because of the waters of the Flood. (8) Of the clean animals, of the animals that are unclean, of the birds, and of everything that creeps on the ground, (9) [two of each] male and female, came to Noah into the ark, just as God had commanded Noah. (10) And on the seventh day the waters of the Flood came upon the earth. (12) The rain fell on the earth for forty days and forty nights. (16b) And Yahweh shut him in.

(17b) For forty days the waters increased and raised the ark so that it rose above the earth. (22) All in whose nostrils was the faintest breath of life, everything that had been on dry land, died out. (23) All existence on earth was wiped out—man, domestic animals, the creeping things, and the birds of the sky; all were wiped out from the earth. Only Noah

that is alive, of all flesh, you shall take two of each into the ark to keep alive with you; they must be male and female. (20) From birds of every kind, beasts of every kind, every kind of creeping thing on earth, two of each shall come inside with you to stay alive. (21) For your part, you are to provide yourself with all the food that that is to be eaten, and store it away to serve as provisions for you and for them." This Noah did. (22) Just as God commanded him, so he did.

(7:6) Noah was six hundred years old when the Flood waters came upon the earth. (11) In the six hundredth year of Noah's life, in the second month, on the seventeenth day of the month—on that day all the fountains of the great Abyss burst forth, and the flood-gates of the sky broke open. (13) On the very same day Noah and Noah's sons, Shem, Ham, and Japheth, and Noah's wife, and the three wives of his sons entered the ark—(14) they and all beasts of every kind, every kind of domestic animal, every kind of creeping thing on earth, and every kind of bird, every winged thing. (15) They came to Noah into the ark, two each of all flesh in which there was the breath of life. (16a) Those that entered comprised male and female of all flesh, as God had commanded him.

(17a) The Flood descended upon the earth. (18) The waters swelled and increased greatly upon the earth, but the ark floated upon the surface of the waters. (19) The waters swelled more and more upon the earth, until all the highest mountains everywhere were submerged, (20 the crest rising fifteen cubits higher than the submerged mountains. (21) All flesh that was left, and those with him in the ark.

(8:2b) Then the rain from the sky was restrained, (3) and the waters receded from the earth steadily. (6) At the end of forty days, Noah opened the hatch of the ark that he had made, (7) and he released a raven; it went back and forth until the waters dried up from the earth. (8) Then (after seven days) he sent out a dove to see whether the waters had decreased from the surface of the ground. (9) But the dove could not find a resting place on which to perch, and returned to him in the ark, for there was water over all the earth. So putting out his hand, he took it into the ark with him. (10) He waited another seven days, and again sent out the dove from the ark. (11) The dove returned to him toward evening, and there in its bill was a plucked-off olive leaf! Noah knew then that the waters had diminished on the earth. (12) He waited still another seven days and then released the dove once more; it did not return to him again.

(20) Then Noah built an altar to Yahweh, and choosing from every clean animal and every clean bird, he offered burnt offerings on the altar. (21) Yahweh smelled the pleasing odor, and Yahweh said to himself, "Never again will I doom the earth because of man, since the desires of man's heart are evil from the start; nor will I ever again strike down all living beings, as I have done. (22) So long as the earth endures, seedtime and harvest, cold and heat, summer and winter, and day and night shall not cease."

stirred on earth perished—birds, domestic animals, wild beasts, and all the creatures that swarmed on the earth, as well as all mankind.

(24) When the waters had maintained their crest over the earth for one hundred and fifty days, (8:1) God remembered Noah and all the animals, wild and domestic, that were with him in the ark. So God caused a wind to sweep across the earth, and the waters began to subside. (2a) The fountains of the great Abyss and the flood-gates of the sky were closed. (3b) By the end of one hundred and fifty days the waters had so diminished that (4) in the seventh month, on the seventeenth day of the month, the ark came to rest on the mountains of Ararat. (5) The waters continued to diminish until the tenth month, and on the first day of the tenth month the tops of the mountains became visible.

(13) In the six hundred and first year (of Noah's life), in the first month on the first day of the month, the waters began to dry up on the earth; (14) and in the second month, the earth was dry.

(15) Then God spoke to Noah, saying, (16) "Come out of the ark, together with your wife, your sons, and your sons' wives. (17) Bring out with you every living thing that is with you—all flesh, be it bird or animal or any creature that creeps on earth—and let them swarm on earth, breeding and multiplying on it." (18) So Noah came out, together with his sons, his wife, and his sons' wives; (19) every animal, every creeping thing, and every bird—everything that stirs on earth—left the ark, one kind after another.

Despite their differences, these two biblical accounts have in common a number of elements not found in the Mesopotamian stories. In both Hebrew sources, monotheism is assumed, the name of the hero is Noah, and man's sin is given as the reason for the Flood. Also, in neither is there any attempt to save craftsmen or the elements of man's civilization as there is in the Mesopotamian traditions. These similarities point to a common origin for the *J* and *P* accounts in an earlier "proto-Israelite" Flood narrative. As this tradition was passed down in oral form among different segments of the Isrealite population or in different areas of Palestine the discrepancies we have noted must have developed.

The exact relationship of this "proto-Israelite" story to the Mesopotamian accounts, however, cannot yet be determined. The Mesopotamian sources are much more ancient than the biblical versions, and most modern scholars acknowledge that they were the ultimate source of the Genesis account.[33] But how many intermediate versions stood between the Sumerian flood story and the *J* and *P* narratives is unknown. A fragment of the *Epic of Gilgamesh* was discovered in debris from the Canaanite layers of Megiddo, an important city in northern Palestine.[34] And it was recently reported that a flood story similar to that from Mesopotamia has been found in the late third millennium archive at Ebla in Syria.[35] Such discoveries indicate that flood traditions related to those of Mesopotamia were known in Syria-Palestine before the Israelite settlement there. Thus, the "proto-Israelite" story of the Deluge could have been based on Canaanite versions that were themselves ultimately derived from Mesopotamia. But other Near Eastern groups like the Hurrians, a people who lived in northern Mesopotamia and Syria, and the Hittites, who lived in Asia Minor, also borrowed Mesopotamian mythology, including the flood story.[36] So it is possible that the Israelites received the account from the Hurrians or some other ethnic group. Or, of course, they could have borrowed the outline of the narrative directly from Mesopotamia itself.

The general agreement between the Hebrew Deluge stories, the Greek legend of Deucalion, and the Mesopotamian flood accounts is not convincing evidence that there once was a historical Flood which all three traditions independently describe. Rather, it is much more likely that the Greek and Hebrew stories are further testimony to the well-documented influence that Mesopotamian civilization, especially literature, had on other eastern Mediterranean cultures. And through these derivative accounts the Sumerian belief in a prehistoric Deluge continues to have influence today.

Evidence for a Worldwide Deluge

Of course many peoples besides the Mesopotamians, Greeks, and Hebrews had flood legends. The existence of these stories in so many different parts of the world is often regarded as confirmation that there once was a universal Deluge.[37] However, when the various stories are subjected to careful scrutiny their value as evidence on this point disappears.

The first problem is that in many cases direct influence from the biblical story of Noah cannot be ruled out. Christian missionaries have been traveling to remote parts of the world for centuries. They were often present on voyages of discovery when Europeans first made contact with peoples of the New World, the Pacific, and East Asia. They were among the first to settle in newly discovered areas, and they often penetrated into the interiors of new lands ahead of adventurers, traders, and colonizers. Moreover, it was often missionaries who first recorded the legends and customs of non-European cultures. It should not be surprising, then, that features of the biblical flood story should appear in legends in different parts of the world.

For example, a Hawaiian account of a flood survived by a man named Nuu and his family is sometimes cited as a parallel to the biblical story.[38] But this "native" legend was recorded long after missionaries had been active in the Hawaiian islands. It is obviously the biblical story of Noah with a local setting and color. Another example comes from South Africa where a "traditional" Hottentot flood story was related to a missionary by a native informant. Subsequently, however, another missionary reported that he had earlier told the story of Noah to that same Hottentot.[39] A flood tradition from southwestern China is almost certainly due to the influence of Nestorian Christians who arrived in that area in the seventh century A.D.[40] Christian influence is also probable in flood legends from Wales and Lithuania, as well as in some of the stories reported from the Americas.

A second point to remember is that "the universality of flood traditions can be explained very easily without requiring a widespread flood of cosmic or any other origin, if we bear in mind that *floods, plural, are a universal geologic phenomenon*."[41] Many flood stories reflect local conditions—river flooding, hurricanes, seismic sea-waves, volcanic activity, and earthquakes—and have little in common with the biblical story. Such legends may have arisen from local inundations caused by normal geological or meteorological forces. Still other stories probably arose to explain local geographical features or natural phenomena.[42]

Flood traditions are rare in Europe (outside of Greece), and are not found in Central Asia or Africa. If one explains all flood stores as memories of a universal Deluge that overwhelmed the earth long ago, it is hard to see why peoples in these areas "forgot" that catastrophic event. Is it just coincidence that the groups which do not have flood stories live in areas which do not normally have disastrous floods?

The absence of a flood tradition in Egypt, the home of one of man's earliest civilizations, seems to be particularly embarassing to modern Diluvialists and catastrophists. Frederick A. Filby, for example, finds it necessary to infer an Egyptian flood myth from Greek accounts supposedly derived from Egypt, and from a statement by the Hellenistic Egyptian historian Manetho that some Egyptian monuments had been erected before the Deluge.[43] But Manetho was writing for Greek readers. It is understandable that he would date Egyptian events in relation to Deucalion's Flood, which he knew his Greek readers accepted and which they dated to a period some three or four hundred years before the Trojan War. Manetho's reference to the Deluge does not prove that the Egyptians had their own traditions of a worldwide flood.

Filby also sees flood traditions in some Egyptian myths. One is the story of how Sekhmet, the goddess of destruction, was prevented from wiping out mankind by having a flood of beer poured in her path, causing her to stop, drink, and become intoxicated. Another is the myth of Atum, the creator sun-god, who rose out of the waters covering the earth. And a third is the legend which told how Osiris, god of the dead, was imprisoned in a coffin and sent down the Nile during a flood.[44] But none of these myths is a true flood story. The flood of beer in the Sekhmet story saves mankind rather than destroying all life, and it is a local affair of small porportions (it is produced by seven thousand jars of beer and covers the fields to a depth of only nine inches). The waters from which Atum rises are not those of a flood, but the waters of chaos which were thought to have been everywhere at the beginning of time before Atum created the gods and the world. This myth parallels Genesis 1, not the story of Noah. And the flood in the Osiris myth is the local, noncatastrophic yearly flood of the Nile.[45] There simply is no trace of a genuine Deluge tradition in the literature, mythology, or historical records of ancient Egypt.

When the flood legends that could have been influenced by the Mesopotamian or biblical flood accounts are eliminated, the remaining stories show little similarity to the story of Noah or even to one another. They are not necessarily varying accounts of *one* Deluge, nor need they all have derived from one early flood narrative. It is far more likely that they are independent creations that utilize material derived from local conditions. And they are found in most parts of the world because disastrous floods, at one time or another, have been part of the experience of virtually all peoples.

A worldwide flood that occurred during man's early civilizations should have left evidence of its existence more tangible than myths and legends. Some believe that such evidence has been found in archaeological deposits in Mesopotamia.[46] In 1929 at Ur in southern Mesopotamia, Leonard Woolley discovered an eight-foot-thick layer of clean, water-laid silt containing no artifacts. This deposit was between strata containing objects characteristic of the prehistoric Ubaid culture, which lasted from c. 4500 to 3500 B.C. Clearly this strange deposit had been produced by a flood, and Woolley estimated that this flood had covered much of southern Mesopotamia.[47] Over the next few years similar flood deposits were found at three other Mesopotamian sites: Kish, Fara, and Nineveh. This evidence seemed to many to be proof of the accuracy of Genesis.

However, the existence of these flood layers does not establish the reality of a universal Deluge in ancient times. The archaeological remains found above and below the Mesopotamian flood deposits indicate that they varied widely in date. And most sites in Mesopotamia, including al-'Ubaid near Ur, have produced no evidence of "the Flood." There is also no sign of destruction by flood at other Near Eastern sites occupied in very early times. The Mesopotamian flood layers are the results of several different *local* floods that did not even cover all of the Tigris-Euphrates valley, let alone the entire world.[48] In fact, the *absence* of contemporaneous flood-caused destruction layers at very ancient settlement sites is very strong, if not irrefutable, evidence against the historicity of a world-wide Deluge.

Vast deposits of remains of mammoths in Siberia are also frequently cited as evidence by supporters of the biblical Deluge as well as by other catastrophists.[49] Tens of thousands of bones as well as four whole mammoths (frozen with their flesh intact) have been found over the centuries. It is argued that these remains prove that a great catastrophe associated with a sudden change in climate overwhelmed herds of grazing mammoths, destroying most of them and quick-freezing a few.

But there is no reason to believe that the bones that have been found were all deposited at the same time. They probably represent the remains of generations of animals, not a single vast herd. Neither do the four frozen carcasses demand a catastrophic explanation. Despite claims to the contrary, the flesh of the best preserved of these beasts had begun to rot before it was frozen.[50] This indicates that the dead mammoth was frozen by a normal, gradual process. It was not "quick-frozen" by a blast of cold air caused by a sudden shift from a mild to a polar climate.

Dorothy Vitaliano, a geologist, has pointed out other flaws in the catastrophist explanation of the death of the mammoths:[51]

One thing the catastrophists usually neglect to explain when using the frozen mammoths as evidence of a stupendous upheaval is, why have no human remains been found too? Any disaster which could wipe out tens of thousands of woolly mammoths at one fell swoop would have been equally hard on the cave men who hunted them. As for the arguments for an overnight shift into a colder climatic zone: if, prior to their demise, the mammoths were living in a mild climate, why were they all wearing such heavy wool coats? And why are the other animals whose remains are found with theirs also overwhelmingly of species which are at home in a cold climate, like the mastodon, moose, deer, bear, musk-ox, yak, bison, and wolf, to name a few?

Conventional uniformitarian hypotheses fit the evidence better than theories relying on the Flood or some other gigantic cataclysm.

Some individuals still interpret most geological phenomena and fossil deposits as results of the Deluge,[52] while other believers in the Flood reject this approach.[53] But both groups find it necessary to challenge geological and archaeological dating in order to maintain that the Flood occurred sometime during man's early history, c. 4000–2500 B.C.[54] Especially questioned is radiocarbon dating, a method used to establish early dates for settlements like Jericho, which show no signs of a flood.

The radiocarbon dating method relies on the fact that carbon-14 (C^{14}), a radioactive form of carbon, represents a small proportion of the carbon in the atmosphere, rivers, lakes, and oceans, and thus in all living things. As long as an organism is alive, the proportion of radioactive carbon it contains remains constant. But when an organism dies it ceases to receive new carbon-14, causing the ratio of C^{14} to nonradioactive carbon (C^{12} and C^{13}) to decrease gradually as the radioactive carbon decays into nitrogen. It takes about 5,700 years for half of the carbon-14 in a once-living object to become nitrogen, another 5,700 years for half of the remaining C^{14} to decay, and so on. By determining the percentage of radioactive carbon remaining in material of animal or vegetable origin and comparing it with the percentage found in living organisms, scientists can tell how long the carbon-14 has been decaying and, thus, how long it has been since the organism in question died.[55]

In theory such a computation should reveal the exact age of a specimen. However, there are a number of factors that complicate the process and make carbon-14 dates less reliable than one might suspect. First, the amount of radiocarbon in any object is so minute that present-day equipment cannot measure it exactly. Scientists must make a number of measurements for each object dated, then average the differing results. Thus, the date finally arrived at is only probable, not certain. To indicate this fact, carbon-14 dates are usually written with a plus or minus factor representing one standard deviation from the average date obtained. For example, a specimen might be dated 1425 B.C. ±75. This means that there are about two chances out of three that the date of the object being tested falls somewhere between 1500 B.C. and 1350 B.C. (Many people misunderstand this point and assume that such notation means that 1425 B.C. is the most probable date for the object with the chances for correctness decreasing as one approaches 1500 on one hand, or 1350 on the other. In fact, *any* date within that range is as probable as any other—the correct date is as likely to be 1500, 1475, or 1350 as it is to be 1425 B.C.) If one doubles the standard deviation given with any radiocarbon date, the chances that the correct date of the object is within the resulting range of dates goes up to better than nine out of ten.

Another problem with carbon-14 dates results from the fact that the amount of C[14] in the atmosphere has varied over the ages. Recent tests using long-lived bristlecone pines have shown that radiocarbon dates for some of the more ancient parts of the trees were hundreds of years younger than the true age determined by tree-ring count.[56] A carbon-14 date will also be erroneous, of course, if the sample is contaminated by modern carbon, either on the site (by water seepage or intrusion of modern plant rootlets, for example) or during the excavation, handling, or processing of the sample. Naturally, those who believe in the Deluge emphasize these problems and maintain that they make radiocarbon dating totally unreliable.[57]

However, checks provided by tree-ring chronology, thermoluminescence dating (a scientific method for dating pottery by measuring accumulated radiation damage), and objects dated by textual evidence show that the error in radiocarbon dates for the past 1200 years is less than 2 per cent.[58] The error is greater for earlier material, especially for the period before 2000 B.C. For objects dated between 3000 and 4000 B.C. by the radiocarbon method, the difference between the C[14] date and the tree-ring date is as much as 800 to 1,000 years.[59] But even a 1,000-year error is not enough to make the dates of all early settlements later than 3000-2000 B.C. (that is, after the Flood) in order to harmonize them with the chronology of Genesis. Early levels of Jericho, for example, have been radiocarbon dated to c. 6250 and c. 5850 B.C.,[60] while the lowest strata of Çatal Hüyük and Hacilar in Anatolia have yielded dates of 6385 ± 101 and 5614 ± 92, respectively.[61] Furthermore, the tree-ring evidence shows that radiocarbon dates for the pre-Christian era are too recent, not too ancient! That is, an object dated to c. 3500 B.C. by radiocarbon dating actually dates from c. 4300 B.C. and is thus much older than the carbon-14 date indicated. So, the error in carbon-14 dates doesn't help supporters of the Flood; it increases their problem.

While all of the geological and archaeological dating methods based on radioactivity may contain a small degree of error, their agreement in dating man and the earth's physical features to periods much more ancient than anything suggested by Genesis is difficult to explain away. One must assume that God created the world with its "atomic clocks" already set to indicate erroneously a much earlier time for the creation.[62] Such an explanation is an admission that acceptance of the Deluge is still primarily a *religious* belief. "Scientific Creationists" and others who continue to accept the Flood as a factor in man's early history do so *despite* the scientific evidence provided by geology and archaeology not because of it.

The Quest for Noah's Ark

But what if Noah's Ark were to be found on Mount Ararat? That would certainly justify belief in the Flood and support the historicity of the early chapters of Genesis. Thus, over the past thirty years many individuals and expeditions have searched for the remains of the great vessel described in Genesis 6:15. Ark sightings reported recently in articles, books, and motion pictures have convinced many that the Ark will soon be revealed to confound an unbelieving world.[63]

The modern search for Noah's Ark has centered on Agri Dagi, the "Mount Ararat" of Armenian tradition, which is located in northeastern Turkey near the Iranian and Russian borders. Ancient and medieval writers are often quoted to prove that this site for the Ark's landing has been known from before the time of Jesus. And some of these early authors mention that the Ark was still visible in their day.[64]

But are these traditions as uniform as Ark-seekers believe? The Bible doesn't designate the specific spot where Noah's Ark came to rest. Genesis 8:4 states only that the Ark landed on "the *mountains* of Ararat." Ararat was an ancient mountainous kingdom (called "Urartu" by the Assyrians) that occupied most of the area later called "Armenia." This region is now divided between Turkey, Russia, Iran, and Iraq. Agri Dagi is in the northern part of ancient Ararat/Armenia, and many believers in the Ark uncritically assume that any early mention of "Mount Ararat" or Armenia as the resting place of the Ark refers specifically to this mountain. But, in fact, few ancient or medieval authors placed the Ark on or near Agri Dagi.

Josephus, a Jewish historian who lived during the late first century A.D., as well as Hippolytus and Julius Africanus, two third-century authors, indicate that the Ark was in Iraq near the Lower Zab river.[65] This is roughly the area where the Mesopotamian tradition embodied in the *Epic of Gilgamesh* placed the landing of Utnapistim's ship. Other ancient writers locate the Ark's landing place in southern Armenia, the area called "Gordyene" in antiquity, or in central Asia Minor, the district known as Phrygia in Classical times.[66] Muslim tradition places the Ark on Jebel Judi, a mountain in Arabia according to the Koran, but located near Mosul in northern Mesopotamia according to medieval writers.[67] Agri Dagi does not seem to have been designated as the mountain of the Ark earlier than the eleventh or twelfth century A.D.[68]

Modern Ark-searchers, however, have ignored these variations in the early traditions and have concentrated their efforts on Agri Dagi. Some theorize that an 1840 earthquake, which changed the topography of the

FIGURE 1: Traditional sites for the Ark's landing place

1. Adiabene (Josephus, first century A.D.; Hippolytus and Julius Africanus, third century A.D.)

2. Phrygia (cited by Julius Africanus, third century A.D.)

3. Gordyene (Epiphanius, fourth century A.D.; Medieval Muslim location of Jebel Judi)

4. Jebel Judi (The Koran, seventh century A.D.)

5. Agri Dagi (Armenian tradition, twelfth century A.D.)

mountain, may have uncovered the Ark,[69] for there have been a number of reported sightings of the vessel since that time:

1. About 1856, a young Armenian Seventh-day Adventist named Haji Yearam and his father were supposedly hired by three atheistic British scientists to take them up to Agri Dagi to prove that the Ark was *not* there. But the Armenians led the scientists directly to the intact remains of Noah's ship. The atheists tried to destroy the Ark, but the wood was as hard as stone and could not be burned. They threatened the boy and his father with death if they ever told anyone what they had seen, and Haji Yearam remained silent until 1920 when he was on his death-bed in America. The man to whom he told the story did not publicize it himself until 1952! Supposedly a year or two before Yearam died there were newspaper reports of a death-bed confession by a British scientist who told a story identical to that of the Armenian. However, no copy of this article has been found and the scientist has never been identified.[70]

2. In 1876, Sir James Bryce, a well-known British historian, statesman, and jurist, climbed Agri Dagi. At a height of over 13,000 feet he found a piece of hand-tooled wood, about four feet long and five inches thick, lying on some loose stones. It was easy to cut, so he broke off a piece with his ice-axe and took it back to London.[71]

3. Newspapers in 1883 quoted a news release from Turkey stating that a government expedition surveying earthquake damage on Agri Dagi had found the Ark protruding from a glacier. Members of the expedition claimed that the Ark was well preserved, though a good deal broken and filled with ice. They entered the vessel and noted that the interior was divided into compartments by fifteen-foot-high partitions.[72] However, the original Turkish news release cited in Western newspapers (which picked up the story from one another) has never been produced.[73]

4. John Joseph, a Nestorian Christian who also called himself "Prince Nouri," claimed that he discovered the Ark in 1887. He reported that the vessel, the beams of which were held together with long nails, was intact, though half-filled with snow. He hoped to remove the Ark from Agri Dagi, but his plans were never realized.[74]

5. An elderly Armenian-American, Georgie Hagopian, in 1970 claimed that when he was about ten years old (sometime between 1902 and 1910—the accounts vary) his uncle took him up Agri Dagi to the Ark. There were no holes or doors in the side, so he climbed to the top by means of a pile of stones. The wood of the Ark was rock-hard, but it was covered with green moss which made its surface feel soft. Hagopian noted that no nails were visible; it seemed as if the entire vessel was made of one piece of petrified wood.[75]

6. A Russian aviator flying over Agri Dagi shortly before 1917 allegedly saw the Ark beached on the shore of a lake. It had a stubby mast,

was rounded on top with a five-foot-wide catwalk down the center, and had large doorways on one side (one nearly twenty-four feet square). An expedition sent to investigate his report discovered the ship and spent some time exploring it. The records of the expedition were lost during the Russian Revolution, but some relatives of members of the expedition later claimed that they had heard stories relating the discovery.[76]

7. About 1936 a New Zealander named Hardwicke Knight found large timbers projecting from a glacier near the snow line. The rectangular pieces of wood were "soggy and dark," and they extended in more than one direction. Only later did he decide these may have been part of Noah's Ark.[77]

8. During World War II American and Russian pilots reportedly spotted the Ark from the air. It is claimed that the Russians took photographs that clearly showed the Ark, and some of these photos are reputed to have been published in various newspapers in the United States. The account of one of the American sightings is supposed to have appeared in a 1943 Tunisian theatre edition of the Army paper *Stars and Stripes*. However, repeated searches have failed to locate copies of these newspaper photographs or articles.[78]

9. In 1948 a Kurdish farmer named Resit reported that he had seen the prow of the Ark jutting from the ice on the north face of Agri Dagi about two-thirds of the way up the mountain. Its wood was so hard that Resit could not break off a piece with his dagger. Peasants from villages in the area are said to have climbed to the spot and verified the discovery. They agreed with Resit that the object was part of a large ship.[78] However, when the dean of a small North Carolina Bible college arrived the following year, he could not locate Resit. Nor did a search of villages for a hundred miles around Agri Dagi turn up anyone who had seen the Ark or who had heard the story of Resit's discovery.[80]

10. George Greene, a mining engineer, took six aerial photographs of an object he believed to be the Ark in 1952. Unfortunately, these photos disappeared ten years later when Greene was murdered by thieves in British Guiana. However, about thirty people claim to have seen the photographs, and they state that a boat-like object was clearly visible in them.[81]

11. A five-foot piece of hand-worked timber was pulled from a water-filled pocket in a glacial crevasse by Fernand Navarra in 1955. More beams were recovered from the same spot (elevation about 13,500 feet) in 1969. A Spanish laboratory dated the partly fossilized wood to about 3000 B.C., but radiocarbon tests indicate a medieval date.[82]

12. The Ark supposedly appears in three recent photographs. Eryl Cummings took a 35mm slide of terrain on Agri Dagi in 1966. Later, he noticed a strange object in the picture near the base of a cliff. However, it

cannot be positively identified as the Ark. In 1973 an orbiting U.S. Earth Resources Technology Satellite took photographs of Agri Dagi from an altitude of 450 miles. These show a number of dark spots in the ice fields, and some think one of these anomalies represents the remains of the Ark. Finally, in 1974 or 1975 the Holy Ground Mission Changing Center revealed a photograph supposedly taken with a telephoto lens high on Agri Dagi. It shows an object with lines like planking on its side.[83]

This volume of material indicating the presence of Noah's Ark on Agri Dagi seems impressive until one examines it more closely. Then it becomes clear that many of the stories are heresay accounts that cannot be verified. And some of them contradict one another. John Joseph and Georgie Hagopian both claimed that they had spent some time examining the Ark, inside and out (items 4 and 5). Yet John Joseph said it was held together by long nails, while Hagopian specificially denied seeing nails. Hagopian claimed there were no holes or doors in the side of the Ark, but the Russian aviators (item 6) supposedly saw more than one opening in the side, the largest at least twenty-four feet square. The Ark was half encased in a glacier according to accounts 3, 4, and 9, but the Russians saw it on the shore of a lake (6), and no glacier is visible in Cummings's photograph (12). (If a glacier had repeatedly advanced and retreated over the spot where the Ark was standing, the ship would have been almost totally destroyed). Some claim the wood of the Ark was as hard as stone (1, 5, and 9), while others found it soggy and easy to cut (2, 7, and 11). Many of the accounts state that the Ark was largely or completely intact, but the beams found by Bryce (2), Knight (7), and Navarra (11) could only have come from a vessel that had been broken into pieces. Also, for the Ark to appear as an anomaly on the satellite photographs, it would have to be broken up and its remains spread over a fairly large area.[84] Thus, the weight of the "evidence" of Ark sightings is not cumulative. If some of them are true, then others are necessarily false. Unless, of course, there is more than one "Ark" on Agri Dagi.

Much of the above "evidence" is inherently unlikely,[85] and it is strange that so many alleged newspaper articles and photographs cannot be located. The only evidence which can be subjected to objective scrutiny and analysis is the wood brought back by Navarra (item 11) and the photographs taken since 1966 (item 12), and they do not prove that the Ark is on Agri Dagi.

Pieces of Navarra's wood were subjected to radiocarbon analysis at five different laboratories, and the results indicate the wood is far too recent to come from Noah's Ark. The dates ranged from A.D. 260 to A.D. 790 ± 90 years, with most of the results centering around the century from A.D. 650 to 750. The divergence in dates was not really as great as it appears, for the A.D. 260 date was obtained from a test run on a sample only half the minimum size needed.[86] Ark-searchers have rejected these tests and the carbon-14 dating method itself as unreliable.[87] But for the period indicated for Navarra's wood (the last 1,700 years) C[14] dates have proven to be accurate within about fifty years.[88] The dating methods used to date the wood to c. 3000-2500 B.C.—color and density change, degree of lignite formation, cell modification, and degree of fossilization—are all far less reliable than radiocarbon dating. Furthermore, to produce even moderately accurate results by these four methods, the environmental factors to which the wood has been subjected must be known and control specimens must be available.[88] These conditions were not met for Navarra's samples, so attempts to date them by such methods are fruitless. Navarra seems to have found the remains of some wooden structure (perhaps a chapel, a replica of the Ark, or a hut for climbers) built near the snow line on Agri Dagi during the Middle Ages.[90]

The photographic evidence for the Ark is also weak. The anomalies in the satellite photographs are too large to be the Ark. They probably represent natural features.[91] The object in the Cummings slide is also probably a natural rock formation. In 1972 a group of Ark-searchers tried to find the area shown in the slide. They located a place that had all the features in the photograph and were sure it was the right spot. But when the Ark-like object in the slide turned out to be a rock formation, they decided that they had made a mistake and were in the wrong location.[92] The object in the Holy Ground Mission photograph could also be a natural feature, but many individuals (including some ardent Ark-searchers) believe that this photo has been retouched or altered.[93]

All of this "evidence" for the existence of Noah's Ark on Agri Dagi will convince only those who already believe and do not need to be convinced. But the lack of persuasive evidence for Noah's Ark and the Deluge and the existence of strong geological and archaeological evidence against a worldwide Flood will not convince everybody. Many individuals and groups believe that the Bible is literally the Word of God, verbally inspired and incapable of error. For such persons acceptance of the historicity of the Deluge is not an intellectual choice; it is an act of faith.

Most Christian denominations, however, have made their peace with science, abandoning literal belief in a six-day creation and in the Deluge. Leaders of these churches accept the historical-critical approach to interpreting the Bible. They understand the Scriptures in terms of the times in which they were written and, while acknowledging the theological truths which the Bible conveys, they recognize the possibility that some portions of it might contain scientific or historical errors. Yet even in these denominations, many (possibly even most) laymen continue to believe in the historical reality of Noah's Flood. It is one popular belief about man's ancient past that archaeologists and historians will probably never succeed in eradicating.

Atlantis, the Sunken Continent

Argument over the reality of Atlantis, a continent that supposedly vanished thousands of years ago, has raged since ancient times. Over two thousand books have been written on this subject, and the number continues to grow each year. But all of this great volume of material actually rests on the writings of one man, the Greek philosopher Plato, who recounted the story of Atlantis in two of his latest dialogues, *Timaeus* and *Critias,* written about 350 B.C.

Plato's Story of Atlantis:

The *Timaeus* describes a discussion between Socrates, Timaeus, Hermocrates, and Critias which Plato sets during the Panathenaic festival in Athens around 421 B.C. On the previous day Socrates had been discoursing on the nature of the ideal state, outlining the institutions that are described in greater detail in Plato's *Republic.* Socrates' speech reminded Critias of a story he had heard as a young boy from his aged grandfather, and he briefly outlines the story to his friends:[1]

> Listen, then, Socrates, to a story which, though strange, is entirely true, as Solon, wisest of the Seven, once affirmed. He was a relative and close friend of Dropides, my great-grandfather, as he says himself several times in his poems; and he told my grandfather Critias (according to the story the old man used to repeat to us) that there were great and admirable exploits performed by our own city long ago, which have been forgotten through the lapse of time and the destruction of human life. . . . I will tell you the story I heard as an old tale from a man who was himself far from young. At that time, indeed, Critias, by his own account, was close upon ninety, and I was, perhaps, ten years old. . . .
> "In Egypt," said Critias, "at the apex of the Delta, where the stream of the Nile divides, there is a province called the Saitic. . . . Solon said that, when he travelled thither, he was received with much honour; and further

that, when he inquired about ancient times from the priests who knew most of such matters, he discovered that neither he nor any other Greek had any knowledge of antiquity worth speaking of. . . .

'Ah, Solon, Solon,' said one of the priests, a very old man, 'you Greeks are always children; in Greece there is no such thing as an old man.'

'What do you mean?' Solon asked.

'You are all young in your minds,' said the priest, 'which hold no store of old belief based on long tradition, no knowledge hoary with age. The reason is this. There have been, and will be hereafter, many and divers destructions of mankind, the greatest by fire and water, though other lesser ones are due to countless other causes. . . . To begin with, your people remember only one deluge, though there were many earlier; and moreover you do not know that the bravest and noblest race in the world once lived in your country. From a small remnant of their seed you and all your fellow-citizens are derived; but you know nothing of it because the survivors for many generations died leaving no word in writing. Once, Solon, before the greatest of all destructions by water, what is now the city of the Athenians was the most valiant in war and in all respects the best governed beyond comparison; her exploits and her government are said to have been the noblest under heaven of which report has come to our ears. . . .

Many great exploits of your city are here recorded for the admiration of all; but one surpasses the rest in greatness and valour. The records tell how great a power your city once brought to an end when it insolently advanced against all Europe and Asia, starting from the Atlantic ocean outside. For in those days that ocean could be crossed, since there was an island in it in front of the strait which your countrymen tell me you call the Pillars of Heracles. The island was larger than Libya and Asia put together; and from it the voyagers of those days could reach the other islands, and from these islands the whole of the opposite continent bounding that ocean which truly deserves the name. For all these parts that lie within the strait I speak of, seem to be a bay with a narrow entrance; that outer sea is the real ocean, and the land which entirely surrounds it really deserves the name of continent in the proper sense. Now on this Atlantic island there had grown up an extraordinary power under kings who ruled not only the whole island but many of the other islands and parts of the continent; and besides that, within the straits, they were lords of Libya so far as Egypt, and of Europe to the borders of Tyrrhenia. All this power, gathered into one, attempted at one swoop to enslave your country and ours and all the region within the strait. Then it was, Solon, that the power of your city was made manifest to all mankind in its valour and strength. She was foremost of all in courage and in the arts of war, and first as the leader of Hellas, then forced by the defection of the rest to stand alone, she faced the last extreme of danger, vanquished the invaders, and set up her trophy; the peoples not yet enslaved she preserved from slavery, and all the rest of us who dwell within the bounds set by Heracles she freed with ungrudging hand. Afterwards there was a time of inordinate earthquakes and floods; there came one terrible day and night, in which all your men of war were swallowed bodily by the earth, and the island Atlantis also sank beneath the sea and vanished. Hence to this day that outer ocean cannot be crossed or explored, the way being blocked by mud, just below the surface, left by settling down of the island.'"

Now, Socrates, I have given you a brief account of the story told by the old Critias as he heard it from Solon. When you were speaking yesterday about your state and its citizens, I recalled this story and I was surprised to notice in how many points your account exactly agreed, by some miraculous chance, with Solon's.

After Critias has completed this summary of Solon's story, it is agreed that Timaeus will describe the creation of the universe and the nature of man (which takes up the rest of the dialogue). Then, in the following dialogue, *Critias,* the story of the conflict between Athens and Atlantis is taken up again, this time in detail.

Critias describes how, more than nine thousand years before Solon's time (which is the date he gives for the destruction of Atlantis), the gods divided up the earth with Hephaestus and Athena receiving Athens as their portion. They created wise and courageous people to live there and guided them in creating an ideal society. The military class lived on the Acropolis, apart from the rest of the population. Owning no private property, they were supported by their fellow citizens, but they received no more than they needed for sustenance. They were, in fact, exactly like the guardians described in the *Republic.*[2] The land of Attica was more fertile in that long-distant time and the climate was ideal, so most of Athens's citizens were farmers or craftsmen. There is no mention of merchants or trade. The number of citizens was kept close to twenty thousand, and they gained a reputation throughout Europe and Asia for their good looks and virtuous character.[3]

Poseidon took Atlantis as his share, dividing the island into ten parts, one for each of his sons. The largest and most fertile part of the island went to Poseidon's oldest son, Atlas, who reigned as king over his brothers who, in turn, were princes controlling large territories and populations. These rulers and their descendants gradually extended their control over other islands in the ocean and over Africa and Europe as far as Egypt and Tyrrhenia (the area of Tuscany in north-central Italy).

The successors of Atlas became the wealthiest kings ever to rule, for in addition to the tribute from their captive lands, they controlled the great natural resources of Atlantis itself. The island contained deposits of every kind of metal, including orichalcum (probably a natural alloy of copper), which was considered more valuable than any other metal except gold. There were forests to supply wood, all types of wild and domesticated animals (including elephants), and a variety of grains, spices, fruits, canes, vegetables, olives, and grapes.[4]

This great wealth made it possible for the kings to construct a capital city of unrivaled splendor. Its center was situated fifty stadia (almost six miles) from the sea and consisted of an inner island or citadel surrounded by three concentric rings of water separated by two rings of land. A canal connected the outer ring of water to the sea, and tunnels through the circles of land (which were raised much above sea level) allowed access to the inner waterways and the central island. Each of the islands was protected by a metal-plated stone wall with towers and fortified gates. The wall around the outermost ring of land was covered with bronze, the second with tin, and the innermost with orichalcum.

In the center of the citadel, surrounded by a gold wall, was a temple to Cleito and Poseidon. The citadel also contained another temple to Poseidon that was covered with silver, except for the statues on its pediments, which were sheathed in gold. The interior was roofed with ivory decorated with gold, silver, and orichalcum ornaments, while the columns, walls, and floor were covered with orichalcum. Inside was a colossal gold statue of Poseidon in a chariot drawn by six winged-horses. The royal palace on the citadel was decorated in a similarly luxurious fashion. Nearby were hot and cold baths, a sacred grove containing all sorts of beautiful trees, and numerous costly statues.

On the two outer circular islands were many temples to various gods, gardens, gymnasiums, and a racecourse. There were also shipyards filled with triremes and their equipment. Houses of citizens and merchants surrounded the outermost ring of water for almost six miles, and around these habitations was still another circular wall running right down to the sea.

The capital city was located in a large plain (about 345 miles long and 230 miles wide) surrounded by high mountains. The mountains contained many villages which supplied enough men to field a military force of 120,000 hoplites (heavily-armed infantry soldiers), a like number of both archers and slingers, 240,000 light-armed troops, 10,000 chariots and 1,200 warships. Every one of the other nine sections of Atlantis had similar wealth and manpower.[5]

Each of the ten rulers had absolute authority within his own territory, but their relationships with one another were governed by laws laid down by Poseidon. Alternately at four- and five-year intervals they assembled in the citadel of the capital city to discuss affairs of state and pronounce judgment on any who had broken the law. These sessions were preceded by a ritual in which the ten rulers, using only clubs and lassoes, captured a bull that they then sacrificed to Poseidon.

For many generations, the kings ruled wisely and in obedience to Poseidon's laws. But as their divine strain became increasingly diluted by marriage to mortals, they grew greedy and power-hungry. When Zeus saw this he called a council of the gods to decide how to discipline them. Here the account ends in mid-sentence as Zeus begins addressing his fellow gods.[6] Possibly the ending of the dialogue was lost, but it is more likely that Plato, for unknown reasons, decided not to finish it. If he had, perhaps much of the subsequent argument over Atlantis would have been unnecessary.

Development of the Atlantis Theme

Debate over Plato's account began soon after his death. Aristotle, Plato's most famous and most gifted student, did not believe there ever had been a real Atlantis. In a work that is now lost but which was quoted by Strabo, a first-century geographer, Aristotle compared Plato's use of the Atlantis story to fictional elements employed by Homer to further his plot. Aristotle is said to have remarked, concerning the sinking of the island continent, that "the one who created it also destroyed it."[7] On the other hand, Crantor, a contemporary of Aristotle and the first author of a commentary on the Platonic dialogues, accepted the Atlantis narratives as straight history.[8]

A variety of ancient writers such as Strabo, Philo Judaeus, Tertullian, and Ammianus Marcellinus agreed with Crantor that Atlantis had been a real place, while others such as Origen, Amelius, Porphyry, and Longinus were certain the story was a myth or an allegory. A few, like Pliny the Elder and Plutarch, discussed the question without committing themselves to one side or the other. The only conclusion that can be drawn from this ancient debate with any certainty is that Plato's writings were the sole source for the Atlantis story. All of the ancient authors who mention Atlantis either credit Plato with the story or display dependence (directly or indirectly) on his dialogues. There is no valid evidence of any other ancient traditions about a sunken continent.[9]

Little that was new was added to Atlantis speculation during the Middle Ages, but the early modern era saw renewed interest in the story. As early as 1530 a poet named Giralamo Fracastoro suggested that the Indian cultures that the Spanish explorers had discovered in Central America were remnants of Atlantean civilization. Other sixteenth-century Spanish authors agreed, including the historian Francisco Lopez de Gomara, who repeated the suggestion in his *General History of the Indies* (1553). Sir Francis Bacon used this theory as the basis of his unfinished utopia, *The New Atlantis* (1627), and in succeeding centuries the Atlantis-in-America idea was supported by leading scholars such as Georges Buffon, Jacob Krüger, and Alexander von Humboldt.[10]

Identification of American Indian cultures as Atlantean led to widespread adoption of a belief about Atlantis that was not supported by Plato's account—the idea that Atlantis was the source of *all* civilization. Alleged similarities between the New World cultures and the civilizations of ancient Egypt and Mesopotamia were cited to prove that all early civilization had its origin in Atlantis. It was thought that civilization had been carried to Old and New World centers by Atlantean colonists or survivors of the catastrophe that destroyed the lost continent.

One of the most ardent supporters of this hypothesis was Flemish scholar Abbé Charles-Étienne Brasseur de Bourbourg. For years Brasseur traveled in the Americas, searching out old documents and learning Indian languages in order to understand the origins and history of the Indian civilizations. Then, in 1864, he discovered in Madrid an abridged copy of an early Spanish description of Mayan culture written in the 1560s by the then bishop of Yucatan, Diego de Landa. Landa's work, based on information from native informants, recounted the history of Yucatan, described Mayan customs and ceremonies, and attempted a decipherment of Mayan hieroglyphic writing. His interpretation of the glyphs for the days and months of the Mayan calendar proved to be accurate and has provided the key for reading dates on Mayan monuments. However, Landa mistakenly assumed that the rest of the writing system was alphabetic like European writing, when in reality it seems to consist of a complex combination of ideographs (glyphs representing individual words) and syllabic signs denoting sounds. The readings he gave for the Mayan "alphabet" have since been shown to be incorrect.[11]

Of course, Brasseur was unaware of Landa's error. He used the supposedly alphabetic signs and a lot of imagination to "read" the *Troano Codex* (one of only three Mayan books to survive destruction by Spanish missionaries), interpreting it as an account of a great cataclysm that had engulfed a large island in the Atlantic in the year 9937 B.C. According to Brasseur the Indian name for this lost continent was Mu, but it was obviously the same island which Plato had called Atlantis.[12]

Other scholars' attempts to use Landa's "key" to read Mayan texts soon proved that the "alphabet" was worthless and that Abbé Brasseur's translation of the *Troano Codex* was invalid. Though Mayan writing still is not fully decipherable (only about one-third of the signs can be understood), it is now generally recognized that this codex is really an astrological treatise, not an account of Atlantis. But believers in Atlantis continued to use Brasseur's interpretation to support their theories long after scholars had shown them to be without merit. Even today some works accept ideas drawn from this long discredited "translation."[13]

Augustus Le Plongeon, the first person to excavate Mayan sites in Yucatan, further developed Brassuer's ideas about Mu/Atlantis in the 1880s and 1890s.[14] He claimed to be able to decipher Mayan inscriptions, interpreting four of them as records of the destruction of Mu. Among these was the *Troano Codex,* which he "re-translated," adding details to Brasseur's intepretation and making it more readable:[15]

> The year six Kan, on the eleventh Muluc, in the month Zac, there occurred terrible earthquakes, which continued without intermission until the thirteenth Chuen. The country of the hills of mud, the "Land of Mu," was sacrificed. Being twice upheaved, it suddenly disappeared during the night, the basin being continually shaken by volcanic forces. Being confined, these caused the land to sink and rise several times and in various places. At last the surface gave way, and the ten countries were torn asunder and scattered in fragments; unable to withstand the force of the seismic convulsions, they sank with their sixty-four millions of inhabitants, eight thousand and sixty years before the writing of this book.

Le Plongeon further claimed that certain Mayan texts recounted the story of a princess named Moo. She married her brother Coh and together they ruled Yucatan. But another brother, Aac, killed Coh and seized the throne. Queen Moo tried to find refuge in some remnant of Mu, her ancestral home, but she could find no trace of it. She then continued on to the Muvian colony in Egypt where she built the Sphinx as a memorial to her dead husband. The Egyptians loved Queen Moo and eventually came to worship her as the goddess Isis.[16]

Both Brasseur de Bourbourg and Le Plongeon claimed that Mu was the Mayan name for Atlantis. But it soon came to be regarded as a shortened form of Lemuria, a lost continent in the Pacific. The idea of Lemuria was first suggested in the 1880s and 1890s by scientists trying to explain the distribution of lemurs, primitive monkey-like primates. They posited a continental mass embracing Africa and South America with a large peninsula extending from South America across the Indian Ocean to India. This continent was supposed to have existed millions of years ago and to have disappeared near the beginning of the Cenozoic Era, about one million years ago. It was Helena P. Blavatsky, however, who was responsible for bringing Lemuria into the orbit of Atlantists.[17] In *The Secret Doctrine* (6 vols., 1888-1936) Madame Blavatsky, a leading exponent of the occult, described Lemuria as the home of the Third "Root Race" to appear on earth. The Lemurians supposedly were apelike, egg-laying creatures, some with an eye in the back of their heads and some with four arms. The Fourth Root Race was the human-like population of Atlantis, and we are the Fifth. A later writer, James Churchward, moved Mu from the Indian Ocean to the central Pacific and claimed that Atlantis was just a colony of this older parent civilization.[18] Thus, many people came to believe in *two* lost continents, one in the Atlantic and one in the Pacific.

Ignatius Donnelly, a contemporary of Le Plongeon, also made use of Brasseur's translations, but Donnelly's book, *Atlantis: The Antediluvian World* (1882), became more famous than any of the works of Le Plongeon or of Brasseur himself. There were thirteen propositions whose validity Donnelly tried to demonstrate:[19]

1. That there once existed in the Atlantic Ocean, opposite the mouth of the Mediterranean Sea, a large island, which was the remnant of an Atlantic continent, and known to the ancient world as Atlantis.

2. That the description of this island given by Plato is not, as has been long supposed, fable, but veritable history.

3. That Atlantis was the region where man first rose from a state of barbarism to civilization.

4. That it became, in the course of ages, a populous and mighty nation, from whose overflowings the shores of the Gulf of Mexico, the Mississippi River, the Amazon, the Pacific coast of South America, the Mediterranean, the west coast of Europe and Africa, the Baltic, the Black Sea, and the Caspian were populated by civilized nations.

5. That it was the true Antediluvian world; the Garden of Eden; the Garden of the Hesperides . . . ; the Elysian fields . . . ; the Gardens of Alcinous . . . ; the Mesomphalos . . . ; the Mount Olympos . . . ; the Asgard . . . ; the focus of the traditions of the ancient nations; representing a universal memory of a great land, where early mankind dwelt for ages in peace and happiness.

6. That the gods and goddesses of the ancient Greeks, the Phoenicians, the Hindus, and the Scandinavians were simply the kings, queens, and heroes of Atlantis; and the acts attributed to them in mythology, a confused recollection of real historical events.

7. That the mythologies of Egypt and Peru represented the original religion of Atlantis, which was sun-worship.

8. That the oldest colony formed by the Atlanteans was probably in Egypt, whose civilization was a reproduction of that of the Atlantic island.

9. That the implements of the "Bronze Age" of Europe were derived from Atlantis. The Atlanteans were also the first manufacturers of iron.

10. That the Phoenician alphabet, parent of all the European alphabets, was derived from an Atlantis alphabet, which was also conveyed from Atlantis to the Mayas of Central America.

11. That Atlantis was the original seat of the Aryan or Indo-European family of nations, as well as of the Semitic peoples, and possibly also of the Tauranian races.

12. That Atlantis perished in a terrible convulsion of nature, in which the whole island was submerged by the ocean, with nearly all it inhabitants.

13. That a few persons escaped in ships and on rafts, and carried to the nations east and west the tidings of the appalling catastrophe, which has survived to our own time in the Flood and Deluge legends of the different nations of the Old and New Worlds.

In support of these theses Donnelly pointed to the existence of a mountain range below the Atlantic, the Mid-Atlantic Ridge, whose highest peaks rise above the surface of the sea to form the Azores. This submerged ridge, he claimed, was all that remained of the former continent of Atlantis. To prove that it was possible for an entire continent to vanish, he cited geological evidence that the present continents have been above and below the sea a number of times in the past, and that entire islands have been created or destroyed in a matter of hours by volcanic eruptions. Earthquakes have also caused great devastation and have been responsible for submerging coastal areas.[20]

Similarities in the flora and fauna of the Old and New Worlds, Donnelly argued, pointed to a place of common origin or to the existence of easy land communication between Europe and America such as would have existed when Atlantis occupied most of the area now covered by the Atlantic Ocean. He claimed that cotton, potatoes, maize, tobacco, guavas, and other plants were grown in both the New and Old Worlds before the time of Columbus.[21]

Deluge legends from around the world were compared and used to prove the historicity of the cataclysm that destroyed Atlantis.[22] And the origin of all civilization in Atlantis is supposedly demonstrated by cultural similarities between New and Old World civilizations and by anomalies within the individual civilizations. Donnelly claims that Egyptian civilization appeared suddenly in the Nile valley and was higher at its first appearance than at any subsequent period in its history; that the traditions of the Central American Indians point to an eastern origin for the peoples of Yucatan; that Central American monuments portray bearded men and negroes; that metallurgy, pyramids, obelisks, the arts, astronomy, and other cultural elements were the same in Old and New World civilizations; and that the Phoenician alphabet can be shown to be related to that of the Maya as recorded by Diego de Landa. He also stated that languages of the New and Old Worlds are related. Quichua (the language of the Incas of Peru) is supposedly an Indo-European tongue, and Le Plongeon was favorably quoted as saying that "one third of this [Mayan] tongue is pure Greek." Chiapanec (a Central American language) resembled Hebrew, according to Donnelly; Chinese he related to Chaldean (ancient Assyrian and Babylonian) as well as to the Otomi language of Mexico; the Choctaw, Chickasaw, Muscogee, and Seminole tongues seemed similar to the Ural-Altaic family of languages in Europe; and so on.[23]

Even though virtually all of Donnelly's theses and the arguments supporting them have been shown to be wrong, they have remained at the heart of almost all later works championing the existence of Atlantis. Moderate Atlantists, such as Lewis Spence, abandoned Donnelly's linguistic "evidence" and concentrated on the arguments stemming from flora and fauna, as well as those based on cultural similarities between different civilizations. But Donnelly's influence has been so great that some modern works continue to repeat his claims about connections between New and Old World languages even though these have been totally disproved by linguistic study. For example, Alexander Braghine states that the Otomi Indians of Mexico "speak the old Japanese idiom [*sic*. Donnelly claimed it was Chinese], and once when the Japanese ambassador to Mexico visited this tribe he talked with them in this old dialect."[24] And Otto Muck agrees with Braghine in relating both Japanese and Otomi to Basque and to the Georgian dialect of southern Russia.[25] Even Charles Berlitz, a writer who recognizes that almost all of Donnelly's linguistic claims are invalid, argues that the occurrence in different languages of a few words with similar sounds and meanings indicates that many languages contain dim traces of the antediluvian speech of Atlantis.[26]

Did an Atlantic Continent Sink?

How valid is the evidence used to prove the existence of Atlantis? Was Plato's account of Atlantis an essentially factual recollection of a historical situation, a confused and legendary reflection of earlier events, or an allegorical myth created by Plato's imagination?

Modern geological and archaeological evidence makes the first of these alternatives untenable. Geologists have discovered that the ocean bottoms are composed primarily of basalt, while continental land masses are essentially granite.[27] A sunken continent, therefore, should be detectable by its geological composition. But after much testing and study, geologists have concluded that "nowhere in the ocean basins is there any sign of a large mass of continental-type crust which could represent a submerged continent."[28] This statement rules out the existence of a Pacific Mu as well as Atlantis.

The Mid-Atlantic Ridge is not evidence of a sunken land mass, as Donnelly and other Atantists have argued. Rather, it is a relatively recent feature, still being built up from the ocean floor. There is now much evidence showing that the present continents are slowly drifting apart. As the huge "plates" on which the land masses rest move away from one another, new material from deep within the earth's mantle surges upward through the crack between them. This process has produced the Mid-Atlantic Ridge.[29]

In 1898, some five hundred miles north of the Azores, a ship dredged up splinters of basaltic glass called tachylite from a depth of 1700 fathoms

(10,200 feet). At that time it was believed that this type of vitreous lava could be formed only under atmospheric pressure. Thus, the lava from which the samples had come must have been extruded at the surface and only later submerged. Atlantists use this evidence to show that the Mid-Atlantic Ridge was once above the ocean's surface, but has sunk nearly two miles in relatively recent times.[30] However, it has been proved that it is the rate of cooling, not pressure, that is significant in determining whether or not tachylite will form from a basaltic lava flow. Lava extruded into cold water forms glassy rock (tachylite) just as lava meeting cold air does. There is no reason to suppose that the tachylite dredged up in 1898 was produced anywhere other than where it was found, under 10,000 feet of water.[31]

If Atlantis had occupied much of the North Atlantic until some 11,600 years ago, the ocean bottom that was once the continent should be covered by only a very thin layer of marine sediment. But samples of the Atlantic's floor obtained by drilling show deposits 2,600 feet thick. And study of organisms in the lowest layers of these sediments indicate that they were deposited before the end of the Cretaceous Period, some 63 million years ago. The Mid-Atlantic Ridge itself has been part of the ocean floor for at least the last 72,500 years. This date was obtained from deposits found 812 miles east of Newfoundland.[32] It is also interesting that all of the sampling and dredging of the North Atlantic floor has produced no artifacts, traces of buildings, or other signs of civilization.

There is also no known geological force that could destroy a continent in the short time described by Plato. Atlantists point out that there is much evidence that the present-day continents have risen and sunk many times in the past. And they note examples of land being suddenly submerged as a result of earthquakes or volcanic activity. However, these points, while valid, do not support the theory of a sudden collapse of an extremely large island. Geological evidence, particularly the fossil record, indicates that the rise and fall of large land masses is a very slow process occurring over millions of years. On the other hand, the sudden destruction or submergence of land areas by earthquakes or volcanoes is limited in extent. Past examples have seldom caused a loss of more than fifty or sixty square miles of territory at a time.[33]

The rise in sea level due to the melting of glaciers at the end of the Ice Age was also too slow to account for Plato's story of the destruction of Atlantis. The retreat of the glaciers and the slow rise in sea level took place over a few thousand years.[34] This was certainly no catastrophic event. Many areas which had been dry land were flooded as the level of the oceans rose. But even if there had been a low-lying island in the Atlantic at the time, its inhabitants would have had lots of time to flee the waters that rose at a rate of only a few inches a year. Recent theories that rapid melting of one or more glaciers produced a surge of melting water that suddenly raised sea level by a foot or so a year have been shown to be groundless. The evidence indicates that the melting took place over several years (which is "rapid" by geological standards), and that the added rise in sea level was probably no more than a fraction of an inch a year.[35] Even a sudden rise of a foot or two in ocean levels, however, would not account for Plato's story of the complete destruction of Atlantis, which contained high mountains as well as large plains.

No known geological forces can account for the sudden destruction of a continent, but astronomical forces might. Through the years a number of writers have suggested that a collision or near-collision between earth and a heavenly body (variously described as an asteroid, meteorite, moon, or comet) caused the destruction of Atlantis.[36] The evidence that earth has experienced cosmic collisions in historical times is usually drawn from interpretations of myths, legends, and folklore of many peoples around the world. This evidence is highly suspect and will be considered in Chapter 3. Here we need only note that there is doubt whether any life on earth would have survived a collision powerful enough to sink a continent-sized island. But since there are no traces of a sunken continent in any of the ocean basins, the question is moot.

Geological evidence against an Atlantic site for Atlantis also negates arguments based on cultural similarities and connections between the flora and fauna on both sides of the ocean. However, scholars have long recognized that these arguments are not valid proofs of the existence of Atlantis. Many of the supposed connections simply do not exist. No American Indian language is directly related to Chinese, Japanese, Basque, Hebrew, or any other Old World tongue. Native New and Old World cotton-plants do not belong to the same species. The hieroglyphic writing of the Maya of Central America was not alphabetic. It is totally unrelated to the ancient Phoenician alphabetic script, yet both were supposedly derived from Atlantean writing. The Inca culture of Peru also supposedly descended from Atlantean civilization, but the Incas did not have any writing system at all![37] Atlantists point to cultural features that seem similar, and they assert connections, but they usually ignore differences that are far more significant that the supposed similarities.[38] If civilization in both hemispheres derived from the original (and higher) civilization of Atlantis, why did Old World Cutures have the plow and potter's wheel, while both were unknown in the Americas? And if the pyramids of the Mayas, Aztecs, Egyptians, and Mesopotamians all go back to Atlantean prototypes, why did the American examples appear hundreds of years later than the ancient Near Eastern structures? Whatever similarities there are between the cultures or the flora and fauna of the New and Old Worlds can be explained without recourse to the hypothesis of a lost continent and a vanished parent civilization.[39] Chapter 1 has already discussed the supposed interrelationship of flood stories from around the world; other alleged connections between the eastern and western hemispheres will be treated in Chapters 5 and 6.

Atlantis and the Eruption of Thera

There is no valid evidence supporting the existence of an Atlantic island civilization, and the geological evidence is strongly opposed to such a hypothesis. But if Plato's account cannot be accepted as literally true, could it not be a legendary reflection of earlier happenings? Could it not contain a kernel of truth, overlaid with anachronistic details or errors due to the faulty knowledge of those who transmitted the tale?

Many Atlantists have taken this position, changing one part or another of Plato's account to suit their theories. Lewis Spence, for instance, recognized that no bronze-using civilization such as that described in the *Timaeus* and *Critias* existed c. 9600 B.C., the date Plato gives for the destruction of Atlantis.[40] Instead, he identified the Atlanteans with the Cro-Magnon Aurignacian culture of the Paleolithic Period (the Old Stone Age), positing a series of migrations from Atlantis to Europe starting 25,000 years ago and ending some 10,000 years ago when Atlantis was destroyed.[41] The American Indians, he claimed, also migrated from Atlantis by way of Antilia, supposedly a southern remnant of the continent, portions of which survive today as the West Indies.[42]

But changing Plato's dates and demoting the Atlantean civilization to an advanced Stone Age culture while leaving Atlantis in the Atlantic does not meet the geological objections. Other writers have chosen a different course. They usually retain the concept of a highly civilized Atlantis, but change the location. North America, Central America, South America, North Africa, South Africa, Palestine, Crete, Malta, Spain, central France, Spitsbergen, Sweden, the British Isles, Belgium, East Prussia, Greenland, Mongolia, Australia, Ceylon, and the Arctic are among the places that have been proposed as the real site of Atlantis.[43] Bimini and the Bermuda Triangle are the lastest additions to the list.[44] Such theories, of course, are very subjective and selective. Proponents choose whatever parts of Plato's account they wish to believe or whichever ones fit their chosen location and reject the rest as distortion or myth.

Recently, however, one such theory has attracted considerable scholarly support because it includes the essentials of Plato's tale—a vanished civilization and a sunken island—as well as providing an explanation for the way the story might have come to be misunderstood by Plato. This hypothesis states that the Atlantis legend derives from Egyptian accounts of the explosion of the volcanic island of Thera in the Aegean and the destruction of Minoan civilization on Crete caused by this catastophe.[45]

Thera (or Santorini as it is also known), the southernmost of the Cyclades, lies about seventy miles to the north of Crete. The island—or group of islands, since it now consists of one large and four smaller islands around and within a great bay—was once a single, large volcanic cone ten or twelve miles in diameter. At some time in the past it exploded, blowing out millions of tons of material from its interior. The central part of the crater then collapsed into the empty chamber beneath the volcano, creating the bay (or caldera, as it is known to science) surrounded by a broken circle of cliffs—the remnants of the volcano's flanks (see Figure 2).

It has long been known that about 1450 B.C. a great calamity befell the Minoan civilization on Crete. The towns and palaces, with the exception of Knossos, were burned, and most were abandoned.[46] Early in the twentieth century, the classical scholar K. T. Frost suggested that this sudden destruction of the Minoan civilization formed the reality behind the later legend of Atlantis.[47] This theory was strengthened in 1939 by the hypothesis of Spyridon Marinatos, a Greek archaeologist who argued that the ancient eruption of Thera and the earthquakes and tidal waves that must have accompanied it had caused the destruction of the palaces and towns of Crete.[48] It was an attractive idea, but there was little hard evidence to back it up, and few scholars were convinced.

In the two decades following World War II, however, evidence supporting Marinatos's theory about Thera began to accumulate. Swedish and American oceanographic research teams studying the sediments on the sea bottom in the eastern Mediterranean discovered two layers of volcanic ash, which they traced to Thera. The lower layer was dated to an eruption that had taken place about 23,000 B.C. But the upper layer came from an eruption that radiocarbon dating placed later than 3000 B.C., that is, at some time during the Aegean Bronze Age. The ash from this second eruption was found covering a large area of the eastern Mediterranean, including the Cyclades and most of Crete. Only the westernmost fourth of the island seems to have escaped the ash-fall.[49]

Scientists studying cores from the Mediterranean floor and the volcanic deposits on Thera itself noted that a series of minor eruptions had preceded the great explosion and collapse of the volcano. The closest parallel to the Thera eruption they could find in modern times was the 1883 eruption of Krakatoa in the Sunda Strait between Java and Sumatra. Like Thera, much of the island of Krakatoa collapsed during its eruption, creating a deep caldera surrounded by small islands.

The well-documented Krakatoa eruption enabled vulcanologists to draw conclusions about what might have happened during Thera's explosion. Severe earthquakes jolted the area around Krakatoa for six or seven years prior to the eruption. Then on May 20, 1883, the volcano burst into life. From May until August there were a series of violent eruptions that showered pumice and ash over a large area. The climax came on August 27 with four tremendous explosions that were heard 2,000 miles away in Australia. A great pall of darkness (caused by the vapors and fine ash ejected from the volcano) spread outward over large areas of Java and Sumatra. Shock waves of the blasts broke windows and cracked walls of masonry buildings a hundred miles away. In its final paroxysm, two-thirds of Krakatoa collapsed into the sea, sending fifty to a hundred-foot high *tsunamis* (or tidal waves) racing through the straits to destroy nearly three hundred villages and drown 36,000 people.[50]

Thera's caldera is four times larger than that of Krakatoa and more than 30 percent deeper. Thus, the explosion of Thera might well have been considerably more violent than that of the Pacific volcano. Certainly such an eruption could have damaged areas of Crete, only seventy miles to the south. But did the explosion occur at the same time as the destruction of the Minoan centers? The answer lay hidden in the ruins of a Minoan town on Thera buried by the eruption.

Marinatos began excavating at Akrotiri on Thera in 1967. He uncovered a number of houses and much pottery, including some imported vases from Crete. The style of pottery in use on Thera at the time of the eruption is called by archaelogists "Late Minoan I A,"[51] and it is generally dated to the period between c. 1550 and 1500 B.C. Such a date for the eruption also seems indicated by a radiocarbon date of 1559 B.C. ± 44 years, which was obtained from the remains of a tree killed during the first stage of the volcano's activity.[52]

Thus, some time around or shortly before 1500 B.C. Thera burst from its dormant state. At that time the settlement on the island was abandoned and a layer of pumice nearly fifteen feet thick was spread over the ruins (Figure 2, B). Then the volcano quieted down for an unknown length of time—at least long enough for the pumice layer to show some signs of erosion. Thera resumed its activity with five small eruptions over a period of some weeks or months. Finally, the great explosion occurred, depositing a layer of fine white volcanic ash up to two hundred feet thick over the island (Figure 2, C). At the end of this explosion a large portion of the volcano fell into its empty chamber beneath the sea (Figure 2, D-E). This last eruption was the one thought to be responsible for the destruction of the Minoan centers on Crete.[54]

During the Minoan period, Egypt was engaged in trade with Crete (which the Egyptians seem to have called "Keftiu"). When news of the eruption and collapse of Thera reached Egypt, along with stories about draw conclusions about what might have happened during Thera's explosion. Severe earthquakes jolted the area around Krakatoa for six or seven years prior to the eruption. Then on May 20, 1883, the volcano burst into life. From May until August there were a series of violent eruptions that showered pumice and ash over a large area. The climax came on August 27 with four tremendous explosions that were heard 2,000 miles away in Australia. A great pall of darkness (caused by the vapors and fine ash ejected from the volcano) spread outward over large areas of Java and Sumatra. Shock waves of the blasts broke windows and cracked walls of masonry buildings a hundred miles away. In its final paroxysm, two-thirds of Krakatoa collapsed into the sea, sending fifty- to a hundred-foot-high *tsunamis* (or tidal waves) racing through the straits to destroy nearly three hundred villages and drown 36,000 people.[50]

Thera's caldera is four times larger than that of Krakatoa and more than 30 percent deeper. Thus, the explosion of Thera might well have been considerably more violent than that of the Pacific volcano. Certainly such an eruption could have damaged areas of Crete, only seventy miles to the south. But did the explosion occur at the same time as the destruction of the Minoan centers? The answer lay hidden in the ruins of a Minoan town on Thera buried by the eruption.

Marinatos began excavating at Akrotiri on Thera in 1967. He uncovered a number of houses and much pottery, including some imported vases from Crete. The style of pottery in use on Thera at the time of the eruption is called by archaelogists "Late Minoan I A,"[51] and it is generally dated to the period between c. 1550 and 1500 B.C. Such a date for the eruption also seems indicated by a radiocarbon date of 1559 B.C. ± 44 years, which was obtained from the remains of a tree killed during the first stage of the volcano's activity.[52]

Thus, some time around or shortly before 1500 B.C. Thera burst from its dormant state. At that time the settlement on the island was abandoned and a layer of pumice nearly fifteen feet thick was spread over the ruins (Figure 2, B). Then the volcano quieted down for an unknown length of time—at least long enough for the pumice layer to show some signs of erosion. Thera resumed its activity with five small eruptions over a period of some weeks or months. Finally, the great explosion occurred, depositing a layer of fine white volcanic ash up to two hundred feet thick over the island (Figure 2, C). At the end of this explosion a large portion of the volcano fell into its empty chamber beneath the sea (Figure 2, D-E). This last eruption was the one thought to be responsible for the destruction of the Minoan centers on Crete.[54]

During the Minoan period, Egypt was engaged in trade with Crete (which the Egyptians seem to have called "Keftiu"). When news of the eruption and collapse of Thera reached Egypt, along with stories about the destruction of Minoan towns and palaces, the Egyptians possibly got the mistaken idea that the entire island of Crete had vanished. Later the story could have been related to Solon, and a translation error might have caused all of the numbers to be increased tenfold. So instead of 900 years before Solon's time, that is, c. 1500–1450 B.C., the date of the destruction was handed down to Plato as *9,000* years before Solon, and the size of the island was similarly enlarged.[55] Perhaps the location of the lost island civilization also became confused due to differences between the Egyptians and Solon over the meaing of "west".[56] Or Plato, realizing that such a large island could not have existed in the Mediterranean, himself might have moved Atlantis outside the "Pillars of Herakles" (the Strait of Gibraltar) into the Atlantic Ocean.[57] In addition, the Greeks possibly retained dim memories of the effects of the Thera eruption in traditions about a great flood survived by Deucalion and his wife, about Poseidon flooding Attica, the Argolid, and other parts of Greece, about floating islands, and about a bronze giant named Talos who hurls fragments of stone at approaching ships.[58]

This theory is very attractive, but it has problems that are difficult to overcome. The first difficulty is that while the explosion of Thera must have had some harmful effects on Crete, it was not necessarily as catastrophic as Galanopoulos, Luce, Marinatos, and others have claimed. The evidence from sea cores indicates that an average of only 0.5 to 2.5 inches of ash fell on eastern Crete (Figure 3). But the ashfall would not have been uniformly thick. It would have collected in drifts, like snow, and eventually it would have been washed into the sea by rain. This ashfall must have ruined some Minoan crops and disrupted life for a time, maybe for as long as a year or two, but it probably was not enough to cause long-term damage to the Minoan agricultural economy.[59]

Furthermore, the earthquakes accompanying the eruption were probably not as severe as theorized. Volcanic earthquakes are usually very weak and are felt only in the vicinity of the erupting volcano. Damage to the Minoan centers on Crete would have had to be caused by a movement of the earth's crust which happened to coincide with the eruption of Thera. But it is unlikely that a single strong earthquake shock could have damaged virtually every site in eastern Crete, but spared Knossos.[60]

The most frightful destruction on Crete, though, is usually credited to *tsunamis*. These sea waves produced by the sudden displacement of large volumes of water must have accompanied the eruption, but they probably did not cause the amount of damage often attributed to them. Estimates that gigantic *tsunamis* were produced by Thera are based on the assumption that all of the material from the central part of the volcano collapsed into the sea at the same time. But that assumption is not likely to be correct.[61] It is unknown how rapid the collapse was, and

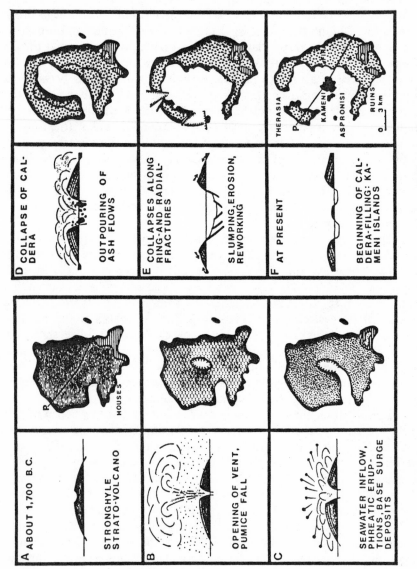

FIGURE 2. Phases of the Minoan eruption of Thera (after Pichler and Friedrich 1980: 17)

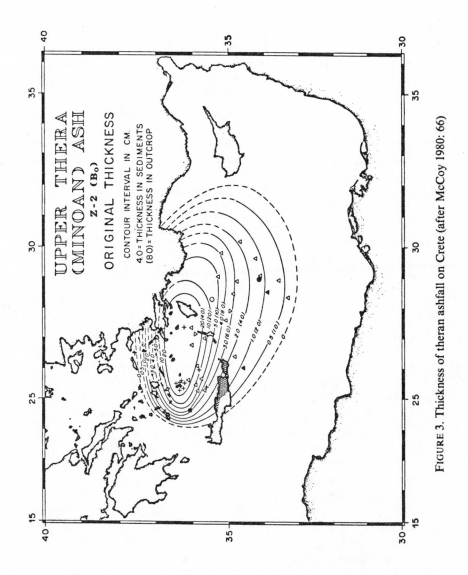

FIGURE 3. Thickness of theran ashfall on Crete (after McCoy 1980: 66)

the size of any *tsunamis* generated depends upon the amount of material falling into the sea at any given time. If the collapse occurred in stages spread out over a number of hours, days, weeks, or even months or years (and experience with other volcanoes has shown that this is more probable than a sudden total collapse), the effect of any waves produced could have been almost imperceptible on Crete. Even if the waves were quite large, they would not have attained the same height at all points along the Cretan shore. Phaistos on the south coast, for instance, should have had little damage from *tsunamis*. Even on the north coast evidence from Amnisos indicates that the *tsunamis* reached a height of only 19.5-26 feet.[62] Thus, it is highly improbable that *tsunamis* could have been responsible for destroying all of the Minoan ports and the entire fleet.[63]

There are also questions about the alleged similarities between Plato's description of Atlantean civilization and the Minoan culture on Crete. The bull-catching ritual described by Plato is more like a ceremony depicted on Egyptian reliefs than like Minoan bull-leaping or the capture of wild bulls shown on two Minoan cups found at Vaphio.[64] And acceptance of a connection between Plato's account of imperialistic, maritime Atlantis and Minoan Crete requires that one believe that the Minoans controlled a sea empire. This view, once widely held, has come under greater and greater attack.[65] There is little solid evidence for a Minoan thalassocracy (rule of the sea), so it can no longer be confidently assumed that this is one area where Minoan civilization clearly fits Plato's picture of Atlantis. Plato's physical description of Atlantis does not fit Crete, the date he gives is wrong, and his account of the Atlantean capital city does not resemble Thera, Knossos, or any other Minoan site. "Just what is supposed to be left of the original Plato after the Thera proponents finish with their 'corrections' of the text? Certainly nothing in Plato's accounts relates explicitly or directly to the volcano theory at all; only by radically *altering* Plato can his two texts be made to correspond here and there to the preformed Thera hypothesis."[66]

The greatest problem for the Thera hypothesis, however, is a chronological one. The Late Minoan I B "Marine Style"—a type of pottery characterized by lively decoration featuring dolphins, starfish, shells, octopuses, and other sea creatures—was not found on Thera. However, the mature phase of this type of pottery was in use in Crete when the palaces and towns were destroyed. Since the development and spread of a pottery style takes some time, the end of Late Minoan I B is usually placed about 1470-1450 B.C., thirty to fifty years after the end of Late Minoan I A. Thus, those who credit the destruction of Minoan civilization to the eruption of Thera must spread that eruption over a generation or two. But recent studies of Thera by vulcanologists have led them to assert that the quiescent phase between the beginning of the eruption and the renewed activity that culminated in the final explosion lasted only a few weeks or months. It possibly might have been as long as a year or two, but no more. The pumice layer deposited in the initial eruption shows signs of erosion, but no top-soil had yet been formed. Therefore, it is unlikely that the pumice layer was open to the elements and undergoing active weathering for as much as thirty or fifty years before being covered by ashfall from the climactic phases of the eruption.[67] As with Krakatoa, the whole volcanic episode from the initial blast to the final cataclysm probably occupied a time-span of six months or less.

John Luce and Phyllis Forsyth have attempted to deal with this geological evidence by suggesting that the Late Minoan I A pottery found on Thera was contemporaneous with the Late Minoan I B material on Crete. A few vessels that were excavated on Thera were decorated with dolphins. Luce and Forsyth argue that these represent the vanguard of the "Marine Style" of Late Minoan I B pottery. The developed Late Minoan I B style had already appeared on Crete (though it was rare even there), but no examples of it had yet reached Thera when the eruption occurred. Or, perhaps the few Late Minoan I B vessels on Thera were deemed so precious that they were carried away when the inhabitants fled the island. Thus, there would have been only one eruption, as the vulcanologists contend, but it would have occurred c. 1470 or 1450 B.C. rather than 1500 B.C.[68]

This revised Thera hypothesis is not very convincing. It is difficult to believe that there would have been much of a time lag between the development of a pottery style on Crete and its appearance on Thera, only seventy miles away. Pottery, frescoes, and other artifacts uncovered on Thera point to a close relationship and frequent contact between the settlement on the volcanic island and the Minoan centers on Crete. Moreover, "Marine Style" pottery has been found on Keos, an island smaller than Thera, and on Rhodes, which is much further away from Crete.[69] The Minoan settlements on those islands were destroyed while Late Minoan I B pottery was in use, as was the case with the palaces and towns of Crete. If the Thera eruption destroyed the Minoan towns on Keos and Rhodes as on Crete, why did they contain Late Minoan I B vessels while the settlement on Thera did not?

But a more telling point against any equation of the Theran Late Minoan I A period with the Cretan Late Minoan I B era comes from material once used by supporters of the Thera hypothesis to prove a two-phase eruption of the volcano. At Zakros, in extreme eastern Crete, one room of the palace was found filled with pieces of pumice and votive offerings. A similar deposit had been found earlier at Amnisos.[70] Another votive deposit was uncovered at Nirou Khani, a site on the coast some eight miles east of Heraklion: A number of Late Minoan I A cups filled with lumps of pumice had been buried under the threshold of a doorway into a shrine.[71] These collections of pumice indicate that an eruption of Thera had occurred, and it had given people in Crete reason to fearthe wrath of the gods. Now if the theory of Luce and Forsyth was correct—if the eruption took place c. 1470-1450 B.C., when Late Minoan I B pottery was in use on Crete but Late Minoan I A vessels were still being used on Thera—one would expect that at least one or more Late Minoan I B objects would be found with these offerings on Crete. But they were not. These votive deposits were in pure Late Minoan I A contexts. Further-more, geologists have identified volcanic ash particles in a Late Minoan I A deposit at Zakros sealed *beneath* Late Minoan I B remains.[72] The inescapable conclusion to be drawn is that the eruption of Thera occurred when pure Late Minoan I A pottery was in use on Crete as on Thera, and that the Late Minoan I B style developed *after* the collapse of the volcanic island.

The dates for the eruption and for the destruction of the palaces in Crete simply do not coincide. Thera exploded at the end of Late Minoan I A, about 1500 B.C. While some of the palaces seem to have been damaged at that time, the destruction was not final. The damage was soon repaired and the Minoan towns and palaces continued to exist for at least another generation—until the end of the Late Minoan I B Period, c. 1470-1450 B.C., Whatever destruction the eruption of Thera caused in Crete, it could not have been as extensive nor as final as the supporters of the Thera hypothesis claim.

Since Minoan civilization did not suddenly vanish at the time of the eruption of Thera, it is difficult to see how or why the Egyptians would have created an account connecting the two events. Furthermore, nothing in Egyptian texts that mention Keftiu indicates that Egyptians had the kind of detailed knowledge of the Aegean and its cultures to form the background for an account like that of Atlantis. The Egyptians seem to have lumped the Minoans and Mycenaeans together, and probably both were designated as Keftiu people. Men from Keftiu continued to appear as tribute-bearing vassals in lists from the reigns of Amenhotep III (c. 1405-1367 B.C.) and Rameses II (c. 1304-1237 B.C.), long after the destruc-tion of the Minoan centers. It has been argued that these late lists are simply copies of more genuine lists of earlier times.[73] But even so, they prove that there could have been no tradition in Egypt that Keftiu (Crete/Atlantis) had been destroyed by natural convulsions at the time of Thutmose III (c. 1504-1450 B.C.). Propagandistic lists of vassals, even if semi-fictional, were *meant* to be believed! How could anyone be expected to believe that men of Keftiu had brought tribute to Amenhotep III or Rameses II if it were known that Keftiu had ceased to exist long before that time? Egypt obviously had no tradition of a lost civilization in the

Aegean.

When the Greek historian Herodotus visited the Nile valley in the fifth century B.C., he questioned the priests about ancient events. Yet none of the stories he claims they told him resembles a tradition about the end of Minoan Crete or the destruction of Atlantis. He almost certainly would have recorded such an account if he had heard one.

Like other theories attempting to demythologize Plato's account of Atlantis, the Thera hypothesis should be abandoned. While it is a bit more plausible than most theories that argue for a core of ancient tradition in the Atlantis narratives, its primary contentions are not supported by the evidence. Minoan civilization was not destroyed by the effects of the volcanic eruption of Thera, and if it had been, the Egyptians probably wouldn't have noticed. We are left with the third possible explanation for Plato's story—he made it up.

Atlantis in the Context of Plato's Writings

Would Plato have invented the entire tale of Atlantis and then claimed it was true? No, say Atlantists, both those who believe in the absolute validity of Plato's account and those who accept it as a legend which developed around a historical core. John Luce's statement is typical: "'Listen to my story,' says Critias (*Timaeus* 20d), 'it is strange but absolutely true.' Would Plato have introduced the tale in such a way if he had known it to be entirely without historical foundation? I do not think he would."[74]

But such statements ignore the fact that Plato used myths throughout his works, and openly defended the practice. In the *Republic,* while discussing falsehood as foreign to the gods, Plato has Socrates accept the occasional necessity of using literal falsehood to attain some good end. For example, he argues, it is certainly acceptable to deceive enemies during wartime, or to lie to keep a madman from injuring himself. Then he goes on to defend the use of literal falsehood in edifying myths: "In the fables of which we were just now speaking, owing to our ignorance of the truth about antiquity, we liken the false to the true as far as we may and so make it edifying."[75]

Virtually every myth Plato relates in his dialogues is introduced by a statement claiming it is true. As J. A. Stewart has pointed out, "it is of the very essence of a Myth to represent as having a history in time what in itself is out of time."[76] By the use of statements which are literally false, Plato intends to convey to his readers concepts that he regards as true.[77] So his insistence on the truth of the stories he tells is a normal literary device on the surface, but at a deeper level it represents Plato's conviction of the symbolical validity of the accounts.

In introducing a story about final judgment, the Isles of the Blessed and Tartarus (the Greek equivalents of Heaven and Hell), in his dialogue *Georgias,* Plato has Socrates say: "Give ear then, as they say, to a very fine story, which you, I suppose, will consider fiction, but I consider fact, for what I am going to tell you I shall recount as the actual truth."[78] At the end of the Myth of Er, which relates how a man returned from the dead to tell of the afterlife, Plato's Socrates states that "the tale was saved, as the saying is, and was not lost. And it will save us if we believe it."[79] Elsewhere, while describing the place above heaven where immortal souls go, Plato writes that "assuredly we must be bold to speak what is true, above all when our discourse is upon truth."[80] And Plato gives still another myth about the immortality and reincarnation of souls in *Meno* where he has Socrates introduce the story by saying that it is "something true . . . and fine" which he received on the authority of "priests and priestesses of the sort who make it their business to be able to account for the functions which they perform."[81]

Plato also tells of cycles in history interrupted by changes in the earth's revolution; they produce earthquakelike tremors that only a remnant of the human race survive. When the earth runs on its own, men grow old and die. But at the end of that cycle God rewinds the earth in the opposite direction, and those who survive the change in direction become progressively younger until they return to the earth from which they are resurrected to begin life anew. The era before the present one was such a Golden Age—there were no political constitutions, there was no need to work, the gods ruled and provided for man's needs.[82] At the end of that era descendants of the resurrected individuals "passed on to us these stories of the earthborn, and it is an unsound judgment to disbelieve them as so many do nowadays."[83] Another picture of the Golden Age is given in Plato's last dialogue, *Laws.*[84]

Did Plato expect his readers to accept *all* of these stories as historical fact or reliable tradition? He usually describes them with the term *muthos* (myth), which meant an invented story, fable, tale, or legend. Yet he makes the same kinds of statements about their truth that he does about the Atlantis narratives. And he often credits these accounts to reliable sources just as he does with the story of Atlantis. But taken on a literal basis, many of these stories contradict one another. The details in the story of the final judgment in *Georgias* are not the same as those in the much longer Myth of Er in the *Republic.* And both disagree with descriptions of the afterlife given in the *Phaedrus* and *Meno.* The accounts of man's primeval past in *Timaeus* and *Critias* (the Atlantis story), *Statesman,* and *Laws* are all different.

Surely Plato was aware of such discrepancies, yet he insists on the truth of each story. Either he deliberately lied to his readers (and thought they would be too stupid to notice the contradictions), or he expected them to recognize that these stories were parables or allegories whose "truth" did not rest on literal acceptance of the accounts themselves. The Atlantis story is of the same type as the others. Like them it includes supernatural events and describes the actions of divine as well as human beings. On what basis, then, is one justified in insisting on the historical reliability of the Atlantis narratives, while treating the others as myths or creations of Plato's imagination?

But why would Plato invent the tale of Atlantis? The answer lies in the context in which it was placed. The Atlantis story occurs in two dialogues of a projected trilogy. The purpose of this trilogy seems to have been to place Plato's ideal state in a historical setting and to show the superiority of its institutions in action. At the beginning of *Timaeus,* Socrates briefly outlines the nature of the ideal state (which he supposedly had been discussing with Timaeus, Critias, and Hermocrates the day before), and then comments that he would like to observe such a state in a real situation: "I should like to hear an account of her putting forth her strength in such contests as a city will engage in against others, going to war in a manner worthy of her, and in that war achieving results befitting her training and education, both in feats of arms and in negotiations with various other states."[85] It is then that Critias announces that the previous day's discussion had caused him to remember Solon's story of early Athens and its conflict with Atlantis.

The *Timaeus* forms the general introduction to the trilogy and provides background by describing the creation of the world and man. Then the *Critias* takes up the main theme by relating the events of primeval history supposedly told to Solon by an Egyptian priest. Here was a kind of Golden Age with two different types of states founded by different gods. One state, Athens, is just like the ideal commonwealth described by Socrates. It is a small, virtuous, agricultural community ruled by Guardians who live a totally communistic life. The other government, Atlantis, is a large, commercial, imperialistic monarchy. Atlantis became progressively degenerate (as Plato believed any imperialistic and mercantile state must) until the gods decided it had to be destroyed. The dialogue was not completed, but the outline of the story in *Timaeus* indicates that Athens alone would have stood up to this gigantic evil power, and by its valor prevented the conquest of the entire eastern Mediterranean. Then natural catastrophes would have destroyed Atlantis and ended this era of man's past. Only a few shepherds in the mountains would have survived the floods (except in Egypt), and all Greek civilization would have been lost.

The last volume in the series, *Hermocrates,* was never written, so its proposed contents can only be surmised. But F. M. Cornford's conjecture is probably not far off the mark: "Taking up the story at this point, what could Hermocrates do, if not describe the re-emergence of culture in the Greece of prehistoric and historic times?"[86] However, instead of finishing the *Critias* and writing the *Hermocrates,* Plato wrote *Laws.* Perhaps he had written himself into a corner with the Atlantis tale and didn't know how to end it in a way that furthered his overall scheme.[87] Or perhaps he felt death stalking him and realized he didn't have time to finish the *Critias* and then write another dialogue. So he abandoned the *Critias* and scrapped the trilogy, writing instead the *Laws,* which in one dialogue realized the purposes of the proposed three.[88]

In *Laws* Plato presents a theory of recurrent catastrophes which only a few men survive. After the last Deluge man had to start over again, first going through an idyllic "noble savage" phase before gradually discovering metals, agriculture, and sedentary existence. After describing the emergence of cities and different kinds of governments, Plato arrives at the beginning of history as the Greeks knew it. He then analyzes this account of man's development to determine what laws should go into the makeup of an ideal, but realizable, city-state. This is probably the end he had intended for the *Hermocrates.*[89]

Through the ages it has been Plato's description of Atlantis that has captured readers' imaginations, but Athens was supposed to be the star of the account. Atlantis was intended to be the villainous foil that, by contrast, would show off early Athens's virtues. But most of those who claim some truth for the Atlantis story ignore Plato's picture of prehistoric Athens. The fact that early Athens was so similar to Socrates' ideal state was supposedly what reminded Critias of the entire story that he had been told as a child. Thus, without Athens's part in the narrative there would have been no Atlantis account. Yet few would claim that there really was a civilized Athens in 9600 B.C., with a government like that delineated in the *Republic.* For some reason, Plato's description of early Athens can be considered imaginary, while his account of Atlantis is accepted as fact!

Plato's Sources for the Atlantis Story

It is sometimes claimed that the account of Atlantis is so realistic that Plato could not have invented it. But there is nothing in the story which cannot be credited to the work of a creative imagination utilzing the geographical and scientific knowledge of Plato's time.

Plato's belief in periodic catastrophes that destroyed civilization was a rationalistic approach to ancient myths and legends like the story of Deucalion and the Flood or of Phaethon bringing the sun too close to the earth. It was part of the "scientific" approach of Plato's day.[90] And during Plato's lifetime, local natural disasters had been responsible for devastating small islands and cities. In 426 B.C. severe earthquakes rocked much of Greece.[91]

> At Orobiae in Euboea the sea subsided from what was then the shore and afterwards swept up again in a huge wave, which covered part of the city and left some of it still under water when the wave retreated, so that what was once land is now sea. Those of the inhabitants who were unable to escape in time by running up to the high ground were lost in the flood. An inundation of the same kind took place at Atalanta, the island off the coast of Opuntian Locris; here part of the Athenian fortifications were swept away and one of two ships that were drawn up on the beach was broken to pieces.

Then in 373 B.C. Helice, Bura, and Aegira, three communities on the Gulf of Corinth, were submerged as a result of an earthquake. Knowledge of such disasters combined with the theory of catastrophism could easily have been responsible for Plato's account of the sudden destruction of Atlantis by earthquakes and floods.[92]

Plato's description of the Atlantic was also based on the limited information available in his time. Greek knowledge of the world had steadily expanded until by the fourth century it embraced most of the Near East and Mediterranean, but the Altantic was still an unknown area.[93] The Carthaginians, who controlled the western Mediterranean from the sixth through the third centuries B.C., kept most Greek ships away from Spain and the Strait of Gibraltar. Probably Carthaginians also were responsible for spreading stories among the Greeks that the Atlantic was not navigable. A contemporary of Plato who wrote under the name of Scylax of Karyanda described the area outside the Pillars of Herakles as a great gulf ringed with reefs just below the surface. And the sea beyond, he claimed, was not navigable because it was too shallow due to mud and seaweed.[94] Aristotle agreed with this view, remarking that the sea beyond the Pillars was shallow and windless.[95] Such statements about the Atlantic prove "how little it was known to the Greek mariners."[96] So Plato could situate an island-continent in the Atlantic without fear of contradiction, and he could use the destruction of the island as an explanation for the mud and shallow seas which he and his contemporaries believed to exist outside the Strait of Gibraltar.[97]

Much of the physical description of Atlantis was probably based on Plato's own memories of Sicily.[98] Plato toured Sicily in 388-387 B.C., and he was invited back in 367 to tutor Dionysius II, the young tyrant of Syracuse. His final visit to the island was in 361 B.C., some ten years before he wrote *Timaeus* and *Critias*. Sicily was a large, populous island "in the west" (from a Greek perspective). Its major city, Syracuse, was situated on the shore at the edge of a great fertile plain that was ringed by impressive mountains. Sicily was rich in mineral resources and timber; it was noted for its abundant harvests, especially of wheat. It was also prone to violent earthquakes. Syracuse, one of the largest cities in the Mediterranean world at Plato's time, was a mercantile center that contained four distinct zones or sections, each with its own wall. (However, these zones were not arranged in concentric rings as in the capital city of Atlantis.) Moreover, the citadel of Syracuse was on a peninsula between two harbors equipped with numerous shipyards and docks. Possibly Plato intended the entire Atlantis story as an object lesson for his former pupil, Dionysius II, who despite Plato's teaching was following the despotic and expansionistic policies for which his father, Dionysius I, had been noted.[99]

It is possible that Herodotus's accounts of Ecbatana and Babylon,[100] as well as stories of contemporary Carthage also influenced Plato's description of the capital city of Atlantis.[101] Carthage was the primary rival and enemy of Syracuse, and Plato must have heard much about this North African city during his visits to Sicily. Carthage had a great circular harbor or cothon surrounded by docks that could accommodate 220 ships at a time. On an island in the center of the harbor was the headquarters of the admiral of the Carthaginian fleet. The circular harbor, in turn, was connected by a narrow channel to a rectangular one. An outer wall protected the two harbors and most of the city, and an inner wall encircled the Byrsa, a hill which served as a citadel.[102] The fact that Carthage was an imperialistic mercantile state also may have inspired Plato to borrow some of its features for Atlantis.[103]

When we consider, in addition, a traditional Greek myth about Poseidon mating with a woman named Kelaino and settling their son in the Isles of the Blest[104] and the example of Athens standing alone against a great autocratic power (Persia) at the beginning of the Persian Wars, it is clear that Plato had ample sources from which to build his account of Atlantis. The search for any *one* prototype for Atlantis—Crete, Tartessos, Sicily, Carthage, etc.—is likely the quest of a chimera. Plato seems to have called upon the entire range of his knowledge and experience in writing the story. He blended mythological material, elements from history and literature, and conventional science and geography with his own ideas about government and the relative merits of commerce and agriculture to produce one of the most intriguing narratives ever written. But Plato did his job too well. He made his description of Atlantis seem so authentic that it came to be regarded as history, eclipsing the moral and philosophical message of the tale. It is ironic that today many people have heard of Plato only as the person who first recorded the Atlantis story. And many more are familiar with Atlantis but know nothing of the philosopher who, as Aristotle said, created the fabulous island, then sank it beneath the sea.

III
CHAPTER

Cosmic Catastrophism

A large comet or asteroid hurtles through space on a collision course with the earth. As the impact nears, the earth is racked by cataclysms: Volcanoes erupt simultaneously; earthquakes shatter what was once firm land; mountain-high tidal waves destroy continents and change the earth's topography. A science fiction plot? Not according to many authors who have presented a similar scenario as historical fact over the years.

A supposed collision or near-collision between earth and an asteroid, comet, or planet in ancient times has been used variously as the explanation for the destruction of Atlantis,[1] the Deluge recorded in Genesis,[2] or the miraculous events connected with the Israelite Exodus from Egypt.[3] Immanuel Velikovsky has provided the most detailed arguments for such cosmic catastrophism, and his theories have a large and very vocal following among the general public.

Worlds in Collision?

Immanuel Velikovsky was a medical doctor (with a specialty in psychoanalysis) who also read very widely in the natural sciences, history, and law. In the spring of 1940, while studying the biblical account of the Exodus, he became convinced that some natural upheaval had occurred at the time of Moses and that it should have been noted by Egyptian authors as well as in the texts, myths, epics, and folklore of other ancient peoples. So, over the next few years he searched the records of one ancient nation after another locating what he thought to be references to the same catastrophic events described in the Bible.[4] The results of Velikovsky's research were published in *Worlds in Collision* (1950), which presented his theories of cosmic upheavals within the solar system during historical times, and *Ages in Chaos* (1952), which argued for revised historical synchronisms between Egypt and the rest of the ancient world. He provided more detailed treatment of the geological evidence supporting catastrophism in *Earth in Upheaval* (1955) and continued his revisions of ancient history and chronology in *Oedipus and Akhnaton* (1960), *Peoples of the Sea (1977),* and *Ramses II and His Time* (1978).

According to Velikovsky, during the second millennium B.C. a large cometlike object (which later became the planet Venus) was ejected from Jupiter.[5] Around 1450 B.C., as Moses prepared to lead the Israelites out of Egypt, this comet approached the earth. Earth passed through the comet's tail, receiving a fall of red meteorite dust which made rivers and seas appear to turn to blood. Then ashlike dust, burning meteorites, and petroleum rained down upon terror-stricken nations. Fires raged everywhere.[6] As the earth plunged more deeply into the tail and approached the comet's head a pall of darkness occurred that lasted for days. The earth's rotation was slowed, causing earthquakes around the globe. Hurricane-force winds swept across the terrain, and huge tidal waves piled mountains of water on some areas, while leaving some former seabeds (such as that of the Red Sea) uncovered for a time.[7]

When the earth emerged from the tail, the comet looked like a pillar of smoke during the day and a pillar of fire at night. Violent electrical discharges flashed between the earth and the comet and between the comet's head and its own tail, creating the appearance of a great battle raging in the sky.[8] The disturbance of the earth's rotation generated so much heat that rocks melted, lava flowed from new as well as old volcanoes, new mountain ranges rose, and the seas boiled. This heat also made frogs, flies, and other vermin propagate at a feverish rate. In addition, vermin hatched from eggs and larvae carried in the trailing atmosphere of the comet probably infested the earth.[9] Clouds of water vapor and dust covered the earth for years, and in these clouds reactions between the carbon and hydrogen from the tail of the comet produced carbohydrates that rained down as "heavenly food," manna or ambrosia.[10]

Gradually the comet receded, but fifty-two years later its erratic orbit again brought it very close to colliding with the earth. This time the earth's rotation was gradually slowed to a complete stop for a time, enabling Joshua and the Israelites to defeat their enemies while the sun appeared to stand still. Once again meteorites rained from the sky, earthquakes split the surface of the ground, volcanoes erupted, and tidal waves overwhelmed portions of the earth. When this crisis passed, people accepted the comet as part of the solar system and began worshipping it as a divinity (Venus, Ishtar, etc.), carefully observing its movements.[11]

For the six hundred years between c. 1400 and 800 B.C., the solar system was spared from further cataclysms. But, in the eighth century B.C., Venus collided with Mars, knocking the red planet out of its long-established orbit. Mars approached earth a number of times (776, 747, 717 or 702, and 687 B.C.), creating further catastrophes that supposedly destroyed Mycenaean citadels in Greece as well as the Assyrian army that was beseiging Jerusalem. As a result of these contacts, both Mars and Earth settled into their present orbits. The earth's year—the time it takes to make one revolution around the sun—was lengthened from 360 days to approximately 365¼ days. Meanwhile, Venus had already had its elliptical orbit modified to its present nearly circular pattern by its collision with Mars. The solar system had at last attained the stable arrangement observable today. Catastrophes ended, and a collective amnesia gradually developed to protect mankind from traumatic memories of these events. References to the upheavals in myths, legends, folklore, and the Bible were veiled by poetic language and explained as miracles or magic. The world chose to forget how close it had come to annihilation.[12] This, in brief, is Velikovsky's claim.

Scientists Confront Velikovsky

When *Worlds in Collision* was published, it caused a storm of controversy. It was denounced by leading scientists, especially astronomers, and a few even tried to prevent the book from being stocked in bookstores and libraries. These individuals thought they were protecting the public from erroneous ideas, from fiction masquerading as fact. But all they accomplished was to make Velikovsky a martyr in the eyes of his followers. Today, scientists not only admit that cosmic collisions could have taken place at some time in the distant past, but some even theorize that the impact of a large meteorite about sixty-five million years ago caused the extinction of the dinosaurs.[13] It has also been suggested that the solar system weaves upward or downward across the galactic plane of the Milky Way about every thirty or thirty-six million years, increasing the likelihood of a collision between the earth and a comet or large meteor.[14] Yet the vast majority of scientists continue to reject Velikovsky's theory. Their objections center on the improbability of a number of such collisions occurring within historical times and around questions about the scientific validity of many elements in the scenario.

Carl Sagan, a well-known astronomer, has argued that the odds against a comet grazing the earth in any given millennium are 30,000 to 1, and that the odds against a series of such encounters in the *same* millennium become so high that they make the theory untenable.[15] Furthermore, an object moving on an orbit between Jupiter and the sun (as Velikovsky proposed for Venus) would likely be ejected from the solar system altogether (as the Pioneer 10 spacecraft was) due to a close encounter with Jupiter.[16] Velikovsky and his supporters argue that the odds against repeated collisions are not quite as high as Sagan claims they are, and they correctly point out that statistics show only that multiple collisions are *unlikely,* not that they could not have occurred.[17] But even if the exact odds are disputed, it is clear that the sequence of events postulated by Velikovsky would constitute an extremely rare and improbable happening. Scientists are used to evaluating explanations of data in terms of probability rather than possibility, so the evidence would have to be clear and unambiguous to convince them that a theory like Velikovsky's was valid. And that condition is simply not fulfilled.

A similar problem arises over Velikovsky's claim that the sun seemed to stand still during Joshua's battle due to the close passage of Venus. Such an illusion could have been caused by a cessation of the earth's rotation or by a tilting of the terrestrial axis.[18] The chances that either of these possibilities would actually happen, however, are quite small. In addition, whatever forces caused the rotational stoppage or tilting of the axis had to be reversed or counteracted soon afterward to return the earth approximately to normal. The probability of this happening is even smaller.[19] So not only is Velikovsky's hypothesis of a series of collisions within the solar system during the span of some eight hundred years very unlikely, but it also includes effects of those collisions that are extremely improbable. The chance that the entire theory is correct becomes so minute that most scholars will not consider it further.

Scientists also argue that the scientific evidence available today does not support many elements in Velikovsky's scenario. For example, Velikovsky stated that Venus originated in Jupiter. It would be expected, then, that the two planets would have a similar composition. But such is not the case. Jupiter's density is low, indicating that most of its mass is in the form of light elements such as hydrogen and helium. However, Venus has a density close to that of the earth and four times higher than that of Jupiter. There is no way that Venus could contain large amounts of hydrogen, helium, or other light elements. Like Earth, Venus must have a core of heavy metals and a mantle of rocky minerals.[20] There are similar discrepancies between the atmospheres of the two planets.[21]

It is also difficult to account for Venus's hypothetical change in orbit from a very elongated one to a nearly circular one as the result of a collision with Mars.[22] Such a change "would have required the application of outside forces thousands of times more powerful than those needed to tilt the earth's axis, disturb the rotation, and destroy the landscape. There is no agent available to provide those outside forces."[23] There are also features of the orbits of both Venus and Mars which suggest a long period of relative stability.[24]

Velikovsky uses the two small moons of Mars to support his case. These satellites were not discovered until 1877, but Velikovsky claims that they were known to the ancients because they had been seen clearly when

Mars passed close to the earth.[25] Not only does evidence of ancient knowledge of these tiny moons fail to stand up under careful scrutiny, but their very existence on nearly circular orbits is strong evidence *against* Velikovsky's contention that Mars collided with Venus and repeatedly had close encounters with Earth. If such near-misses had occurred the orbits of the moons would have been severely disturbed, and the probability is that Mars would have lost them to either Venus or Earth, both of which are larger than the red planet.[26]

Another problem arises from Velikovsky's suggestion that some of the vermin which infested the earth at the time of the Exodus might have come from larvae carried in the tail of the comet Venus. He concluded that "the ability of many small insects and their larvae to endure great cold and heat and live in an atmosphere devoid of oxygen renders not entirely improbable the hypothesis that Venus (and also Jupiter from which Venus sprang) may be populated by vermin."[27]However, if such vermin existed they certainly would have been incinerated by the tremendous heat produced when Venus left Jupiter and again when Venus approached Earth. Those in the tail would have been fried and atomized like small meteors when they entered the earth's atmosphere.[28] If by a miracle, some Venusian vermin did survive to propagate on Earth, they should have left offspring that could be easily detected because of their differences from the products of terrestrial evolution.[29] Velikovsky responded that he had indicated that vermin infestation from Venus was only a *possibility,* yet his statements seem to indicate that he continued to regard it as a "not improbable" theory.[30]

Scientists find other problems with Velikovsky's theories: Velikovsky's explanation of the craters and geology of the moon is questionable: relief features observed on the surface of Venus seem to indicate too thick a crust for a planet which supposedly was molten only 3,500 years ago; and evidence for the composition of the polar caps of Mars seems to contradict Velikovsky's claims about them.[31] Velikovsky and his supporters have responded vigorously to scientific arguments against his work in numerous articles in the Velikovskian journals *Pensée, Kronos,* and *Society for Interdisciplinary Studies Review.*[32] They frequently point to the accuracy of some of Velikovsky's predictions as evidence of the validity of his theory: strong "fossil" magnetism on the moon, the extremely hot surface of Venus and its backward rotation, radio noises from Jupiter, and the magnetic field around the earth. But while these arguments have sustained the faith of Velikovskians, they have not converted the scientific community. Carl Sagan has pointed out that none of Velikovsky's correct astronomical predictions are so precisely described in *Worlds in Collision* or so intimately linked with his theory that they cannot simply be lucky guesses.[33] There are alternative explanations of these "predicted" phenomena which scientists regard as far more likely than the reasons for them suggested by Velikovsky's writings.

And so the debate continues. But while most public attention has been focused on the scientific implications of Velikovsky's theory, it should be remembered that it is essentially a *historical* thesis, not a scientific one. The primary evidence for Velikovsky's view was drawn from ancient texts, myths, and legends. Much of the same material had been used earlier by Alexander Braghine to support the theory that a comet hit the earth.[34] But Velikovsky expanded this material and presented his case more persuasively. He claims that ancient sources indicate that Venus almost collided with Earth, then forced Mars out of its orbit and into several near-collisions with Earth. If scientific theory cannot be reconciled with the historical evidence, he asserts, then the scientific theory is wrong.

But is Velikovsky's understanding of these ancient sources correct? Do they tell a uniform tale of worldwide catastrophes? Or is the entire scenario of clashing planets built on an imaginative interpretation of vague myths and legends?

The Ancient Evidence for Catastrophes

The first question that must be asked of Velikovsky's evidence is, "Are the various sources approximately contemporaneous?" If various legends, myths, and writings are supposed to be describing the same worldwide catastrophe, it must be demonstrated that they originated at about the same time. This does not mean that all of the sources had to be committed to writing immediately after the events they describe took place (though that is an ideal situation for which every historian longs). However, if written accounts appeared only a considerable time after the events they narrate, the origin and accuracy of the traditions upon which the written versions are based should be discussed. A historian should find out as much as possible about the background and transmission of the sources he uses. Velikovsky generally ignores this fundamental principle of responsible historical scholarship.

He often uses details from Jewish writings of the Roman and medieval periods to supplement descriptions found in the Bible written many hundreds of years earlier.[35] Yet he provides no arguments or reasons to persuade the reader that the authors of these relatively late writings had access to accurate historical traditions not included in the earlier biblical accounts. In fact, he also fails to question the accuracy of the biblical stories, themselves sometimes written centuries after the events they describe.

On another occasion Velikovsky claims that Mexican Aztec legends about the ferocity of their war god originated in catastrophes of the eighth and seventh centuries B. C. when Mars supposedly had several encounters with Venus and Earth. He also asserts that these cataclysmic events caused the Aztecs to change their homeland and that the appearance of heavenly warfare between Venus and Mars led the Toltecs and Aztecs to engage in conflict with each other, each tribe fighting on behalf of its patron deity.[36] But there is no evidence to indicate that the Aztec tribe even existed in the seventh century B.C.[37] And there were no wars between the Toltecs and Aztecs as claimed by Velikovsky. The Toltec empire came to an end in the twelfth century A.D ., while the Aztec empire was not created until the fifteenth century.[38] The Aztec migration from their place of origin (Aztatlan) to Mexico City (Tenochitlan) seems to have occurred between A.D. 1111 and 1345.[39] How can legends relating to this movement possibly provide information about a cataclysm that supposedly took place more than 1,700 years earlier, in 687 B.C.? Velikovsky doesn't say.

Questions of applicability also surround Velikovsky's use of the *Popul-Vuh* and other Mayan manuscripts. These accounts of Mayan mythology and history were only written down following the Spanish conquest of Yucatan in the sixteenth century A.D., many centuries after the end of the most flourishing period of Maya culture, the era between c. A.D. 300 and 900.[40] They represent a late stage in Mayan tradition, after it had been influenced by the Toltec-Itzá rulers of Yucatan, who arrived in the ninth or tenth century A.D. It is highly unlikely that these sources describe accurately or even allude to events that really happened in the fifteenth or eighth and seventh centuries B.C.

Velikovsky's use of references to Nergal, the ancient Mesopotamian god of pestilence and the Underworld, presents a different kind of dating problem. The Mesopotamians equated the planet Mars with Nergal. So Velikovsky quotes Babylonian hymns and prayers describing the ferocity and power of Nergal as evidence of the catastrophes and resulting terror caused by the close approaches of the planet Mars in the eighth and seventh centuries B. C .[41] But Nergal was originally a Sumerian deity borrowed by the later Babylonians and Assyrians. His fierce character as god of pestilence and the Underworld, a fearsome "fighter without peer," is already evident in texts of the eighteenth, fifteenth, and fourteenth centuries B.C.[42] This is long before the planet Mars is supposed to have caused any problems according to Velikovsky's scenario. Descriptions of Nergal in the eighth-century-B.C. texts Velikovsky quotes are natural outgrowths of the long-established characteristics of this ancient god. They cannot be used as evidence of a change in the character of the planet Mars or as references to catastrophes supposedly produced in the eighth and seventh centuries B.C.

A further problem with Velikovsky's methodology concerns his somewhat arbitrary identifications of mythological persons with the planets Mars or Venus. He often provides no evidence that the people who created the myths he quotes meant them to refer to these specific planets. For example, he claims that the Aztec war-god Huitzilpochtli was the planet Mars.[43] But the Aztecs identified Huitzilpochtli with the *sun* according to leading students of Aztec mythology.[44] Velikovsky provides only a very lame argument to support his unorthodox identification: The Aztec Huitzilpochtli and the Roman Mars were both gods of war and are similar in character (both become enraged and destroy cities); both are depicted holding spears or bows and arrows, and a shield. Therefore, since Mars was the planet Mars, Huitzilpochtli was the same planet-god.[45] But all of these similarities between the two gods stem from their natures as war gods! They have nothing to do with possible connections between the gods in question and some heavenly body. The similarities simply do not demonstrate that Huitzilpochtli was the Aztec name for the planet Mars.

In another section of *Worlds in Collision,* Velikovsky claims that a Greek myth describing how Athena sprang full-grown from the forehead of Zeus derived from observation of the birth of the planet Venus from Jupiter.[46] But the ancient Greeks equated Aphrodite, not Athena, with the Roman goddess Venus and with the planet Venus. Athena's Roman counterpart was Minerva, who was not one of the planets. (Velikovsky is under the mistaken impression that Aphrodite was the Greek name for the moon rather than for the planet Venus.[47] However, the Greek name for the goddess of the moon was Selene, not Aphrodite.[48]) Velikovsky maintains his identification of Athena with the planet Venus despite strong ancient testimony to the contrary (which he acknowledges in *Worlds in Collision.*[49]). The Greek writer Lucian and the Roman statesman Cicero both identified the planet Venus with the Greek goddess Aphrodite, not Athena. And St. Augustine stated that the Greeks "did not find even a star in which to place" Athena.[50] These ancient writers knew Greek religion firsthand and had much better sources for their statements about Greek identifications of Athena or Aphrodite than we now have. Yet Velikovsky tosses aside their testimony in favor of his own unsupported claim that the early Greeks really equated the goddess Athena with the planet Venus.

The Greek myth of Zeus's battle with the giant Typhon also supposedly derived from the catastrophes connected with the fifteenth-century-B.C. approach of the comet/planet Venus. According to Velikovsky, the Greeks were so confused that they didn't know which planet, Jupiter (Zeus) or Venus (Athena), was really involved in the fearful incidents taking place.[51] But it is Velikovsky who seems to be confused in his identifications. He argues that Typhon was recognized by the ancients as a comet.[52] This would seem to equate Typhon with the comet/planet Venus. But, when Zeus battles typhon, Zeus is supposed to be the proto-planet Venus and Typhon just the tail (the "pillar of cloud").[53] Another myth about Athena killing Pallas supposedly refers to the same perceived battle between the comet and its tail, since Pallas "was another name for Typhon."[54] Velikovsky provided no justification for his equation of Pallas and Typhon and, when Carl Sagan took him to task for this,[55] Velikovsky responded: "That Pallas and Typhon are the same I need not have supported with a note—any dictionary will tell this."[56] However, leading dictionaries and studies of Greek mythology do not tell that! In the Greek myths Pallas and Typhon are quite distinct.[57] The reader of *Worlds in Collision* is expected to believe that, while the ancient Greeks and Romans were thoroughly confused (they thought Aphrodite was the planet Venus when really Athena was; they thought Pallas and Typhon were unrelated individuals when really they were the same; and they couldn't always distinguish between Zeus and Athena), Velikovsky could clearly read the whole story of cosmic catastrophes from their myths.

Velikovsky also equates the Persian god Mithra, the Egyptian goddess Isis, and the Canannite god Baal with the planet Venus and the Iranian Gokihar and Germanic Fenrir or "Fenris-Wolf" with the planet Mars. Most of these identifications are questionable, yet he gives no evidence or arguments to support his assertions. But enough has been said on this point. Velikovsky does not properly establish the connection between particular planets and characters in myths. And without such unquestionable identifications, his interpretations of the myths cannot stand.

Further problems arise from Velikovsky's interpretations of many of the myths and legends. He seems to assume "that any mythological references, by any people, to any god which also corresponds to a celestial body represent a direct observation of that celestial body."[58] For example, Ares and Athena are Greek deities. Velikovsky believes that they were also the planets Mars and Venus, respectively. So when the *Iliad* speaks of these gods fighting on opposite sides during the Trojan War, the planets they represent must have been observed actually engaging in conflict.[59] But such a view contradicts almost everything learned over the past fifty or sixty years about the complex nature of mythology.[60] Some myths do arise as explanations for historical events or physical phenomena, but others provide answers for psychological or social problems. Still others describe the origin of and provide the justification for traditional cultic practices. Myths about deities like Mars, Venus, and Jupiter had a variety of origins. And different myths about a single god served a variety of purposes. The assumption that most, or even many, of the myths about Mars, Venus, and Jupiter refer to actions of the planets with the same names is simplistic and totally unjustified.

Not only does Velikovsky regard references to some deities in myth as literal descriptions of planets by the same names; he also adopts a literalistic interpretation of much mythological descriptive imagery. If different peoples believed that their planet-gods had the form of wolves, scorpions, mice, dogs, pigs, fish, dragons, or other creatures, then such figures must have been seen in the sky. The atmosphere of the planet Mars became so distorted by its close approach to earth that it took on these various shapes.[61] But even if Mars had approached near enough for such distortions to be seen by the naked eye, it is not likely that the images produced could have been so clear that different people would have interpreted them the same way, even within the same culture. As Sagan points out, "our experience with Rorschach and other psychological projective tests gives clear proof that different people will see the same nonrepresentational image in different ways."[62] That people who envisioned their gods as serpents, wolves, fish, or other animals ever actually saw a heavenly body (Mars) in such forms is unlikely in the extreme!

Many poetic scriptural passages are also interpreted literally. "The voice of the Lord is powerful. . . . The voice of the Lord breaketh the cedars. . . . The voice of the Lord shaketh the wilderness; the Lord shaketh the wilderness of Kadesh."[63] "The kingdoms were moved; he uttered his voice, the earth melted."[64] Cosmic discharges and earthquakes are supposedly commemorated in these passages from the Psalms.[65] The psalmist is obviously using such lines to emphasize the power and glory of Yahweh, the God of Israel. But is he describing catastrophic physical realities that he or his people actually experienced? Most modern biblical scholars would say no. Even most fundamentalists who insist on the absolute veracity of Holy Scripture do not interpret such poetic passages literally. Other psalms state that God "has made the world firm, not to be moved."[66] This phrase even occurs in the context of a recital of the Exodus events, indicating that the psalmist recognized that the catastrophes associated with the flight from Egypt were local, not worldwide.[67] Another psalm compares the endurance of God's Truth to the firmness of the earth that He established.[68] Could such lines have been written by men who knew that all over the world at the time of the Exodus mountains melted, firm land heaved and cracked, the seas boiled, hurricane-force winds swept the surface, and the earth seemed to be rent asunder?

Poetic exaggeration or metaphorical meanings are not considered by Velikovsky as explanations for the passages he quotes. If one took the same literalistic approach to modern poetry as exemplified in popular songs, references to catastrophes could be found on every hand—"Blue Moon" describes the moon changing color from blue to gold (a passing "comet" heated it and made it incandescent?), "The First Time Ever I

Saw Your Face" states that the earth moved like the trembling heart of a captive bird (earthquake?), and "On The Street Where You Live" implies that the pavement will not stay beneath the poet's feet and claims that suddenly he is swept into the air to a height of several stories (tornado or hurricane?)!

Such problems with Velikovsky's methodology and with his interpretations of various texts are enough to cause almost all mythologists, anthropologists, and ancient historians to reject his thesis. But isn't there more objective evidence? Can't it be determined whether or not major catastrophes occurred in the fifteenth and eight to seventh centuries B.C.?

One approach would seem to be through geology. Physical upheavals of the kind described by Velikovsky should have left their mark on the surface of the earth. Geologists find no evidence of such catastrophes in relatively recent times, though they are willing to admit that a collision between the earth and an asteroid may have occurred about sixty-five million years ago.[69] But Velikovsky and his followers claim that the evidence is plentiful—features that geologists claim took millions of years to develop were really the result of the cosmic collisions Velikovsky recounts.[70] According to this view, fossils are the remains of the species exterminated by these recent upheavals.[71]

However, according to Velikovsky's theory, the oceans came to a boil in the fifteenth century B.C. as a result of the close approach of Venus. This situation coupled with immense tidal waves must have destroyed most sea creatures. The few marine survivors of the catastrophe might have restocked the oceans in time, but one would expect the numbers of species to be limited. It is difficult to understand how the great variety of marine life present today survived the kinds of cataclysms that supposedly took place less than 3,500 years ago. Even a rapid "cataclysmic evolution" caused by radiation from cosmic discharges[72] could not replace many types of life that would have been destroyed in the catastrophe Velikovsky described.

Coral is a case in point. These small marine creatures build up reef structures (which are actually the accumulations of their skeletons) at a slow rate that can be measured. The growth rings of some species even reflect accurately the number of days per month and the number of days per year.[73] But living coral polyps can survive only in water temperatures between 61° and 97° F. So all coral polyps would have been destroyed in a catastrophe that caused the seas to boil. If, by some miracle, coral polyps did survive, their numbers would have been few, certainly much smaller than they had been before the cataclysm. Most reefs, then, should exhibit a cessation of growth about 3,500 years ago with only limited renewed growth in a few areas. But this is not the case. Furthermore, study of coral growth rings shows that, despite Velikovsky's claims to the contrary, no major changes have occurred in the length of the year in recent millennia.[74]

Archaeological discoveries should also be able to provide evidence for ancient catastrophes. Velikovsky cites a couple of examples that he claims show that the earth's axis shifted in the catastrophes of the eighth and seventh centuries B.C. Discrepancies in Babylonian astronomical tablets seem to indicate that Babylon was once some 250 kilometers (about 155 miles) further north than it is today. [75] And errors in a sundial found in the Faiyum in Egypt and a water clock found at the Egyptian city of Thebes also supposedly prove that the earth's axis has moved in historical times.[76] But this archaeological evidence does not demonstrate the correctness of Velikovsky's theories. The errors in the Babylonian texts and the Faiyum sundial require a shifting of these locations *southward,* while the Theban water clock's error indicates that Thebes has moved 1,000 kilometers (c. 621 miles) *northward.*[77] Not only are two parts of the Near East required to move in opposite directions, but also Egypt is divided internally. The Faiyum in north-central Egypt would have been moving to the south while Thebes in southern Egypt would be shifting northward! Obviously, if the axis shifted, it could shift in only one direction or the other, not both at the same time. It is far more likely that the objects responsible for these discrepancies were not made at the sites where they were found. Such a situation would account for their errors without requiring a shift of the earth's axis.

But what of other archaeological evidence? Immense cataclysms should have left more direct signs on man's handiwork. Mankind might have survived devastation of the kind Velikovsky recounts, but civilization would have been severely damaged. Architectural constructions would have been especially hard hit. Buildings would have crumbled due to earthquakes, tidal waves, hurricane-force winds, and heat hot enough to melt rocks. Virtually everything would have been destroyed—it is questionable whether even the pyramids could have endured such catastrophes. Velikovsky does credit some destruction of ancient cities to the cataclysms,[78] but the powerful forces involved would lead one to expect more signs of wholesale devastation around the globe. Minoan sites on Crete were destroyed around 1450 B.C., but most Egyptian and Mesopotamian buildings were not. There is also no evidence of widespread destruction in the eighth and seventh centuries B.C. in the Near East, Europe, or the New World. Individual sites were destroyed during those periods, but there are no signs of the universal conflagration one would expect from Velikovsky's writings. However, Velikovsky negates some of this archaeological evidence by questioning the dating of the remains (see "Reconstructing Ancient Chronology" below).

Finally, radiocarbon dating does not support Velikovsky's claims.[79] He has questioned the validity of this scientific dating method because it was based on the assumption that the amount of carbon-14 in the atmosphere did not change over time (see above, pp. 20-21). Velikovsky's theory of cosmic catastrophes, however, suggests that new carbon (including some C^{14}) was added to the atmosphere by the "comet" Venus in the fifteenth century B.C.

and still more carbon was added by the eruptions of numerous volcanoes in the fifteenth and the eighth to seventh centuries B.C. This would have changed the ratio between normal carbon and radioactive carbon in the air and thus in living things. So any dates obtained by the radiocarbon method would be inaccurate for periods before the last alleged catastrophe in 687 B.C.[80] But radiocarbon dates have been calibrated by testing a sequence of tree rings stretching over the past 7,000 years. If major catastrophes had occurred c. 1450-1400 B.C. and again c. 800-687 B.C., the rapid addition of much new carbon to the atmosphere at those times should cause radiocarbon dates for tree rings added during those periods to deviate wildly from the expected dates. However, they do not. All of the radiocarbon tests of material earlier than the third century B.C. produced dates that were more recent than the tree-ring chronology showed they should be. But the C[14] dates for tree rings formed between 1450 and 1400 B.C. deviate from the true dates by no more than those for 1600 B.C. or for 1300 B.C. The errors in radiocarbon dates for the eighth and seventh centuries B.C. are also not as great as they should be if Velikovsky were correct.[81]

There is thus no firm evidence in favor of cosmic catastrophes in the past 3,500 years. The myths and texts Velikovsky claims describe these disasters do not all relate to the same time. And many of them can be connected with astronomical bodies or read as records of catastrophes only by adopting Velikovsky's eccentric and highly questionable methodology. Furthermore, geology and archaeology give no support to theories of recent cataclysms. It is easy to see, then, why ancient historians, anthropologists, archaeologists, and mythologists have joined scientists in rejecting Velikovsky's hypothesis.

Reconstructing Ancient Chronology

When Velikovsky first began searching for other references to the catastrophes supposedly recounted in the biblical book of Exodus, he came across an Egyptian text that seemed to describe the same "plagues."[82] This papyrus manuscript is known as "the Admonitions of Ipuwer," and in the 1940s it was generally thought to reflect the turmoil in Egypt following the collapse of the Old Kingdom around 2100 B.C. or during the invasion of the Hyksos at the end of the Middle Kingdom, c. 1750 B.C. Velikovsky thought that the second of these two periods, that of the Hyksos invasion, was the correct era for the Ipuwer papyrus.[83] So, if the "Admonitions of Ipuwer" belonged to the beginning of the Hyksos Period in Egypt, and if it reflected the catastrophes mentioned in the biblical account of the Exodus, then the Exodus must have occurred at about the same time as the Hyksos invasion of Egypt.

Table 1. Conventional Chronology Compared with Velikovsky's Revisions

Date	Conventional Synchronisms — Other Areas	Conventional Synchronisms — Egypt	Israelite History	Velikovsky's Synchronisms — Egypt	Velikovsky's Synchronisms — Other Areas	Date
1500-	KASSITE PERIOD IN BABYLON	DYNASTY XVIII Hatshepsut Thutmose III		MIDDLE KINGDOM		-1500
1450-			THE EXODUS (?) (I Kings 6:1)			-1450
1400-	Kadashman-Enlil Burnaburiash (II)	Amenhotep III Akhenaton				-1400
1350-						-1350
1300-	HITTITE EMPIRE MYCENAEAN PERIOD IN GREECE	DYNASTY XIX Rameses II				-1300
1250-			THE EXODUS (?)	HYKSOS RULE		-1250
1200-	DESTRUCTION OF MYCENEAN SITES AND HITTITE EMPIRE	DYNASTY XX Rameses III defeats Sea Peoples				-1200
1150-			PERIOD OF THE JUDGES			-1150
1100-	DARK AGE IN GREECE	DYNASTY XXI				-1100
1050-			UNITED KINGDOM Saul David			-1050
1000-		DYNASTY XXII		DYNASTY XVIII BEGINS		-1000
950-		DYNASTY XXII (LIBYAN RULE) Shoshenk I (Shisak)	Solomon	Hatshepsut		-950
900-	ASSYRIAN EMPIRE		DIVIDED KINGDOM	Thutmose III (= Shishak) Amenhotep III Akhenaton		-900
850-	Shalmaneser III		Ahab of Israel & Jehoshaphat of Judah		Shalmaneser III (= Burnaburiash)	-850
800-		DYNASTY XXIII				-800
750-	Shalmaneser V			LIBYAN DYNASTIES (XXII-XXIV)		-750
700-	Sargon II Sennacherib	DYNASTIES XXIV-XXV	Fall of Samaria Hezekiah of Judah	ETHIOPIAN DYNASTY (XXV)	MYCENAEAN SITES DESTROYED	-700
650-	Esarhaddon Asshurbanipal	DYNASTY XXVI (SAITE PERIOD) Necho II		DYNASTY XIX (= DYNASTY XXVI)		-650
600-	NEO-BABYLONIAN EMP. Nebuchadnezzar		Josiah Fall of Jerusalem THE EXILE	Rameses II (= Necho II)	Nebuchadnezzar (= Hattusilis III)	-600
550-						-550

Today, many Egyptologists would agree with the first of these contentions, that the "Admonitions of Ipuwer" dates from the Hyksos Period.[84] It is the second premise in the argument that is highly questionable. The "Admonitions of Ipuwer" deals with laments about a chaotic situation that has engulfed Egypt. Most of the lines describe social and economic upheaval—bandits are everywhere, foreigners have invaded the land, commoners have usurped the positions and wealth of nobles, no one is ploughing or tending the land, crops have been destroyed, houses and palaces have been burned, and death is everywhere from either violence or plague.[85] In such a context, few would take literally (as Velikovsky does)[86] statements like "the land spins around as a potter's wheel does" or "the River is blood." In fact, the metaphorical meaning of the first of these phrases is indicated by its following line: "The robber is (now) the possessor of riches."[87] Clearly the Egyptian scribe's world was topsy-turvy figuratively, not literally. Like the Exodus story, the "Admonitions of Ipuwer" describes a period of confusion and disaster. But there is no necessity to see the two as accounts of the *same* events, nor do they clearly indicate that the "plagues" they describe had the same causes (a cosmic catastrophe).

Thus, the link between the Exodus and the beginning of the Hyksos Period is not firmly established. But assuming this connection, Velikovsky goes on to argue that the Hyksos were the Amalekites who fought against the Israelites in Sinai during the Exodus, and who later were defeated by Saul and David.[88] Saul and David were successive kings of Israel in the late eleventh and early tenth centuries B.C. That date can be determined from connections between biblical events and Assyrian history that can be accurately dated through reliable Mesopotamian king and eponym lists reaching to later times. On the other hand, the end of the Hyksos era in Egypt is usually dated c. 1580 B.C. For Velikovsky's synchronism of the end of the Hyksos Period with the reigns of Saul and David to be correct, Egyptian chronology has to contain an error of about six hundred years.[89]

Velikovsky goes on to synchronize the post-Hyksos Eighteenth dynasty of Egypt (usually dated c. 1580–1320 B.C.) with the Hebrew monarchy and Assyrian Empire of the tenth to seventh centuries B.C. He argues that the Egyptian Queen Hatshepsut, who is thought to have reigned c. 1503–1482 B.C. was really the Queen of Sheba who visited Solomon in the tenth century B.C.[90] And the fourteenth century B.C. Egyptian pharaohs Amenhotep III and Akhenaton he makes contemporaries of the mid-ninth-century-B.C. rulers Ahab of Israel, Jehoshaphat of Judah, and Shalmaneser III of Assyria.[91]

In later works, he carried on this revision of ancient history by claiming that the sixth-century-B.C. Neo-Babylonian Empire of Nebuchadnezzar and the supposedly much earlier Hittite Empire were really one and the same.[92] Traditional history records that about 1190 B.C. the Egyptian pharaoh

Rameses III defeated a collection of invaders from the Aegean area known as the "Peoples of the Sea." But Velikovsky argues that these "Sea Peoples" were really the Persians and their subjects and that the battles with Rameses III took place in the fourth century B.C.[93] All of these arguments are bolstered by an extensive (and, to the layman, a very impressive) array of textual and archaeological evidence.

However, Velikovsky's arguments and evidence have not persuaded the vast majority of specialists in various fields of study relating to the ancient Near East. His interpretations of ancient texts are especially questionable. For example, there are a number of letters written on clay in Akkadian (the language of the ancient Babylonians and Assyrians) that were found at El-Amarna in Egypt in the nineteenth century. These Amarna letters, as they are called, were written mainly to the Egyptian pharaohs Amenhotep III and Akhenaton. As just mentioned, Velikovsky synchronizes the reigns of these two pharaohs with those of the mid-ninth-century-B.C. rulers of Judah, Israel, and Assyria. The people, places, and events mentioned in the Amarna letters, therefore, must match biblical accounts of the period of Ahab and Jehoshaphat in I and II Kings and II Chronicles as well as the Assyrian records of Shalmaneser III. This would seem to supply a simple and straightforward test for Velikovsky's thesis—compare the three sets of texts and see whether or not they agree.

The Amarna letters contain the names of a number of Near Eastern rulers, but they are not the same as those of the ninth century B.C. (Table 2). In place of the ninth-century kings Jehoshaphat of Judah and Ahab of Israel, the Amarna correspondence names individual rulers for many Palestinian cities.[94] I Kings 16:31 states that Ethbaal was king of the Phoenician city of Sidon at the time of Ahab, but the ruler of Sidon in the Amarna letters is named Zimreda.[95] The names of the mid-ninth century rulers of Assyria and Babylonia also differ from those listed for these areas in the Amarna texts.[96]

Velikovsky explains the failure of these names to agree by pointing out that ancient Near Eastern kings usually bore many names. Thus he claims that Shalmaneser III was also Burnaburiash (his name as ruler of Babylon). Jehoshaphat, King of Judah, he equates with Abdu-Hepa, ruler of Jerusalem in the Amarna letters, and Ahab of Israel with Rib-Addi, King of Gubla. He also asserts that Abdi-Ashirta and Azaru (successive rulers of a part of Syria in the Amarna texts) are different names for Ben-Hadad (I) and Hazael, ninth-century-B.C. rulers of Damascus.[97]

While it is true that Near Eastern kings often had more than one name, it is extremely unlikely that Shalmaneser III always would have used one name when writing to the Egyptian pharaoh and another in his inscriptions. It is also difficult to believe that virtually every name in the Amarna letters would be different from those used in ninth-century Mesopotamian and biblical sources if the Amarna correspondence belonged to the ninth century

B.C. as Velikovsky claims. There are also problems with some of the specific identifications Velikovsky makes between individuals in the various sets of texts. It is possible that Jehoshaphat of Judah had another name that we don't know about, but it is very improbable that it was Abdu-Hepa, as Velikovsky asserts. The Bible indicates that Jehoshaphat was a dedicated worshipper of Yahweh who attempted to suppress idolatry in Judah.[98] Could he have received such favorable notice from the biblical authors if he had chosen the throne name Abdu-Hepa, which (despite Velikovsky's claims to the contrary[99]) means "Servant of [the goddess] Hepa"? Furthermore, in the Amarna letters, Azaru is the son of Abdi-Ashirta. Velikovsky declares that these two individuals are the same as the ninth-century rulers Hazael and Ben-Hadd (I), but both the Bible and Shalmaneser III's inscriptions indicate that Hazael was *not* the son of Ben-Hadad (I). Hazael was a commoner who usurped the throne—Shalmaneser's inscription calls him "son of a nobody."[100] Velikovsky's attempts to explain away these problems[101] are not convincing.

TABLE 2. Near Eastern Rulers in the Amarna Letters and Ninth-Century Texts

Rulers in Armana Letters	Place	Rulers in Mid-Ninth-Century B.C.
Abdu-Hepa	Jerusalem	
Mikilu, then Ba'lu-shipli	Gezer } Judah	Jehosaphat
Zimreda	Lachish	
Lab'ayu	Shechem	
Biridia	Megiddo } Israel	Ahab
Abdu-Tirshi	Hazor	
Rib-Addi	Byblos (Gubla)	
Zimreda	Sidon	Ethbaal
Abdi-Ashirta then Azaru	Syria	Ben-Hadad (I), then Hazael
Asshur-uballit	Assyria	Shalmaneser III
Kadashman-Enlil, then Burnaburiash	Babylon	Nabu-apal-iddin, then Marduk-zakir-shumi

For Velikovsky's synchronization to be valid, not only must his improbable explanation for the differences in the royal names be correct, but also his interpretation of certain place names. In the Amarna letters,

Rib-Addi is king of Gubla, which Velikovsky argues was the original name of Jezreel in Israel before Ahab changed it.[102] He rejects the traditional equation of Gubla (Gebal in Hebrew and Phoenician) with Byblos, a city in Lebanon that is still called Jebeil in Arabic. Yet not only does the Bible refer to Byblos as Gebal (Joshua 13:5; Ezekiel 27:9; Psalms 83:8), but also Assyrian texts clearly indicate that Gubla or Gubal was Byblos. An early eleventh-century-B.C. inscription describing an Assyrian campaign in Lebanon refers to Gubal among other Lebanese cities.[103] And ninth-century-B.C. texts recounting the military conquests of the Assyrian monarchs Asshurnasirpal II and Shalmaneser III place Gubal on the coast of Lebanon along with Tyre and Sidon.[104] It should also be noted that in Shalmaneser's inscriptions (which are written in Akkadian just as the Amarna letters are), Ahab is referred to as Ahab of Israel, not Rib-Addi of Gubla![105] It is not only wrong, but wrong-headed, to reject all of this evidence for the identification of Gubla with Byblos and opt instead for its identification with Jezreel, an equation unattested in any ancient text.

There is also no valid reason to identify Sumur, a city in Rib-Addi's territory according to the Amarna texts, with Samaria (*Shomron* in Hebrew), the capital of Israel.[106] Sumur (or Sumura) was not Rib-Addi's capital as Samaria was Ahab's. And eighth-century-B.C. texts of the Assyrian king Sargon II use Samerina (written syllabically *Sa-mir-i-na* or *Sa-me-ri-na*), not Sumur, for Samaria.[107]

Another of Velikovsky's interpretations of the Amarna texts that is almost certainly incorrect is his contention that Mesha, the mid-ninth-century-B.C. king of Moab, is mentioned frequently in the letters. Velikovsky sees Mesha's name in the cuneiform sign that had the syllabic value "mesh."[108] However, this sign was usually written after ideograms to let the reader know that the word represented by the ideographic sign was plural.[109] For example, the sign 𒌉 (DUMU) was read in Akkadian as the ideogram for *māru*, "son." But 𒌉𒈨𒌍 (DUMU.MESH) would have been read *māri*, "sons." If the ancient scribes had intended the "mesh" sign to be read as a personal name they would have placed a single vertical wedge before it (like so, 𒁹𒈨𒌍). This was the normal way to indicate that the word which followed was a masculine name. The cuneiform signs (LÚ.SA.GAZ.-MESH) that Velikovsky translates "the people of the bandit Mesh" really refer to a class of people called the Hapiru (or 'Apiru), a stateless group of individuals who could be slaves, mercenaries, or bandits depending on circumstances.[110] These same signs (LÚ.SA.GAZ.MESH) occur in a letter of Hammurabi, a Babylonian king who lived long before the Amarna Period and long before the time of Mesha of Moab.[111] Obviously, they do not relate to Mesha at all.

One could go on and on, but enough has been said here to make it clear that Velikovsky's synchronization fails the test. The three sets of texts do not describe the same events and people. They can be made to correspond (after a fashion) only if one accepts many extremely questionable identifications of names and places, uses erroneous meanings for some cuneiform signs, ignores evidence that does not fit into the scheme, reads events from the Bible into the Amarna letters where they are not clearly indicated, and also reads elements from the Amarna texts back into the scriptural accounts. It is understandable that such arguments and "evidence" have been rejected by virtually all specialists in the languages and cultures of the ancient Near East.

Archaeology and Velikovsky's Revised Chronology

The ruins of ancient Near Eastern cities form *tells,* that is, mounds composed of debris built up as a result of centuries of occupation and repeated destructions. This debris generally occurs in layers or strata with the remains of the earliest occupation at the bottom and deposits of more recent times on top. Archaeologists study the pottery and other artifacts in these layers and group them into assemblages which have been designated Early Bronze Age, Middle Bronze Age, Late Bronze Age, Iron Age, Hellenistic, etc. Artifacts characteristic of the Middle Bronze Age are found below layers containing Late Bronze Age objects, and these in turn are beneath remains belonging to the Iron Age. As was pointed out a number of years ago, this stratigraphical archaeological evidence from the eastern Mediterranean area cannot be reconciled with Velikovsky's synchronizations.[112]

Archaeologists usually assign the remains of Iron Age levels in Palestine to the period of the Hebrew monarchy, and Velikovsky accepted this dating.[113] The Palestinian Iron Age, then, should also correspond to the Egyptian Eighteenth Dynasty according to Velikovsky's synchronisms.

However, in Palestine and Syria scarabs and other objects bearing the names of Eighteenth and Nineteenth dynasty rulers of Egypt are commonly found with Late Bronze Age material *underneath* layers belonging to the Iron Age.[114] Pharaohs such as Thutmose III, Amenhotep II, and Rameses II whose scarabs are regularly found in Late Bronze Age deposits, may have lived earlier than the Late Bronze Age, but they could not have lived later. To claim otherwise would require that one believe that scarabs could have been made and buried while inscribed with the names of people who had not yet been born. And the occurrence of Iron Age material above Late Bronze Age strata shows that the Late Bronze Age was earlier than the Iron Age (which Velikovsky accepted as the period of the Hebrew monarchy and the Assyrian Empire). Thus, Eighteenth Dynasty rulers of Egypt could not have been contemporaries of Israelite kings.

Velikovsky never really answered this argument, though its validity has been recognized by some of his followers.[115] Since the archaeological synchronism between the Palestinian Late Bronze Age and the Egyptian Eighteenth and Nineteenth dynasties is secure, some supporters of Velikovsky have proposed a radical revision of Palestinan archaeological chronology.[116] They would make the Late Bronze Age contemporaneous with the Hebrew monarchy and radically shorten the Iron Age (see Table 3). This would allow Velikovsky's synchronization of the Egyptian Eighteenth Dynasty with the Hebrew rulers of the tenth to eighth centuries to stand.

But these revised archaeological chronologies present problems of their own. If the Late Bronze Age was the era of the Hebrew monarchy, archaeological evidence from a number of important sites in Palestine cannot be reconciled with Biblical accounts.

The most crucial of these problematic sites is Samaria. The Bible indicates that Omri, king of Israel, built Samaria in the ninth century B.C. and that it remained the capital of Israel until its destruction by the Assyrians in 722 B.C. According to the revised archaeological chronologies, this entire period would fall within the Late Bronze Age. However, no Late Bronze Age remains were uncovered during excavations at Samaria.[117] The Iron Age date of the earliest building levels so far discovered at Samaria fits conventional archaeological synchronisms, but not the revised ones.

John Bimson, at least, is aware of the difficulties Samaria represents for the revised archaeological chronology.[118] The absence of Late Bronze Age strata at Samaria argues against any equation of either the Late Bronze Age I or II Periods with the time of Omri, Ahab, and later kings of Israel. Bimson argues that the limited excavations in the lower city at Samaria may have missed the Late Bronze Age deposits, and that on the citadel the activities of the Iron Age builders (whom he regards as the Assyrians) may have removed all traces of the earlier occupation.[119] In support of his contention he cites the situation on the citadel at Hazor in northern Israel where "Iron Age builders have in places completely removed the remains of the LBA city by massive levelling operations, so that Iron Age remains are found directly above those of the Middle Bronze Age."[120]

The significant words in the quotation above are "in places." Y. Yadin, the excavator at Hazor, found much evidence of Late Bronze Age occupation on the citadel at Hazor as well as in the lower city.[121] The Late Bronze strata on the citadel were seriously disturbed because later builders took stones from the Late Bronze buildings to use in their own structures.[122] But evidence of the Late Bronze occupation, including local pottery sherds and fragments of imported Mycenaean wares, remained. It is extremely unlikely that all traces of an extensive Israelite occupation at Samaria like that which the

TABLE 3. Conventional Palestinian Archaelogical Chronology Compared with Proposed Revisions

Date B.C.	Archaelogical Periods*			Biblical Events	Date B.C.
	Conventional	Courville	Bimson		
1500-					-1500
1450-	LB I	EB III	MB II	The Exodus (?)	-1450
1400-				The Conquest (?)	-1400
1350-	A				-1350
1300-	LB II —	MB I			-1300
1250-	B			The Exodus (?)	-1250
1200-	A		LB I	The Conquest (?)	-1200
1150-		A		The Period of the Judges	-1150
1100-	Iron Age I				-1100
1050-	B	MB II B			-1050
1000-				United King- dom Saul David	-1000
950-	A	C		Solomon	-950
900-					-900
850-	B	I	A	Divided Kingdom: Israel in north,	-850
800-	Iron Age II —	LB	LB II	Judah in south	-800
750-		II	B		-750
700-	C		Iron Age I	Fall of Samaria	-700
650-			Iron Age II & III A		-650
600-		Iron Age	Iron Age III B	Destruction of Jerusalem	-600
550-				The Exile	-550

*EB = Early Bronze Age, MB = Middle Bronze Age, LB = Late Bronze Age

Bible describes could completely disappear over an area as large as that excavated at this site. Buildings could have been demolished, stones re-used, but something (especially pottery sherds) should have remained. Some Early Bronze Age sherds survived under the Iron Age building levels at Samaria. Why didn't at least a few Late Bronze fragments? Bimson's attempt to explain away the failure of the excavators to find Late Bronze remains at Samaria is totally unconvincing. And the lack of the Late Bronze Age strata at Samaria is devastating to any synchroni-zation of the Late Bronze Age with the time of Omri and Ahab.

Almost as important is the archaeological evidence from Dibon. Dibon, located east of the Dead Sea, was the birthplace of Mesha, King of Moab and a contemporary of Ahab in the mid-ninth century B.C. (II Kings 3:4). He rebelled against Israel and established the independence of Moab, recording his victory on a stele found at Dibon in 1868.[123] If the revised synchronisms were correct, there should be Late Bronze Age remains at Dibon just as there should be at Samaria. But modern excavations at Dibon have found no traces of occupation there during the Middle Bronze Age II or Late Bronze Age periods.[124]

A similar situation exists at sites in the Negev, the extreme southern portion of Israel. Arad, which figures in accounts of the conquest of Palestine by the Israelites,[125] was not occupied between the Early Bronze Age and the Iron Age I.[126] And Beersheba, which is mentioned in numerous passages describing incidents from the Patriarchal Age through the period of the mon-archy, did not exist between the Chalcolithic Period and the Iron Age.[127]

Now it must be admitted that the lack of Late Bronze Age remains at these sites in the Negev poses problems for the traditional archaeological chronology as well as for the revised ones. But most Palestinian archaeolo-gists accept the principles and results of modern biblical criticism. They realize that the biblical narratives took form over a long period of time, and that legendary, aetiological, or anachronistic material sometimes got im-bedded in stories of Israel's early days. Accounts of primeval events, the Patriarchs, the Exodus, and the conquest of Canaan are not absolutely his-torical in all details (see pp. 11-15). When the conventional correlation be-tween archaeological periods and biblical history is used, discrepancies between the two are largely confined to the early stages of Israelite history, where biblical criticism indicates we should expect such problems. But with the chronological revisions proposed by Bimson and Courville, discrepancies exist not only for the period of the conquest, but also in the period of the Divided Monarchy (tenth to sixth centuries B.C.), an era for which biblical sources are generally acknowledged to be fairly accurate. If the Late Bronze Age was the period of the Divided Monarchy, then there was no Beersheba to which Elijah could flee (I Kings 19:3), no Dibon in which Mesha could be born, and no Samaria to serve as the capital of Israel or to fall to the

Assyrians!

Both revised chronologies lower the date for the beginning of the Iron Age from c. 1200 B.C. to c. 733–700 B.C. However, archaeological synchronisms between Palestine-Syria and Greece make such a low date for the transition from the Late Bronze Age to the Iron Age I extremely unlikely. Excavations in Greece have produced evidence of a sequence of pottery styles succeeding one another: Mycenaean, Sub-Mycenaean, Proto-Geometric, Geometric, Corinthian, Athenian Black Figure Ware, etc. Imported Mycenaean wares have been found in great numbers in Palestinian Late Bronze Age deposits.[128] So if the Palestinian Late Bronze Age ended c. 733–700 B.C., the Greek Mycenaean Age must also belong to the era just before that date. Greek sources indicate that the earliest Greek colonies in Sicily and southern Italy were founded between 750 and 700 B.C. Thus, the pottery found in the earliest strata at these sites should be Mycenaean according to the revised archaeological chronologies of Bimson and Courville. But it is not! The pottery in the lowest levels of these Greek colonies is in the Late Geometric and Corinthian styles,[129] which come *after* the Proto-Geometric, Sub-Mycenaean, and Mycenaean styles in Greece. Obviously, the end of the Mycenaean Age (which equals the end of Palestinian Late Bronze Age II) and the beginning of the Sub-Mycenaean style cannot be placed as low as 733–700 B.C.

At Al-Mina in Syria and Sarafand in Lebanon Greek Geometric and Cypro-Geometric pottery was found in Iron Age II contexts.[130] Yet, in Greece, pottery of this type is found stratified *below* the types of wares noted in the earliest levels of the Sicilian colonies founded between 750 and 700 B.C. Thus the Syro-Palestinian Iron Age II Period must have begun before 700 B.C., and the Iron Age I must have been even earlier. Any attempt to move the entire Iron Age into the period after 733 B.C. is untenable.

Near-Eastern archaeological chronology is a complex chain of interlocking links constructed through generations of careful, scholarly labor. Trade items relate archaeological deposits of one area with those of another, and texts supply further synchronisms as well as absolute dates at a number of points. One cannot move historical personages and events from one age to another without consideration of their archaeological contexts. The Egyptian Eighteenth and Nineteenth dynasties belong to the Palestinian Late Bronze Age. And Rameses III of the Twentieth Dynasty ruled at the time of the transition from the Late Bronze to the Iron Age.[131] These dynasties and individuals cannot be shifted around at will as Velikovsky does.

But if one tries to save at least a part of Velikovsky's system by realigning the Palestinian archaeological periods as Bimson and Courville have done, one runs afoul of archaeological connections linking Palestine to other parts of the Mediterranean world. And one experiences problems in correlating archaeological data with biblical accounts.

There are problems still to be solved in Near Eastern archaeology, and new discoveries will no doubt necessitate revisions in the archaeological synchronisms and chronology now generally accepted. But such revisions almost certainly will be minor compared with the ones we have been considering here. "Ages in chaos" is an apt description for the modifications in ancient historical and archaeological synchronisms advocated by Velikovsky and his followers.

Rejection of Velikovsky's chronological revisions also affects the viability of his theories of cosmic collisions. Without his special dating system, some of the evidence he uses to show that there were catastrophes in the fifteenth and eighth to seventh centuries B.C. is no longer applicable. We have seen that the date for the end of the Mycenaean Period (and the Palestinian Late Bronze Age with which it is associated) cannot be lowered to the seventh century B.C. But if the Mycenaean Age belongs to an earlier time (and it does), then Greek accounts describing incidents which supposedly occurred during the Trojan War at the end of the Mycenaean Period cannot be used to prove collisions between Mars and Venus in the eighth to seventh centuries B.C. And the physical destruction of Mycenaean sites is not evidence of a cosmic cataclysm around the time of Isaiah (c. 750–687 B.C.). Also, if Egyptian chronology is not as error-ridden as Velikovsky has claimed (and it is not), then texts like the "Admonitions of Ipuwer" from the beginning of the Hyksos Period cannot be read as accounts of a fifteenth-century-B.C. catastrophe.

Ancient cultures must have experienced many localized catastrophes such as earthquakes, volcanic eruptions, floods, or pestilence. But the evidence simply does not support Velikovsky's theory of worldwide cataclysms caused by runaway planets in historical times. Whatever rewriting of ancient history may be done as a result of future discoveries, it is a safe bet that it will not resemble the scenario considered in this chapter.

The Search for Ancient Astronauts

Where did mankind come from? Why are human beings superior to all the other animals on this planet? How did man develop knowledge of crafts, architecture, writing, and other elements of civilization? People seem to have been asking these questions since the dawn of history, for they are answered in the holy books, myths, and legends of virtually every nation and tribe on earth.

But the modern era of rockets and manned space-flights has given rise to a new solution to these age-old questions: Astronauts from outer space visited earth in prehistoric times and created man by genetic manipulation (or interbreeding), then taught the new creatures the rudiments of civilization. The idea that spacemen visited earth in ancient times was suggested in a couple of books on UFOs written in the latter part of the 1950s.[1] However, the current widespread popularity of this theory is a result of Erich von Däniken's best-seller, *Chariots of the Gods?* (1968). Since the appearance of that work more than three hundred books advancing its theme have been written.[2] Two motion pictures and two television specials also described von Däniken's theories. And von Däniken himself has continued to defend his claims and add supporting evidence through subsequent volumes: *Gods From Outer Space* (also published under the title *Return to the Stars* (1970), *The Gold of the Gods* (1973), *In Search of Ancient Gods* (1973), *Von Däniken's Proof* (1977), *Signs of the Gods?* (1980), and *Pathways to the Gods* (1982).

Evidence of Extraterrestrial Visitors

The thesis of Von Däniken and his followers that technologically advanced visitors from another world interbred with or altered the genes of apelike creatures on earth to produce intelligent human beings would not seem strange in a science fiction novel. In fact, a number of popular works, including the 1968 film *2001: A Space Odyssey,* have had a similar theme. But von Däniken claims that his assertion is not fiction, but fact. Therefore, some hard evidence must be produced to support his theories.

The evidence he and his followers cite is of two kinds: (1) interpretations of myths, legends, or biblical passages that mention flying beings, gods coming to earth from heaven, sexual relations between humans and gods, etc.; and (2) the existence of archaeological enigmas—artifacts ranging from small seal impressions to huge stone monuments—which supposedly cannot be adequately explained by current archaeological and historical theories. Von Däniken admits that he has no direct or truly "scientific" proof of his beliefs, but he argues that he has provided massive circumstantial evidence, the kind of proof acceptable in a court of law.[3]

The Bible is one of the texts which, it is claimed, supports the ancient astronauts thesis. For example, Genesis 6:1-4 mentions "sons of God" who take human women as wives and produce gigantic heroes known as Nephilim. The account of the destruction of the cities of Sodom and Gomorrah (Genesis 19: 1-28) suggests to von Däniken an atomic explosion set off by spacemen ("angels") to destroy an unpleasant brood of humans.[4] Exodus 25: 10-22 relates the instructions that God gave to Moses about building the Ark of the Covenant. Von Däniken states that this description and the fact that anyone who touched the ark died indicates that it was an electrically charged instrument by which Moses communicated with the astronauts aboard their spaceship.[5] However, he later argues that the Ark of the Covenant was really a mini-reactor which used radiation to produce manna out of dew and green algae.[6] There is also the reference to Elijah being carried to heaven in a fiery chariot (II Kings 2: 11) which may have suggested the title for *Chariots of the Gods?*. And Ezekiel's vision of four creatures and wheels which appear out of a whirlwind (Ezekiel 1: 4-28) supposedly describes a multipurpose vehicle such as an amphibious helicopter.[7]

Von Däniken also cites references to sons of heaven, heavenly chariots, flying wheels and the smoke and light associated with such vehicles in later Jewish works such as the *Genesis Apocryphon* (earlier known as the Lamech scroll, which is the title von Däniken uses), *The Book of Enoch* (or *I Enoch*), *The Apocalypse of Moses*, *II Esdras* (or *IV Ezra*), and *The Apocalypse of Abraham*.[8] These writings, produced between c. 170 B.C. and A.D. 100, expanded upon themes and stories from portions of the Bible such as Genesis, Exodus, and Ezra. They were eventually excluded from both the Jewish and Christian canons of sacred literature, but they were read and widely used as Scripture by many Jews in the first centuries B.C. and A.D.

Other accounts of semi-divine beings (the results of unions between gods and humans), fiery chariots, flying gods, and men carried into the heavens by gods, as well as descriptions of the catastrophic power of the gods' weapons are found in the myths and legends of people around the world. Among the works to which von Däniken refers are the ancient Mesopotamian *Epic of Gilgamesh,*[9] the Maya *Popol Vuh,*[10] Hindu myths about Garuda and Shiva,[11] the Sanskrit epic *Mahabharata,*[12] and the Ethiopic *Kebra Nagast.*[13]

But more persuasive than these interpretations of the Bible and mythology are descriptions of archaeological "mysteries." For example, a map belonging to the sixteenth century Turkish admiral Piri Re'is depicts the Atlantic Ocean with the western coasts of Europe and Africa. Surprisingly, however, it includes the coasts of North and South America as well as a land that might be Antarctica.[14] Von Däniken was amazed by the map's accuracy:[15]

> The mountain ranges in the Antarctic, which already figure on Reis' maps, were not discovered until 1952. They have been covered in ice for thousands of years, and our present-day maps have been drawn with the aid of echo-sounding apparatus. . . . Comparison with modern photographs of our globe taken from satellites showed that the originals of Piri Reis' maps must have been aerial photographs taken from a very great height. How can that be explained?

In Peru gigantic lines visible from the air are etched into the surface of the coastal plain near the ancient city of Nazca. They start from nowhere and lead nowhere. What are they for? To von Däniken, they resemble an airfield and could have been laid out according to directions from a space-ship flying above.[16] In addition to straight lines, there are outlines of huge birds, spiders, monkeys, and other creatures delineated on the Nazca Plain. These and other similar Peruvian figures can be seen in their entirety and comprehended only from the air. Were they signals for the "gods" who flew overhead in their machines? Why would people create signs which could only be seen from high above if they did not know that flying beings actually existed?[17]

Similar evidence is deduced from the name of the Island of Elephantine in the Nile River at Aswan, Egypt. Von Däniken states that the ancients called it "Elephantine" because it looked like an elephant. Yet how did they know that? "This shape can be recognized only from an airplane at a great height, for there is no hill offering a view of the island that would prompt anyone to make the comparison."[18]

Another enigma cited is the existence of a gigantic system of tunnels hundreds or thousands of miles long running beneath Ecuador and Peru. Von Däniken says that in 1972 he explored some of these tunnels with their discoverer, Juan Moricz.[19] Their walls were smooth and seemed to be polished. The ceilings were flat. Passages intersected at perfect right angles. "Obviously these passages did not originate from natural causes—they looked more like contemporary air-raid shelters!"[20]

One of the tunnels led to a large hall which contained a table with seven chairs made of an unknown plasticlike substance, a series of gold animal scupltures, and a library of two or three thousand thin metal plaques. These plaques, each about three feet long by a foot and a half wide, were made of an unknown metal and stamped with signs in an unknown script and language.[21] There was also a pile of gold artifacts in one of the underground chambers, but Moricz would not allow von Däniken to take pictures of the gold, the metal plaques, or the tunnels.[22] However, von Däniken was able to examine and photograph a number of gold objects in the possession of Father Crespi of the Church of Maria Auxiliadora at Cuenca, Ecuador. These objects supposedly came from the tunnels.[23] Von Däniken thinks that the designs on these gold objects and the inscriptions on the plaques as well as the system of underground passages from which they came hold the answers to questions about the origins of mankind and of all civilization.[24]

Those who believe in ancient spacemen also assert that mankind had access to an advanced technology which was later lost and forgotten except for obscure references to it in myths and legends. Without the equipment and engineering know-how of space visitors, how could primitive men have raised the huge stone monuments of antiquity? The stones of the Great Pyramid of Egypt weigh an average of 2½ tons each. At Tiahuanaco in the Bolivian Andes, the "Gateway of the Sun" (nearly 10 feet high and 16½ feet wide) is carved out of a single huge block of stone! On Easter Island in the Pacific Ocean there are many gigantic statues 33 to 66 feet high and weighing as much as 50 tons standing erect far from the quarries from which they were cut. Moreover, they were once topped by "hats" made of a different kind of stone and weighing more than 10 tons apiece. Von Däniken states that such huge stones could not have been cut with stone or copper tools and moved on wooden rollers as archaeologists claim.[25]

Other signs of advanced ancient technology supposedly abound:[26]

Electric dry batteries, which work on the galvanic principle, are on display in the Baghdad Museum. . . . Parts of a belt made of aluminum lay in a grave at Yungjin, China. At Delhi there is an ancient pillar made of iron that is not destroyed by phosphorus, sulphur, or the effects of the weather.

In addition, on an ancient wreck near the Greek island of Antikythera, sponge divers found an "inexplicable" first-century-B.C. bronze machine with gears and dials that could be used to predict movements of various heavenly bodies.[27]

Von Däniken believes that the source of this advanced technology in antiquity was spacemen, and that they were depicted many times by the ancients. Among the Tassili frescoes in the Sahara is a drawing of a being with a large round head. According to von Däniken's interpetation, this picture represents a man in a space or diving suit.[28] Other Stone Age carvings and paintings in the Sahara, Australia, California, Italy, Peru, and Russia are also interpreted as depictions of men in spacesuits with helmets, antennae, and other accessories.[29] And at Palenque in Yucatan a stone relief of a "space-god" (Figure 4) was supposedly found.[30] Here is how von Däniken describes it:[31]

> There sits a human being, with the upper part of his body bent forward like a racing motorcyclist; today any child would identify his vehicle as a rocket. It is pointed at the front, then changes to strangely grooved identations like inlet ports, widens out, and terminates at the tail in a darting flame. The crouching being himself is manipulating a number of indefinable controls and has the heel of his left foot on a kind of pedal. His clothing is appropriate: short trousers with a broad belt, a jacket with a modern Japanese opening at the neck, and closely fitting bands at arms and legs. With our knowledge of similar pictures, we should be surprised if the complicated headgear were missing. And there it is with the usual indentations and tubes, and something like antennae on top. Our space traveler—he is clearly depicted as one—is not only bent forward tensely; he is also looking intently at an apparatus hanging in front of his face. The astronaut's front seat is separated by struts from the rear portion of the vehicle, in which symmetrically arranged boxes, circles, points, and spirals can be seen.

With such a mass of circumstantial evidence available, why do scientists and archaeologists still deny that the earth was visited by ancient astronauts?

Astronauts in the Bible and Other Ancient Texts?

Of all the "proofs" von Däniken gives for his thesis, the most difficult to contend with are his interpretations of a number of ancient texts, including the Bible. The difficulty arises from the fact that his approach is so subjective. He usually is content to describe the impression he received from a passage or to simply suggest an interpretation that would explain a text in terms of his theories. Thus, he plants an idea or question in the reader's mind. In many instances, however, these imaginative impressions

FIGURE 4. The Palenque "Astronaut" (after A. Villagra in A. Ruz Lhuillier 1970)

or "suggestions" are later treated as if they were established conclusions drawn after a full analysis of the evidence.

As an example of von Däniken's use of impressions instead of careful analysis, here is his "answer" to questions he raises about the destruction of the biblical cities of Sodom and Gomorrah:[32]

> *Let us imagine* for a moment that Sodom and Gomorrah were destroyed according to plan, i.e., deliberately, by a nuclear explosion. Perhaps—*let us speculate a little further*—the "angels" simply wanted to destroy some dangerous fissionable material and at the same time to make sure of wiping out a human brood they found unpleasant. The time for the destruction was fixed. Those who were to escape it—such as the Lot family—had to stay a few miles from the center of the explosion in the mountains, for the rock faces would naturally absorb the powerful dangerous rays. And—we all know the story—Lot's wife turned around and looked straight at the atomic sun. Nowadays no one is surprised that she fell dead on the spot. [Italics added.]

Characteristically, von Däniken does not examine his interpretation or "speculation" to see if it truly explains all aspects of the text. In the Sodom and Gomorrah story, there is no mention of the shock waves and powerful winds that would have accompanied an atomic explosion and that would have been felt by Lot and his family, even if they were "a few miles from the center of the explosion in the mountains." Furthermore, von Däniken's supposition that Lot and his family would have been shielded by hills from any harmful radiation is incorrect. According to Genesis 19: 18–22, Lot was told to go into the mountains, but *he did not do so.* He persuaded the angels to let him stay at the town of Zoar, which was in the plain. Yet the story claims that Lot and his family survived the destruction of the two nearby cities.

And what of Lot's wife? She supposedly "looked straight at the atomic sun" and died. But while looking at the brightness of an atomic explosion would have blinded her, it would not have killed her. And if she died from other products of the explosion like shock waves, heat, or radiation, these forces would have killed Lot and the others also, regardless of the direction they were facing! The biblical writer does not seem to be describing an atomic explosion. All of the major elements of his story—the fire and brimstone, the rising smoke from the fiery destruction, the pillar of salt—are features which he or his sources could have observed in the Dead Sea region where Sodom and Gomorrah were supposed to have been located. This area was noted for blocks of rock salt, salt-incrusted rocks, sulphur, pools of bitumen and noxious fumes.[33]

A similar failure to carefully check his interpretation against the text is evident in von Däniken's discussions of the Ark of the Covenant. In his early books he claimed that the Ark was an electrical condenser with a voltage of several hundred volts and that it was often surrounded by flashing sparks.[34] "The border and golden crown would have served to charge the condenser which was formed by the gold plates and a positive and negative conductor."[35] However, the Bible states that the entire Ark of the Covenant was to be plated with gold, inside and outside. The carrying poles for it were also plated with gold and placed through gold rings fastened to the Ark.[36] An electrical charge applied to any part of the Ark would have flowed over the entire surface—there was no gap or separation by an insualtor to make possible a positive and a negative pole. The Ark could not have served as a condenser.[37] There is also no reference in the Bible to the Ark being surrounded by flashing sparks.

Von Däniken supports his belief in an electrically charged Ark by reference to II Samuel 6: 2 in which Uzzah, a man who touched the Ark to keep it from falling, died on the spot "as if struck by lightning."[38] However, he forgets that the Ark was often carried by poles placed through the rings in its side.[39] And these carrying poles were covered with gold, making it possible for them to conduct electricity! If touching the side of the Ark could electrocute a person, touching the carrying poles could also. But the Bible does not indicate that any special protective gloves were worn by the Ark's bearers, and none of them seem to have been electrocuted.[40]

In a later work, von Däniken accepted the arguments of George Sassoon and R. Dale that the Ark contained a mini-reactor which produced manna out of dew and green algae. This "manna machine" was supposedly given to Moses on Mount Sinai when he saw the burning bush; the Ark was later made as a carrying case for it. The Ark with its reactor could only be approached by those trained to operate it—all others fell ill or died of radiation poisoning.[41] But the Bible claims that the Israelites were eating manna in the desert before they reached Mount Sinai and for a number of months before the Ark of the Covenant was built.[42] So Moses must have had the "manna machine" with him when he returned to Egypt from his personal exile in Sinai and throughout the early stages of the Exodus. Yet the Bible does not mention Moses having any kind of machine during that time, nor were there attendants to carry it as there later were for the Ark. The mini-reactor interpretation is no better founded than the electrical condenser one was.

Von Däniken's discussion of the "helicopter" of Ezekiel also suffers from a failure to treat the entire text.[43] After quoting the first half of Ezekiel 1:1, he omits the second half of the verse and skips down to 1:4 ff., which describes the whirlwind and the creatures which appear out of it.[44] The omitted portion of the first verse clearly states that what follows was a *vision*. As such, it should be treated symbolically, as are other visions in the book of Ezekiel (like the vision of the Valley of the Dry Bones in Chapter 37). Ezekiel uses the vision of the Cherubim (for this is how the winged creatures are identified in 10:20) and the wheels to emphasize the absolute majesty and transcendence of God "who is not limited by space or gravity."[45] Von Däniken's acceptance of this passage as an historical account of an objective phenomenon ignores the plain statement of the text!

Another problem with von Däniken's use of ancient texts is his failure to utilize scholarly evidence concerning the dates when the works were produced and the cultural environments in which they arose. Not only Ezekiel's vision, but all of the works he discusses are treated as if they were eyewitness reports—sometimes confused and distorted perhaps, since the ancients lacked the technical knowledge to always understand what they saw, but nonetheless descriptions of real things. This practice results in a number of non sequiturs.

There is space here for only a couple of examples. Von Däniken cites a reference in the *Apocalypse of Moses* to Eve seeing a heavenly chariot of light. He then concludes that "chariots of light, wheels, and smoke were spoken of as magnificent apparitions *as early as and in connection with Adam and Eve.*"[46] The *Book of Enoch* contains an astronomical section in which watchmen of the sky tell Enoch about the moon and stars. Von Däniken was amazed: "They give complicated astronomical details which, I feel, nobody could have known *at the time of Enoch, because this whole story happens before the great flood.*"[47] It does not take a specialist in logic to recognize that texts having Adam and Eve or Enoch as major characters do not necessarily date from the beginnings of human history (i.e., "as early as" Adam and Eve or "the time of Enoch"), nor do they necessarily convey any accurate information about such early periods.

The *Apocalypse of Moses* (or *Life of Adam and Eve* as it is now usually titled) was not found for the first time with the Dead Sea Scrolls as von Däniken claims.[48] It has been known to scholars since the 1860s. This book was written in the first half of the first century A.D. Like a number of other works of that time, it amplifies biblical stories with legendary material designed to explain practices, beliefs, or customs not found in the Bible.[49] The *Book of Enoch* (or *I Enoch*) is a composite work produced between 170 and 64 B.C.[50] It thus belongs to the Hellenistic Period, a time when astronomy was quite advanced.[51] Apocalyptic texts from the first two centuries B.C. and the first century A.D., such as *II Esdras* (*IV Ezra*) and the *Apocalypse of Abraham* (both of which von Däniken uses) as well as the *Book of Enoch* were not intended as straightforward historical reports. They present the past in the guise of prophecies and visions given to some very ancient worthy (Enoch, Abraham, Moses, Ezra, etc.), and they utilize elaborate symbolism in presenting their messages. They have much to tell us about the attitudes and beliefs of the time when they were written, but they should not be considered reliable sources of information on pre-history or on the period of Israelite history before about 400 B.C. Also, their references to individuals being taken into the heavens and granted visions should not be taken literally.

Von Däniken's use of non-Jewish literature, myths, and legends is just as faulty. For instance, his discussion of the Mesopotamian *Epic of Gilgamesh* teems with contradictions and errors.[52] Von Däniken claims that the epic's account of the mating of a wild, hairy man named Enkidu and a "semi-divine beauty" is an example of crossbreeding between a female demigod and a half-animal.[53] But the epic actually says that it was a human prostitute who seduced Enkidu.[54] In one place, the epic's story of the Flood is said to be a "first-hand report."[55] However, a bit later von Däniken states that "we now possess an even older description of the Flood than the one in the *Epic of Gilgamesh.*"[56] (How it is possible for any account to be older than firsthand is not explained.) The theme of the *Epic of Gilgamesh* is the mortality of man, and von Däniken notes the warning given to Gilgamesh: "Thou shalt not find the life that thou seekest. When the gods created man, they allotted him to death, but life they retained in their own keeping."[57] A Sumerian poem about Gilgamesh uncovered at Nippur was one of the sources for the later epic, and it has the same theme—man must die; only a great name will survive.[58] Yet, in his discussion of the Sumerians in a subsequent chapter, von Däniken claims that they "looked forward to a new life beyond the grave" and by a rhetorical question he suggests that spacemen must have put the idea into their heads.[59] One wonders whether the hand that wrote Chapter 5 of *Chariots of the Gods?* knew what the hand that wrote Chapter 6 was doing.

When considering the Sanskrit epic the *Mahabharata,* von Däniken states that its core is at least 5,000 years old and possibly goes back as far as 7,016 B.C.[60] Yet specialists in Sanskrit literature place its composition between the sixth and third centuries B.C.[61] The war between two noble families that it describes is probably based on a historical conflict that occurred somewhat earlier, around the begininng of the ninth century B.C.[62] But none of the work, including its "core" (presumably the *Bhagavad-gita*) can be placed earlier than the Aryan invasion of India, which took place c. 1750-1500 B.C.[63] The *Mahabharata* does not provide data from the era between 7,000 and 3,500 B.C., the time during which von Däniken claims his spacemen were active.[64]

Reference after reference is made to myths describing gods traveling through the air on flying devices and possessing awesome weapons.[65] But most of the deities discussed are gods of the sun, moon or stars. What is so surprising about ancient people worshipping these prominent and important natural objects? And why is it amazing that many peoples described the gods associated with heavenly bodies as moving across the sky in chariots or ships (the sun, moon, or stars themselves)? Von Däniken is also surprised that myths tell of divine weapons that reduce entire cities to ashes (nuclear bombs?),[66] or send out lightning flashes or blinding rays (lasers?).[67] Could such descriptions come from imagination? He thinks not. "It must be that the ancient storytellers had a store of things already seen, known, and experienced ready at hand to spark off their imagination!"[68] Von Däniken forgets that Jules Verne imagined and described a space trip to the moon and an electrically powered submarine long before either became a reality. Buck Rogers was flying to other planets and shooting ray guns in fiction decades before scientists developed manned rockets or invented laser beams. The power of imagination—the intellectual faculty von Däniken utilized most in writing his own books—should not be underestimated.

During one interview, von Däniken was confronted with an objection like those we have been raising about his methods of interpreting ancient texts. His response was quite revealing: "It's true that I accept what I like and reject what I don't like, but every theologian does the same. Everyone accepts just what he needs for his theory and to the rest he says, 'Well, that's a misunderstanding.'" "Except," shot back the interviewer, "that you claim to be offering science, not theology. . . ."[69] Unfortunately, von Däniken's treatment of ancient texts provides no justification for assuming that he knows the difference!

The Piri Re'is Map and the Nazca Lines

Much of the archaeological evidence for Erich von Däniken's thesis was derived from two earlier French works, one by Louis Pauwels and Jacques Bergier, and the other by Robert Charroux. These books referred to "mysteries" such as the Piri Re'is Map, Nazca lines, Great Pyramid, Easter Island, Tiahuanaco, Baghdad batteries, Tassili frescoes, and other "proofs" later utilized by von Däniken.[70] And these archaeological enigmas have continued to be stressed in the movies, T.V. specials, and books on the astronaut theme inspired by *Chariots of the Gods?* But archaeological evidence does not support the theory of visits by ancient spacemen any more than ancient textual material does.

The Piri Re'is Map is one of the most often cited and initially persuasive pieces of evidence for the presence of spacemen in antiquity. This map was found in 1929 when the old Imperial Palace in Istanbul was being converted to a museum. It was signed by Piri Ibn Haji Mehmed, better known as Piri Re'is ("Admiral Piri"), and dated in the

Muslim year 919 (which is equivalent to A.D. 1513). It was quickly recognized as one of the earliest maps of America, and surprisingly, it placed South America in its correct longitudinal position in relation to Africa. This was unusual on sixteenth-century maps.[71]

Interest in the map soon died down, but in the mid-1950s, a copy of it came to the attention of Captain A. H. Mallery, a student of old maps. After some study, Mallery suggested that the southernmost bit of land shown on the map represented the coast of Antarctica without its present ice cover. If so, Antarctica must have been mapped in antiquity before it became covered by glaciers.[72]

This theory was developed further and popularized by Charles H. Hapgood. Hapgood arued that the accuracy of longitude on the Piri Re'is map could not be explained in terms of the navigational science available in the sixteenth century.[73] And he agreed with Mallery that the map displayed "striking agreement" with the seismic profile across Queen Maud Land in Antarctica.[74] His conclusion was that the map was based on ancient charts which must have been made by seafarers of an unknown advanced civilization (Atlantis, Mu, or the like) that existed before the Ice Age.[75]

Von Däniken referred to Hapgood's study as the basis for the "shattering information" that the Piri Re'is map must derive from aerial photographs.[76] But Hapgood never made such a claim. Von Däniken seems to have borrowed this idea not from Hapgood, as he says, but rather from Pauwels and Bergier's *The Morning of the Magicians* (1960) and/or Charroux's *One Hundred Thousand Years of Man's Unknown History* (1963), works whose influence on his theories von Däniken did not acknowledge when he wrote *Chariots of the Gods?*[77] Whatever their source, the statements that the Piri Re'is map is "absolutely accurate," that the coasts of North and South America and even the contours of the Antarctic were also "precisely delineated," and that "the maps must have been made with the modern technical aid—from the air,"[78] are simply incorrect.

Careful comparison of sections of the Piri Re'is map with modern maps of the same areas shows the falsehood of claims that the map is fantastically accurate.[79] The Caribbean area on the Piri Re'is map bears little resemblance to reality. Cuba is wrongly labeled "Hispaniola" and is drawn totally out of proportion. The Virgin Islands are shown in the wrong positions, incorrectly shaped and badly out of scale. The eastern coast of South America is also represented incorrectly: The Amazon River appears twice, nine hundred miles of coastline are missing, and there is no sea passage shown between South America and Antarctica. (A drawing of the map illustrated by von Däniken[80] is taken from Hapgood's book[81] and contains notes describing these errors. Von Däniken must not have studied his own illustration.) Finally, despite claims to the contrary, the coast of Antarctica on the map is not in very close agreement with either the present-day coastline or seismic profiles of the area.[82] The explanatory legends on the "Antarctica" portion of the map claim that this land is inhabited by white-haired monsters, six-horned oxen, and large snakes. And the information on this area is explicitly credited to Portuguese sailors and their maps.[83]

Hapgood is able to support his claims for the accuracy of the map's *sources* only by making many corrections, then assuming that these were present in the original maps of small areas compiled to make the Piri Re'is Atlantic map. The errors cited above must have been introduced by the Turkish or earlier compilers, he thinks. Von Däniken doesn't repeat this argument. He wrongly assumes the map is accurate as it stands.

Neither spacemen nor unknown pre-Ice Age seafarers are needed to explain the Piri Re'is map. It seems to be exactly what Piri Re'is stated it was in a marginal note—a composite map based on older Greek and Arab charts, on a map made by Columbus, and charts as well as verbal reports of other New World explorers. Its errors are similar to those that occur on other sixteenth century maps. Considering the limitations with which early mapmakers had to contend, this map is an excellent example of the cartographer's art during the Age of Exploration. But it is a *human* product, not a "mystery" derived from ancient astronauts.

During an interview in 1974, von Däniken was informed about the errors in the map that he claimed was "absolutely accurate." His explanation was that he had not actually checked the map personally; he had based his claims on information he had received. "I must find out about what you say," he promised. "If I find that what I've written is wrong, then I will be the first to correct it. At least in my next book, I'll say this was wrong."[84] Yet in defending his theory in his 1977 book, von Däniken wrote:[85]

I cannot help it if the Turkish Admiral Piri Reis in 1513 made maps of the world showing—before Columbus [sic!]—the coasts of North and South America and even the outline of the Antarctic which were hidden under layers of ice; these are contours which *we* first discovered by echo-sounding during the Geophysical Year, 1957. I really do not know who put an observer-satellite and ultra modern observation apparatus at Piri Reis's disposal.

This passage provides no indication that von Däniken kept his word and checked the Piri Re'is map against modern ones. He does not attempt to refute those who have pointed out the map's numerous mistakes. He simply repeats the erroneous claims that he made in 1968. The objective reader will be forgiven if this incident causes him to doubt the sincerity of von Däniken's frequent assertions that he seeks only the truth. Because of von Däniken's refusal to be bothered with facts once his mind is made up, millions of people remain under the delusion that the Piri Re'is map is so accurate it could have been made only with the help of spacemen.

Unlike the Piri Re'is map, the Nazca lines in Peru *are* a real mystery. These lines were made by removing surface stones to reveal the lighter soil underneath. They remain because the area gets virtually no rain. Archaeologists think the lines were made between c. 200 B. C. and A.D. 600. The animal figures are stylistically similar to representations on Nazca pottery from that era, and fragments of Nazca pottery are strewn across the plain.[86] But no one knows why these lines and figures were created.

The answer originally suggested by von Däniken was that the markings were an airfield.[87] Space visitors laid out an improvised airfield on the plain. After they left, the natives made new lines on the ground like those they had seen to induce the "gods" to return. The animal figures were added later when people had forgotten what the "gods" were really like.[88] Later, however, von Däniken modified this theory somewhat. Spaceships landing and taking off made the marks on the desert floor, he claimed. These tracks were deepened and copied by the natives. When the "gods" failed to return a priest told the people that they had to show sacrificial symbols to the heavenly ones, so the animal figures were created.[89]

Why ancient astronauts in spaceships needed an airfield is never explained. Presumably their space vehicles would have taken off vertically as ours do today, so it is difficult to see how they would have left long straight lines that suggest runways. Von Däniken posits such vertical take-off craft in his account of Ezekiel's vision,[90] but the spacemen at Nazca must have had airplanelike vehicles which had to taxi before taking off. Von Däniken does not seem to have observed that a number of the presumed landing strips run right across hills and ridges formed by dried river beds, or that when its covering of pebbles and stones is removed the soil of the Nazca Plain is too soft for use by aircraft.[91]

In at least one instance, von Däniken gives an interpretation of a group of the lines that goes beyond being merely imaginative and becomes totally deceptive. He published a photograph of some of the lines, describing their appearance as "reminiscent of the aircraft parking areas in a modern airport."[92] Actually, the entire area depicted is only a couple of yards wide, hardly big enough for anything other than toy aircraft.[93] More importantly, however, these lines really form the outline of the right knee-joint and foot of a large bird figure.[94] If von Däniken had shown the whole figure no one would have noted the slightest resemblance to an aircraft parking area!

But if the lines were not meant to mark runways, parking areas, or other features of an airfield, what were they for? A theory supported by many scholars, including Maria Reiche who has studied the Nazca markings for more than thirty years, is that the straight lines indicated the rising or setting points of various heavenly bodies (sun, moon, individual stars, or constellations). Small mounds of rocks found near the lines might have been used to count days, thus making the lines function as a giant astronomical calendar.[95] The animal figures might represent various constellations.[96]

Gerald Hawkins, an astronomer famous for his study of Stonehenge, fed the results of an aerial survey of the Nazca Plain into a computer. He could find no astronomical alignments for the straight lines beyond what would be expected by chance. The computer print-outs did indicate that there was a heavenly body at the end of each of the lines, but the alignments belonged to different periods. That is, there was no single century when most of the lines had significant astronomical alignments. However, Hawkins's study has not convinced all astronomers and archaeologists that the astronomical calendar theory is wrong. If the straight lines were made at different times over a period of centuries, many (if not all) of them might still have had astronomical significance.[97]

Other scholars think the lines had a religious function. Many nonliterate societies use repeated ceremonies or ritual activities to perpetuate knowledge from generation to generation. Walking along various lines (probably while reciting traditional verses) may have been part of such rituals.[98] Or the animal figures may have formed ritual mazes in which a person walking along the line was thought to absorb something of the essence of the creature depicted by the outline.[99]

It has also been noted that the labor necessary to create the Nazca lines must have been equivalent to that utilized by other Peruvian cultures to build pyramids or other monuments. Such communal projects had a definite social value. In order to undertake such large projects, a society had to centralize its food storage so that food could be equitably distributed to those constructing the communal works as well as those engaged in agriculture or herding. This central administration of the food supply would have helped prevent excessive population increases during good agricultural years and the large number of deaths that would have followed during years of ordinary or lean harvests.[100] Of course, this theory of the lines' function does not rule out astronomical or religious reasons for the *form* the lines took. It can be combined with either of the preceding hypotheses.

Whatever their purpose, the lines and figures at Nazca could have been made without directions being supplied by a hovering spacecraft. Recently experiments were undertaken to show that the Nazca people could have constructed hot-air balloons from which work on the lines could have been supervised.[101] But not even hot-air balloons are required to explain how the lines and figures were laid out. Maria Reiche argues that the designs were marked out using pivot rocks and long cords. Near some of the huge animal figures she has also found miniature drawings of the same creatures. These small figures were probably enlarged by placing a grid over them, then copying the features in each square onto a larger grid laid out on the plain with cords.[102]

There are still many questions to be answered about the Nazca lines. But of all the hypotheses attempting to explain these designs, von Däniken's is the least likely to be correct. The plain is simply unsuitable for an airfield. It should also be noted that since the ancient peoples of Peru worshipped the sun, the moon, and other heavenly bodies, the fact that the Nazca figures could be appreciated fully only from the air does not prove that these people knew of ancient astronauts. It is more likely that the designs were meant for these natural gods (sun, moon, and stars) than for spacemen flying above.

Tunnels and Gold in Ecuador

Perhaps the most spectacular evidence for ancient space visitors is von Däniken's description of tunnels in Ecuador containing gold statues and a library of inscribed metal tablets. This sounds like solid evidence, not just a matter of interpretation. Archaeologists can explore the caves; experts can study the writing on the tablets; scientists can test the unknown metal and plasticlike chairs. Unfortunately, this is not the case.

Soon after the appearance of *Gold of the Gods,* in which von Däniken related his visit to one of the tunnels, the German news magazine *Der Spiegel* interviewed Juan Moricz, the man who supposedly discovered the caves and who guided von Däniken on his exploratory trip. Moricz flatly denied that von Däniken had ever been in the caves:[103]

> If he says he personally saw the library and the other things, he's lying. It's a downright disgrace. We never showed him those things. He's even fiddled the photos. The picture on p. 15 of his book *Aussaat und Kosmos* [English version titled *Gold of the Gods*] was taken during our 1969 expedition—it shows a cave entrance eroded by water. As for the amulet on page 20, I didn't find it in a cave, as he claims. . . . We took him on a two-day trip to Cuenca and showed him one of the many cave entrances in the vicinity., You couldn't enter the cave, though, it's blocked.

According to Moricz, the source for von Däniken's descriptions of his "journey" inside the tunnel was a long conversation the two men had in March 1972: "He pumped me for hours on end."[104] Moricz confirmed that he took von Däniken to see Father Crespi's collection of "gold" objects, but said that he warned the Swiss writer that most of the pieces were not authentic. Despite the warning, von Däniken insisted on photographing it all. "And it wasn't the genuine pieces he illustrated in his book," Moricz asserted, "far from it, in my opinion."[105]

Von Däniken later admitted that he had not been inside the main entrance of the caves where the photograph in his book was taken. But he insisted that he had gone into a side entrance (though in the book he lied about its location to keep others from finding it) and he *had* seen the hall containing plasticlike chairs and the library of metal plates.[106] However, some of the events he described had not actually taken place, he confirmed—they were "theatrical effects" to make his writing more interesting.[107] Von Däniken felt Moricz was claiming that the whole account was a hoax because Moricz and the other members of a 1969 expedition to the caves had not received publicity or made money from their experiences as von Däniken had. "But finally," he argued, "the whole controversy over whether I have been down there in those caves or not seems ridiculous. The main question should be: Does the library of gold plates exist or not?"[108]

Geologists familiar with the area von Däniken visited state that there are many caves in the white limestone of the region, but they are all of natural origin. And Father Porras, professor of archaeology at the Catholic University of Quito, has explored caves in eastern Ecuador for twenty-five years without finding any artifacts or other evidence of human use of the caverns.[109] Since the appearance of *Gold of the Gods,* a number of caves in the area have been examined by Fritz Stibane, professor of geology at the University of Giessen, and by a Scottish expedition of which astronaut Neil Armstrong was a member. No gold was found, and there was no evidence that the caves were artificially constructed.[110] The director of Quito's archaeological museum and a United States film-producer have each made very generous offers to Juan Moricz to induce him to produce the inscribed plaques or other evidence he knows about. But he has refused to do so.[111] Finally, Father Crespi's collection has been examined and found to contain mostly tin or brass imitations of the type made for tourists.[112] So efforts *have* been made to determine whether or not the gold plates and other evidence of Ecuadorian astronauts exist. The results have all been negative.

Von Däniken's answer to those who question his theories on the basis of these reports reveals his total failure to comprehend the nature of objective evidence. He argues as if he were presenting his case before a court of law:[113]

> Every expert knows that there are hundreds of different caves in Ecuador. I ask the Court to explain why the expedition crawled about in *any old* cave and not in *my* side entrance to a tunnel? They could not have known its position, because I promised its discoverer not to tell it to anyone. I am

used to keeping my word. [Italics in the orignal.]

It is not the responsibility of scientists and archaeologists to prove von Däniken wrong by searching every cave in Ecuador. For even if that were done, he could always claim that they did not find *his* cave. Scholars have already spent more money and effort trying to verify von Däniken's story than is justified by his flimsy and contradictory statements. The burden of proof is on Moricz and von Däniken. If they expect thinking people to believe that the gold objects and inscribed plates exist, then they must make these artifacts or detailed information about their supposed location available to scholars for inspection. Until they do, the story of tunnels and so-called gold of the gods must be treated as a myth and dismissed as evidence of space visitors.

The Palenque "Astronaut" and Other Portraits of Spacemen

In an earlier section of this chapter, we quoted von Däniken's description of a Mayan relief decorating a sarcophagus lid at Palenque, a site in Chipas, Mexico. This sculpture supposedly depicts a space traveler in his rocket. Close examination of this relief, however, reveals many features that von Däniken omitted or misinterpreted. The illustration he presented in *Chariots of the Gods?* is very unclear,[114] and the photographs in *In Search of Ancient Gods* show only limited portions of the sculpture.[115] The reader should refer to the more accurate drawing given above (Figure 4) or to the excellent National Geographic Society photograph of the entire lid.[116]

One of the first things to be noted is the bird sitting on the nose of the "rocket." Von Däniken failed to mention it in his description of the relief. Why is it there? When asked this question von Däniken answered: "Oh, I don't know. Perhaps it represents flight, you know."[117] So the bird is not a hood ornament. It is allowed to be symbolic while the rest of the sculpture is supposed to depict what the artist actually saw!

The "astronaut" is certainly not suitably dressed for space flight. He is wearing a "helmet" that does not cover his face, yet his head is protruding through an opening in the side of the "rocket." He is not wearing shoes, gloves, long pants or a shirt.[118] Von Däniken seems to have interpreted the anklets and bracelets shown on the relief as the bands at the ends of pants legs and jacket sleeves and the jade necklace as the neck opening of a jacket. However, this figure is dressed like other Mayan nobles portrayed at Palenque (see the figure on the right in Figure 5 and the one on the left in Figure 6, for example). He is naked except for a loincloth, wide belt, and the jewelry on his neck, wrists, and ankles. Jade ornaments like the ones the "astronaut" is shown wearing were found inside the sarcophagus that this lid covered.[119]

The ruler or "astronaut" is half-seated, half-reclining on a symbol that has been designated the "quadripartite badge of rulership," which, in turn, rests on the head of the "Earth Monster," guardian of the underworld.[120] Von Däniken took the "Earth Monster" figure to be the lower part of the space ship and the creature's fleshless jaws reaching upward he took to be the rocket's fins. Above the half-reclining figure rises a cross-shaped object with a double-headed serpent draped over its arms and a quetzel-bird on its top. For von Däniken this cross was the nose section of the rocket. If he had taken the time to compare this relief with others at Palenque, von Däniken would have seen that this cross is a religious object, not part of a space vehicle. It probably is a stylized representation of a maize (corn) plant. In other temples at Palenque it is depicted in much the same fashion as on the sarcophagus lid (Figures 5 and 6). The plant is shown growing from the head of the Earth Monster and a quetzal-bird is perched on its top.[121]

Taken in the context of Mayan art, this scene probably depicts a priest or king at the moment of death suspended between the underworld and the world of the living. Even as the jaws of the Earth Monster reach up to claim him, he gazes upward at the sacred maize plant, symbol of rebirth and life, and at the quetzal-bird, the sun god who is the source of life.[122]

Von Däniken has stated that the inscription around the Palenque "astronaut" relief indicates that the person in the tomb died because of "the hot wind." Naturally he interprets this as the blast from a spaceship.[123] It would be interesting to know the source of this translation of the in-scription, because, except for date formulas, decipherment of Mayan hieroglyphic writing is still very controversial. Experts cannot even agree on the correct reading of the name of the man buried in the tomb.[124] All that is certain is that he died in the late seventh century A.D., a bit late in time for von Däniken's spacemen to be paying a visit.

Other supposed representations of extraterrestrials are even less convincing than the Palenque "astronaut." Round-headed figures painted in caves at Tassili n'Ajjer in Algeria are said to be astronauts with their space-suits and helmets on.[125] But some of these round-headed individuals have pointed breasts. Furthermore, except for bracelets, anklets, and belts, these female "astronauts" appear to be nude. Breasts, fingers, and toes, features which would not be visible under a space suit, are clearly delineated.[126] Why would space travelers wear elaborate space "helmets" with "antennae" while otherwise going completely naked? Von Däniken also neglects to mention that some of the round-headed "spacemen" carry bows and arrows instead of

FIGURE 5. Relief from the Temple of the Cross, Palenque (after Maudslay
1889-1902: vol. 4, Plate. 76)

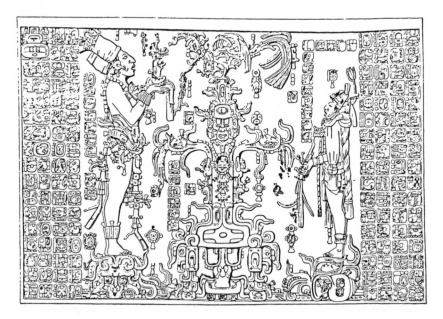

FIGURE 6. Relief from the Temple of the Foliated Cross, Palenque (after
Maudslay 1889-1902: vol. 4, Plate. 81)

ray guns or other advanced weapons.[127] Henri Lhote, discoverer of these paintings, argues that they represent natives in ritual masks and costumes like those still used by many African tribes.[128] Surely this explanation is simpler and more believable than the helmeted astronaut interpretation.

Despite claims that similar representations of spacemen are found all around the world,[129] the specimens illustrated possess a great variety. In fact, von Däniken presents examples of so many different types of supposed "helmets," "antennae," and "spacesuits" that his thesis is actually *weakened* by the abundance of evidence. Some of the figures that he claims are astronauts have plain globular "helmets" with no protuberances at all;[130] others have various types of "aerials" or "antennae" (which usually more closely resemble animal horns) on the sides or top;[131] still other "helmets" cover only the head, not the face,[132] and one has "goggles," but no covering for the lower part of the face.[133] The "spacesuits" these figures wear also vary considerably. It is not very likely that ancient space visitors would have brought with them such a variety of different types of uniforms and helmets. They probably would have had only one or two types of equipment for use outside of the spaceship just as our astronauts do.

So, if the illustrations von Däniken cites are representations of cosmonauts, why are their costumes so different? The only answer that makes much sense within the framework of the space-visitor hypothesis is that the individuals depicted were not all from the same group or from the same planet. Instead of von Däniken's hypothesis of visits by representatives of *one* advanced space-age civilization, we would have to posit a kind of interplanetary convention taking place on earth. Spacemen and women (remember the breasts on some of the drawings) from at least three or four different planets are needed to explain the variety of the supposed extraterrestrials illustrated around the globe. But the odds against numerous visits by spacemen from different sources are so astronomical that no rational person would accept this hypothesis as a viable alternative to traditional explanations of the artworks cited by von Däniken.

Advanced Technology and Other "Mysteries"

What of the claim that the Great Pyramid of Egypt, Easter Island statues, Gateway of the Sun at Tiahuanaco, and other huge monuments are indirect evidence of space visitors? Could such works have been constructed without the aid of advanced knowledge and space-age equipment? The evidence indicates not simply that these monuments *could* have been built without help from spacemen, but that they actually were constructed by peoples with a relatively low level of technology.

Of course, von Däniken does not agree. "Even if people with lively imaginations have tried to picture the Egyptian pyramids being built by a vast army of workers using the 'heave-ho' method," he states, "a similar method would have been impossible on Easter Island for lack of man-power."[134] According to von Däniken, Easter Island is too small to support more than two thousand inhabitants, and even if that number of people worked day and night, they could not have carved and erected all of the statues on the island using only primitive tools.[135]

The evidence for the building techniques used to erect the Great Pyramid of Egypt will be discussed in the next chapter. But study of the remains on Easter Island has yielded similar results. Easter Island receives a constant supply of rainfall and has fairly fertile volcanic soil. In the era when the statues were produced, it probably supported at least three or four thousand (not two thousand) inhabitants.[136] However, even two thousand people would have been sufficient to carve, move, and raise the stone figures.

Around the quarries where the relatively soft volcanic stone for the statues was cut lie hundreds of harder stone hand picks. Descendants of the statues' sculptors showed explorer Thor Heyerdahl how these stone tools were used to carve the huge images. Each man lined up several of the stone picks next to his work station. As the point of one pick became dull, he switched to another. One member of the group sharpened the used tools by flaking away bits of stone to create new points. The stone-cutters hacked out parallel grooves in the rock face about half an inch apart. Then they chipped out the stone ridge left between the grooves. Water was frequently poured on the rock to soften it and to keep dust and splinters from flying into the workers' eyes. In three days a crew of only six men had hacked out the contours of a medium sized statue some fifteen feet long. Two teams working all day in shifts could have finished such a statue in about a year.[137] The largest of the Easter Island statues, an unfinished giant sixty-nine feet long (as tall as a seven-story building), probably required five or six years of work.

One hundred and eighty natives were needed to move a medium-sized statue from the quarry to the place where it would stand erect on its own platform. It was levered onto a Y-shaped sledge made from a forked tree trunk, tied securely, then dragged by ropes to the appointed spot. A greater number of men could have moved the larger statues in the same way.[138] Von Däniken claims that no trees grow on the island, so no wood would have been available.[139] But trees were growing there when Easter Island was discovered by Europeans in the eighteenth century, and analysis of ancient pollen shows that in earlier times the tree cover was much thicker. Therefore, wood for sleds was available.[140]

Raising the twelve- to eighty-ton statues to an erect position was also accomplished without the aid of modern technology. Twelve men using traditional techniques were able to erect a twenty-five- to thirty-ton-figure for Thor Heyerdahl. Their only tools were three long wooden poles, ropes, and a number of boulders of varying size. The wooden poles were used as levers. Their tips were placed beneath one side of the statue and three or four men pulled on the end of each pole. One man slipped stones under the edge of the statue as it moved almost imperceptively. The process was then repeated on the other side. Gradually the statue rose a few inches above the ground on its pile of stones, then still higher as larger stones were inserted under it. In nine days the huge stone figure had been raised nearly twelve feet above the ground on a tower of boulders.

With the bottom of the statue at the level of the high platform on which it would stand, the levers were shifted to the upper portion. Now stones were inserted only under the statue's head and chest, working it into a sloping position. Finally, eighteen days after the work had begun the figure was levered into an upright stance.[141] Using the same method, the red stone "hats" (actually meant to represent hair styled in a topknot) would have been raised and placed atop the flat-headed statues.

The method for cutting, moving, and erecting the Easter Island statues, as well as the songs and dances that accompanied these acts, were passed down among the remaining descendants of the early inhabitants of the island. These people, known as "long ears," now form only a very small minority of the Polynesian population of Easter Island. But the Polynesian invasion occurred only a short time before the island was discovered by Europeans. Accurate traditions could have been preserved during the eleven generations that have elapsed since that time. Excavation has shown that "long ear" traditions about the conquest are grounded in fact,[142] and the stone picks found in great numbers around the quarries tend to substantiate the traditional methods of statue-making demonstrated for Heyerdahl.

The last statues were erected in the 1600s, and carbon-14 dates for material under the earliest stone buildings indicates that the statue-making era could not have begun before c. A.D. 400.[143] Thus, not only is space-age technology not required to explain the Easter Island stone giants, but also, like the Palenque "astronaut," they are too late in time to be credited to von Däniken's space visitors.

The Gateway of the Sun at Tiahuanaco is also of relatively late date. Archaeological evidence shows that it was constructed about 600-800 A.D., during the early stages of the Middle Horizon Period of Peruvian-Bolivian history,[144] not before 1000 B.C., as claimed by von Däniken.[145] Sacsahuamán, a megalithic fortress near Cuzco, Peru, and another of von Däniken's "mysteries,"[146] is even later. It was begun about A.D. 1440 and completed soon after 1500.[147]

The stoneworking technique used at these South American sites was similar to that of ancient Egypt. Wooden wedges were used to split large blocks from the walls of the stone quarries. These huge stones were moved to building sites on sleds or rollers. Then they were pulled up ramps to their proper positions. Once in place, they were smoothed and polished with hard stone tools. Ramps still survive at some sites, and a Jesuit chronicler saw these methods still being used by the Incas of Peru in the seventeenth century.[148]

Other "mysteries" that supposedly show that space-age technology existed in ancient times also fail when they are put to the test:

—Elephantine Island in Egypt did not get its name because observers flying overhead in an aircraft noticed it looked like an elephant (as von Däniken suggested).[149] If he had glanced at a map, he would have realized how absurd this claim is. The island's shape bears no resemblance to an elephant—it actually looks more like an elongated teardrop.[150] The ancient Egyptians called this island "Yeb" or "Yebu" ("ivory") because it was a trade depot for ivory arriving from sub-Saharan Africa. The present name derives from the Greek translation of the Egyptian name: *elephantinos* means "ivory" in Greek.[151]

—The Baghdad batteries[152] are not the products of an advanced technology in which electricity was an important source of power. The use of these ovoid clay jars containing a copper cylinder and an iron rod capped with bitumen is still unknown. They are found in deposits belonging to the Parthian Period (248 B.C. to A.D. 226). If filled with an electrolyte, they might have functioned as simple batteries. However, experiments show that they would have generated only about one-half volt of electricity. That is enough electricity to electroplate silver to copper, and possibly that is the purpose for which they were made.[153] If they were used as batteries, it is clear that their makers did not fully understand the nature and potential of electricity. No signs of any other electrical devices have been found among the remains of the Parthians or other people of ancient Mesopotamia. Surely if knowledge of electricity had been imparted by spacemen, there would have been a more extensive application of it than the production of a few one-half volt batteries! Like the steam engine (whose principle was discovered by ancient Greek scientists), these "batteries" may be examples of discoveries before their time—isolated ideas that did not develop their potential because economic, social, political, or other conditions were not yet ripe. Such discoveries, of which there are many, do not prove the existence of some otherworldly technology.

—Archaeologists know of no pre-Columbian smelted platinum from Peru or belt with aluminum parts from a grave in China.[154] Von Däniken does not say where these artifacts are now located, and he gives no source for his belief that they ever existed.

—The rustproof iron pillar standing near Delhi, India is not made of "an unknown alloy" as von Däniken claims.[155] It is also not four thousand years old as he says—it was erected at the beginning of the fifth century A.D. This column does not rust because its iron is so pure that a thin layer of oxidation on its surface forms a protective coating which prevents further oxidation. It is a tribute to the technological skill of early Indian craftsmen, but it did not require outer-space know-how.[156] Von Däniken himself has admitted that this item should be dropped from his list of "mysteries."[157]

—The Antikythera mechanism[158] is another product of ancient science and technology that does not require an outer space connection. This device, which was made in the first century B.C., contained a series of interlocking gears of varying sizes. As a knob was turned, the gears moved to show the positions of the sun, moon, planets, and constellations in proper relationship to one another.[159] It is certainly a remarkable device, the only one of its kind to survive from antiquity, but it is not "inexplicable." By the late Hellenistic Period, when this mechanism was made, the Greeks had developed an excellent knowledge of astronomy. A Hellenistic scientist named Aristarchus had put forth the idea that the earth and planets moved around the sun, instead of the traditional view that the sun circled the earth, and another astronomer, Hipparchus, discovered the precession of the equinoxes.[160] The Greeks were also skilled in making mechanical gadgets and clever machines, although few of them had a practical purpose.[161] The Antikythera mechanism is a product of Hellenistic science, which in turn had its roots in centuries of Greek philosophy and speculative thought. Only someone ignorant of the many achievements of Greek culture during the Classical and Hellenistic Periods would find it necessary to credit this device directly or indirectly to extra-terrestrials.

As has been stressed, von Däniken's books are riddled with errors of fact as well as unfounded conclusions. But perhaps the most perverse aspect of his theory is that it denies to mankind many of its greatest accomplishments. Time after time he surveys archaeological remains and asks, "How was this done?" And the answer, whether stated or implied, is always "ancient astronauts." But these astronauts must have been busy throughout history, not just at the dawn of civilization, for many of the monuments von Däniken credits to their inspiration or outright help belong to the centuries of the Christian era. The evidence indicates that it was human ingenuity working independently on similar problems that figured out how to move the stones for the pyramids and Stonehenge. And after much observation and study, it was human minds that arrived at the understanding of astronomy displayed in the Antikythera mechanism or *The Book of Enoch*. Only by ignoring the evidence of archaeology can von Däniken claim that the inspiration for the "mysteries" he lists came from outer space.

There is another problem with this theory that von Däniken does not seem to have recognized. He thinks that the evolution of human beings and the development of civilization can be explained only by positing the intervention of advanced extraterrestrials. But how did these hypothetical space visitors evolve and how did they attain their high level of civilization? Did other spacemen "create" them and provide them with the basic elements of culture? One cannot go backward in endless chains of events—one planet's civilization resulting from visits by spacemen who in turn had achieved civilization as a result of visits by other spacemen, etc. There must have been some planet in the universe where intelligent life and civilization developed without outside help. Since indigenous development had to take place *somewhere,* why do von Däniken and his followers find it so hard to accept what the available scientific and archaeological evidence indicates, that it happened on the planet earth?

Mysteries of the Pyramids

For almost twenty-five hundred years the pyramids of Egypt, especially the Great Pyramid and its two major companions at Giza, have fascinated Westerners. And for another two thousand years before that, they were regarded with awe and wonder by the Egyptians themselves. Ancient Greek and Roman authors who visited Egypt rarely failed to describe the Giza triad or to speculate on the cost or purpose of these huge monuments. When the ancients drew up lists of the Seven Wonders of the World, the pyramids of Egypt were always given first place.

Today the spell of the Giza giants continues unabated. How and why were the pyramids built? Could the ancient Egyptians have constructed such marvels? Is the Great Pyramid evidence of a vanished super-civilization? What is the relationship between the pyramids of Egypt and those built in Mesopotamia and the New World? Recent books dealing with such questions can be found in almost any bookstore. Unfortunately, many of these works (often the best-selling ones) are riddled with errors and make fantastic claims which are not justified by the evidence.

The Origins of Pyramidology

New data has proven that the pyramids may be a clue to an ancient, advanced science. . . . This tremendously advanced science ruled the world many thousands of years before Christ was born. The builders of the pyramid knew many secrets of the universe. They understood advanced mathematics. Their knowledge of world geography was amazing. Some of the data built into the pyramid is just now being proven by our space scientists. Ultimately, we will have to revise our textbooks and rewrite the history of mankind.[1]

Such statements reflect the continued influence of a nineteenth-century pyramid theorist named Charles Piazzi Smyth. Smyth, professor of astronomy at the University of Edinburgh and Astronomer Royal of Scotland, wrote two books in which he argued that the Great Pyramid was really a prophecy in stone.

Many authors before Smyth's time had speculated on the purpose of the Great Pyramid of Giza. The conventional theory from the time of Herodotus in the fifth century B.C. had been that the structure was a tomb built for the Egyptian pharaoh Cheops (which is the Greek form of his Egyptian name, Khufu). But many individuals have felt that the tremendous amount of wealth and human energy required to build the Great Pyramid indicates that it was intended to be more than just a sepulcher. Some medieval Muslim writers claimed that the pyramids were erected to preserve elements of man's civilization and wealth from destruction by Noah's Flood. Others mentioned traditions that they were the granaries that the Bible claimed Joseph constructed in Egypt.[2] Early European visitors to Giza argued that the Great Pyramid was an astronomical observatory or a temple used for secret rites.[3]

A very different suggestion was put forth in 1859 by John Taylor, a London publisher. In *The Great Pyramid: Why Was It Built, and Who Built It?* he claimed that the architect of this monument had been inspired by God and that in the dimensions of the pyramid were encoded secrets of the universe. This book so intrigued Piazzi Smyth, a devout Presbyterian, that he went to Egypt himself to independently confirm Taylor's theory. Smyth's measurements, calculations, and conclusions were published in *Our Inheritance in the Great Pyramid* (1864, with revised and enlarged editions in 1874 and 1877) and *Life and Work at the Great Pyramid* (1867).

Smyth fully supported Taylor's assertions. He stated that "the vertical height of that pyramid was to the length of one side of its base, when multiplied by 2, as the diameter to the circumference of a circle, i.e., 1:3.14159+, etc."[4] Thus, the pyramid's measurements yield the scientific value of . Furthermore, according to Smyth, when the length of the base line of one of the Great Pyramid's sides was divided by 366 (the closest approximation to the length of the solar year in even numbers) the result (close to 25 British inches) was one ten-millionth of the earth's semi-axis of rotation. According to Smyth, this proved that the architect "laid out the Great Pyramid's base with a measuring-rod twenty-five inches long in his hand— and in his head, the number of days and parts of a day in a year; coupled with the intellectual and instructive direct intention to represent that number of days in terms of that rod on each base-side of the building."[5]

Using similar logic, Smyth deduced the existence of a "pyramid inch" (equal to .999 British inches) as a basic unit of measurement. And using "pyramid inches" to measure the base-sides of the pyramid as well as the chambers and corridors within the structure, and the sarcophagus in the burial chamber, Smyth discovered figures for the equatorial diameter of the earth, the distance from the earth to the sun, and the density of the earth. He also found dates concealed in the measurements. By equating each "pyramid inch" with one year, Smyth found architectural features marking the date of the Exodus, the birth of Jesus, and other biblical events, including the date for the beginning of the period of trials which would immediately precede the end of the world. That last date was A.D. 1881![6]

Obviously, the world did not end soon after 1881. That fact simply added to the problems for Smyth's theories produced in 1880-81 by W. M. Flinders Petrie, the son of one of Smyth's followers. Petrie went to Egypt at the request of his father to check Smyth's figures and calculations, and he subjected the Great Pyramid to the most thorough scientific measurement it had ever had. This survey proved that the figures with which Smyth had worked had been incorrect.[7] All of the fine calculations were for naught! Others pointed out the circularity of many of Smyth's deductions—he multiplies or divides a measurement by a number he chooses, attains a significant result (the diameter of the earth or something similar), then uses the result as proof that the architect of the pyramid intended to hide these calculations in the measurement itself. And there is no evidence of a "pyramid inch" ever being used as a unit of measurement in ancient Egypt. This unit was created by Smyth for the purposes of his calculations. It has also been noted that if one applied Smyth's methods to the measurements of any building, many of them when multiplied or divided by a suitable unit would yield "significant" figures, such as the distance to Timbuktu or the number of street lights in London.[8]

Smyth's theories and others like them begin with the assumption that the present structure of the Great Pyramid is exactly as it was planned by its builder from the beginning. But this assumption is erroneous. The exterior dimensions of the pyramid are probably close to those intended from the start (though the outer casing stones have been stripped off over the ages). However, the plans for the pyramid's interior chambers and corridors were changed at least twice after construction had begun.[9]

Originally a shaft was cut downward to an unfinished chamber in the bedrock beneath the pyramid (Figure 7, step 1). Then, after the pyramid's lower layers of stone had been laid, the architect decided to place the burial chamber *inside* the pyramid. An ascending corridor had to be cut through the stone blocks already in position until the top level of construction was reached. Then the corridor and chamber could be built into the structure as work progressed. This chamber is now called the "Queen's Chamber," but originally it seems to have been intended to replace the subterranean burial chamber and receive the body of the king. The ventilation shafts for this chamber (or escape shafts for the king's soul) end well within the pyramid, indicating the location of the outer edge of the pyramid at the time the plan was changed once again (Figure 7, step 2). A third, higher burial chamber (the "King's Chamber") was planned, and a majestic twenty-eight-foot-high corridor (the "Grand Gallery") was constructed to give access to it (Figure 7, step 3). The three granite stones which plugged the mouth of the ascending corridor must have been placed in the Grand Gallery while it was being constructed; they are slightly larger than the mouth of the corridor, so they could not have been brought up from below. After the king's burial, these stones were slid down the ascending corridor, completely blocking it. An escape tunnel leading to the descending corridor let the workers who performed the job of moving these stones get out of the pyramid after they had finished. The descending corridor was then plugged from the outside.

Thus, the lengths, gradients, or other measurements of the various corridors in the Great Pyramid are partly the result of necessity—the need to adapt a partially constructed edifice to a new plan. But Smyth bases many of his conclusions on measurements of these corridors. If the architect had planned to hide prophetic messages in the corridors' dimensions, why didn't he build all of these corridors into the pyramid from the start? Why did the lower portions of the ascending corridor have to be cut through stones that had already been laid in place? The evidence that the Great Pyramid's plans were changed during construction makes Smyth's conclusions based on measurements of its internal features very improbable, if not impossible.

Despite Petrie's measurements, evidence for changes in the pyramid's plan, and the logical fallacies in Smyth's methodology, the conclusions of *Our Inheritance in the Great Pyramid* continued to find supporters.[10] The date for the beginning of the "tribulations" of the world was recalculated (still using "pyramid inches") first as 1928, then successively as September 16, 1936, and August 20, 1953.[11] These dates passed without the occurrence of major newsworthy events. But the failure of these prophecies has not convinced many believers that the entire methodology underlying them is wrong. Some recent works still proclaim as fact that cosmic truths are concealed in the pyramid's dimensions.[12]

The Date and Purpose of the Great Pyramid

The Great Pyramid is one of more than seventy pyramids in Egypt. However, those who find esoteric wisdom and advanced scientific knowledge hidden in its design usually regard it as unique. They often claim that it was the first and most perfect of the pyramids—the rest were comparatively crude, inaccurate copies.[13] But Egyptologists see the Great Pyramid

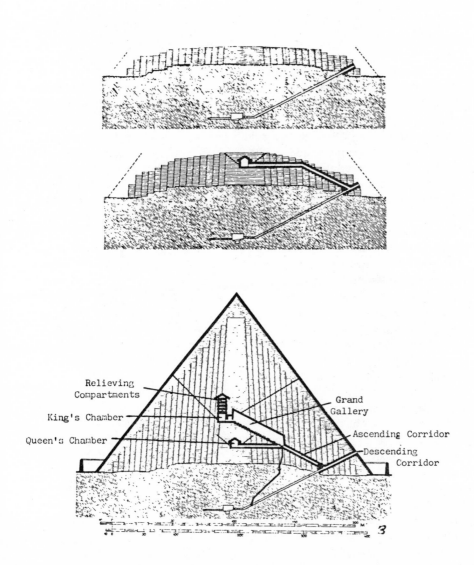

Figure 7. Section of the Great Pyramid, showing successive changes of plan (after Fakhry 1962: 116)

as the culmination of an almost century-long process of pyramid development. What, then, is the evidence for the date of the Great Pyramid and what is its chronological relationship to the other pyramids of Egypt?

The ancient Egyptians believed the Great Pyramid was built by Khufu, second pharaoh of the Fourth Dynasty, who ruled c. 2589-2566 B.C.[14] "But," objects von Däniken, "what if Khufu forged the inscriptions and tablets that are supposed to proclaim his fame? . . . If that was the case, then the pyramid existed long before Khufu left his visiting card."[15] However, Khufu's claim to be the builder of the Great Pyramid does not rest solely on tradition or on inscriptions that could be easily forged. Above the King's Chamber in the center of the pyramid, are a series of five compartments designed to relieve the weight on the ceiling of the chamber (see Figure 7). At some unknown time in the past, a passage was cut into the lowest of these relieving compartments. But the four upper compartments were not discovered until 1837-38 when explorers Col. Richard Howard-Vyse and J. S. Perring forced their way into them from the lowest compartment. On many of the undressed blocks of stone making up the relieving compartments were red ochre quarry-marks that include the name of Khufu.[16] These compartments were constructed when the pyramid was built and were not meant to be seen or entered later. Since they; had remained unknown and unseen from the time the pyramid was constructed to the nineteenth century, Khufu could not have faked the inscriptions. The pyramid must have been built during his reign, as the Egyptians had claimed.

The fact that the Great Pyramid was built by Khufu of the Fourth Dynasty negates claims that it was the earliest pyramid or the model for all other pyramids. The first pyramid to be constructed was the Step Pyramid at Saqqara. Both Egyptian tradition and evidence from within this pyramid indicate that it belonged to the Third Dynasty king, Djoser (or Zoser), c. 2667-2648 B.C.[17] Djoser's architect, Imhotep, originally built a large square tomb (called a "mastaba") similar to the ones in which earlier kings of Egypt had been buried. But he later changed this design, adding layers of stone on top of the mastaba to create a four-stepped pyramid (see Figure 8). Then this structure was enlarged on the north and west and its height increased to six steps.[b1] The development of the Step Pyramid from a traditional mastaba clearly indicates that this monument was intended as a tomb.

The Third Dynasty successors of Djoser were also buried in step pyramids. But at the end of the Third or the beginning of the Fourth Dynasty, an important development occurred (Figure 9): the "steps" in the pyramid were filled in and a true pyramid created.[19] The next two pyramids to be built, the Bent Pyramid and the Northern Pyramid at Dahshur, both belonged to Sneferu, the father of Khufu (Figures 10 and 11). Their size, design, and building techniques continued developments which soon afterwards reached their height in the Great Pyramid.[20] After the time of Khufu, the process

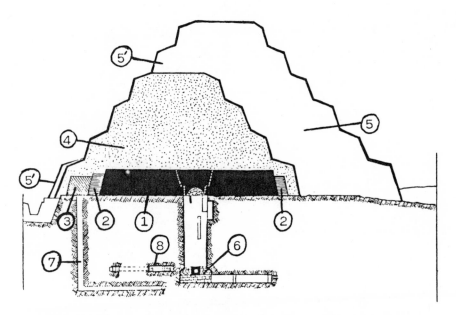

FIGURE 8. The Step Pyramid of Djoser, showing design changes (after Fakhry 1962: 39)

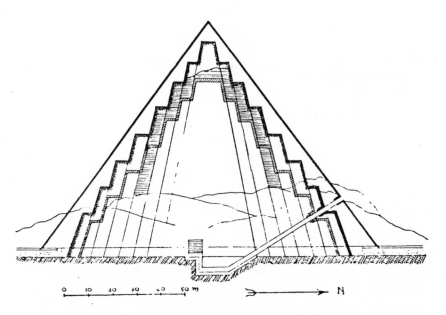

FIGURE 9. Section of the first true pyramid, the Pyramid of Medium, showing the stages of its construction (after Fakhry 1962: 69)

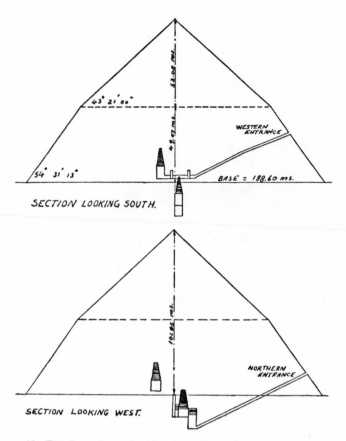

FIGURE 10. The Bent Pyramid (Southern Pyramid of Sneferu) at Dahshur (after Fakhry 1962: 89)

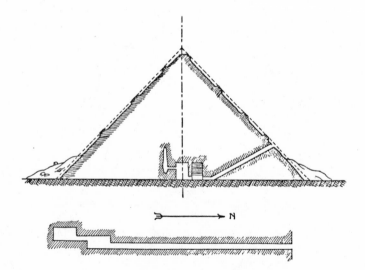

FIGURE 11. The North Stone Pyramid of Sneferu at Dahshur (after Fakhry 1962: 95)

reversed and the pyramids became smaller and smaller.[21] Eventually Egyptian rulers stopped building pyramids, preferring burial in hidden chamber-tombs cut into the hills opposite ancient Thebes.

The evidence of its development shows that the Great Pyramid, like all of the other pyramids, was a tomb. It is almost solid stone, a very impractical design for a granary, and its passages were originally sealed with blocking stones making its use as a temple or an astronomical observatory impossible. Furthermore, we have already seen that the secrets supposedly hidden in the pyramid's measurements exist only in the minds of those who create arbitrary units for measuring it. But many readers will still wonder why the Egyptians devoted so much wealth, time, and effort to create such a huge structure if it were nothing more than a tomb. The answer lies in ancient Egyptian beliefs about the afterlife, the pharoah, and the power of magic.

The Egyptians were convinced that some aspects of the soul could not exist apart from the body. Therefore, for an afterlife to be possible, the body had to be preserved. Those who could afford it had their bodies mummified at death and placed in tombs that would protect them through the ages. Tombs were often called "houses of eternity," and the mastabas of the pharoahs of Dynasties I and II were smaller versions of the palaces they occupied while alive.

Egyptian dogma also asserted that the pharaoh was a god. He not only ruled Egypt, he was the real owner of all its land, people, and resources. How and when this belief originated is unknown, but it is clear that it had become generally accepted by the Fourth Dynasty. As John Wilson, a noted Egyptologist, points out, "If the state had finally succeeded in gaining complete and enthusiastic support for the idea that this pharoah was the state, owned the nation and all that was therein, and that the major hope of eternal reward lay in serving the pharaoh and advancing his immortality, then the supreme energies of the nation would go into the building of the pharaoh's eternal home. As he was incomparably great, wise, and eternal, so his lasting home must be incomparably great, skillfully constructed, and enduring."[22] Ancient Egyptians would not have questioned the use of the bulk of the nation's resources for the construction of a "mere" tomb for their ruler.

Sympathetic magic, the belief that through spells one can make a representation actually become the object it represents, was an important part of ancient Egyptian religion. For example, through magical rites models or paintings of things from this world could become real for the dead in the afterlife. The practice of making the mastabas of the early kings like palaces was more than just symbolism. They became real houses for the dead, magically aiding their occupants to live forever. This belief is probably responsible for the development of the pyramid shape.

Among the Pyramid Texts, a Fifth Dynasty collection of magical incantations designed to help the pharoah live forever, is the following spell: "A staircase to heaven is laid for him [i.e., the king] so that he may mount up to heaven thereby."[23] These same spells or very similar ones were almost certainly in use during Dynasties III and IV. So when Imhotep changed Djoser's tòmb from a mastaba to a step pyramid, he was probably creating a huge magical staircase by which the dead king would climb to heaven.

When the true pyramid form was introduced at the start of Dynasty IV, the staircase symbolism and its magical power was retained, for inside each true pyramid was a step pyramid. (See the diagrams of pyramid construction, Figures 7 and 9). The magical power of whatever was symbolized by the true pyramid shape was added to that of the older step pyramid form. I. E. S. Edwards cites another of the Pyramid Texts, which describes the king as rising to heaven on the sun's rays: "I have trodden those thy rays as a ramp under my feet whereon I mount up to that my mother, the living Uraeus [cobra goddess] on the brow of Re' [the sun god]." Edwards persuasively argues that the smooth sides of the pyramid represent the slanting rays of the sun and thus provide the pharaoh with another magical route to heaven.[24]

In addition, each pyramid probably had another magical identification. It probably represented the mound of earth that first rose above the waters of chaos at the beginning of time according to an Egyptian creation myth. From this mound sprang the gods who then created everything else. Thus, the pyramid, by magically becoming the mound of creation which brought forth all life, would ensure eternal life for the pharaoh buried under or within it.

None of these different conceptions—a staircase, the sun's rays, or the mound of creation—was regarded as exclusive. Embracing one magical symbol did not mean rejecting others.[25] So the step pyramids could be both staircases and creative mounds at the same time, while true pyramids could be both of these and sun-rays as well. Of course, the pyramids also had the practical function of keeping the king's body safe. These various magical and practical functions of the pyramids as tombs were far more important to the ancient Egyptians than providing future generations with encoded knowledge of the universe would have been (even if they had had such knowledge to encode).

How Were the Pyramids Built?

It is sometimes asserted that it was impossible for the Egyptians to have built the pyramids. The Great Pyramid originally contained approximately 2.3 million blocks of stone, each averaging about two and a half tons. The largest of its stones weighs about fifty tons.[26] How could the Egyptians move such huge weights and raise them to the upper portions of the pyramid? The sides of the Great Pyramid are aligned almost exactly to true north-south or east-west, the average error being only about 3'6" (less than 1/15 of a degree). The perimeter of its base sits on an almost level plane, the southeast corner standing only a little more than one-half inch higher than the northwest corner.[27] Could the Bronze Age Egyptians have attained such accuracy? Aren't the pyramids proof of the existence in antiquity of an extremely advanced civilization like Atlantis? Or were the pyramids built with the aid of visitors from outer space?

The fact is that the pyramids were almost certainly built by the ancient Egyptians with the relatively primitive technology available to them—without the use of lasers, anti-gravity guns, space technology, or even pulleys, wheeled-vehicles, or iron tools. We cannot be sure *exactly* how they did it, for the Egyptians left no written descriptions or manuals for pyramid construction. But such an admission does not mean that their building methods are a complete mystery. Analysis of the monuments themselves (especially those left unfinished), the implements used by the builders, and paintings and reliefs from later dynasties enable us to reconstruct the techniques used to erect a pyramid.

Once a site on the west bank of the Nile was chosen (the West was the location of the land of the dead for Egyptians), the bedrock around the outer limits of the pyramid would be leveled. This could have been done by building a low wall around the pyramid site and filling the base area with water. Then a network of trenches could have been cut into the bedrock with their bottoms a fixed depth below the surface level of the water. The stone between these trenches would later have been cut down to the level of the trench floors. The middle of the base area did not have to be leveled; it would be used as part of the core of the pyramid.[28]

After the base was leveled, the orientation of the pyramid's sides was determined. To locate true north, the Egyptians did not need sophisticated equipment. They simply had to choose a star in the northern portion of the sky and bisect the angle formed by its rising position, the spot from which the observations were made, and its setting position. To achieve the degree of accuracy displayed in the Great Pyramid's orientation, an artificial horizon would have been required. A circular enclosure of uniform height, high enough to block out any view of the true horizon, would have been built on the leveled pyramid site where one of the north-south sides was to be located. Then the observation of the star's rising and setting positions would have been made from a point in the center of the circular enclosure.[29] This procedure would have been repeated at the location of the other north-south side. The orientation of the east-west sides could have been easily determined by measuring right angles from the two north-south lines.

While this work on the pyramid's foundations was going on, a causeway would have been built from the site to the point reached by the Nile during its annual flood stage. Many stones for the pyramid would be dragged along this causeway from the Nile once construction began. Most of the limestone used in a pyramid's interior was quarried near the pyramid site. But the fine limestone for the outer casing stones came from Tura, on the east bank of the Nile, and granite for columns, door-jambs, lintels, and other special features came from Aswan in the south.

It has sometimes been asserted that without the use of dynamite or other explosives it would have been impossible for the Egyptians to quarry the stone needed for the pyramids. Also, they supposedly had no means to transport the huge stone blocks to the site. Egypt had few trees, and these were mainly date palms, so there would have been little wood to use for rollers. And, it is argued, too many logs would have been required for it to have been practical to import them.[30]

However, the Egyptian quarries preserve evidence of how the stone blocks were detached. Notches were cut into the rock along the lines desired and wooden wedges were inserted. These wedges were then wet, causing the wood to expand and split the block of stone from the quarry wall. The backs of the slabs roofing the burial-chamber in Menkaure's pyramid at Giza still have the marks made by such wedges. Another method sometimes used was pounding the rock around the desired area with balls of hard stone (dolerite) until a trench was cut. This method took longer, but with it there was less chance that the stone block would crack. Obelisks were later quarried in this way.[31] The men involved in quarrying work often painted the names of their work gangs on the stones they cut. On a block in the Great Pyramid is the notation: "The Craftsmen-gang. How powerful is the White Crown of Khnum Khufu!"[32]

The rough stones as they came from the quarry were suitable for the interior of a pyramid, but those lining corridors or chambers had to be smoothed. This finishing was done with copper chisels or saws as well as stone hammers. A wet abrasive material such as quartz sand may have been employed to aid in sawing the stone.

As early as the beginning of the Old Kingdom, the Egyptians imported large amounts of cedar wood from Lebanon. Some of this wood was used to move stone blocks for construction projects. However, the wood was probably made into sleds, not used as rollers. Since the sleds could be used over and over again, the amount of wood necessary for building a structure like the Great Pyramid was not beyond the capacity of Lebanon to produce or of Egypt to import. Blocks of stone would be tied onto sleds and gangs of men (or, more rarely, teams of oxen) would pull the sled from the quarry to the pyramid site. Those stones coming from distant quarries would be pulled to the river, loaded aboard boats, and floated to the desert's edge near the pyramid site during the Nile's annual flood. They would then be pulled up the causeway to the pyramid. A Twelfth Dynasty tomb painting (c. 1900–1850 B.C.) shows a colossal alabaster statue which must have weighed more than sixty tons being moved in this way (Figure 11). One hundred seventy-two men are pulling on the ropes and others have crowbars to lever the sled forward from behind. Two individuals stand on either side of the sled pouring milk in front of the runners. The fat in the milk would lubricate the runners while the liquid kept them from catching fire from the friction.[33] Von Däniken and others who claim that it was impossible for the Egyptians to move the stones of the Great Pyramid without the aid of advanced technology obviously have not studied this ancient painting. If one hundred seventy-two men could move a sixty-ton statue, only about eight men would have been needed for each two-and-a-half-ton pyramid stone, at least on level ground.[34]

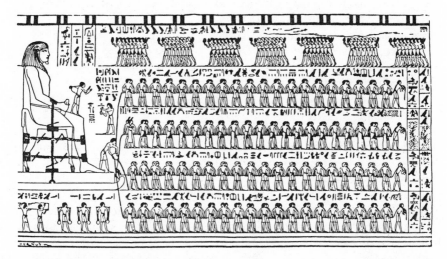

FIGURE 12. Moving a colossal statue of a Twelfth Dynasty Official, Dhutihotep (after Newberry 1898: Plate 15)

After the first layer of stones was in place, one or more ramps of earth and rubble would be built so that the stones of the next layer could be dragged into place. As the pyramid rose, the ramps would have been raised and lengthened. Exactly how the ramps were arranged for reaching the upper layers of the pyramid has been debated, and several possible answers have been suggested. But excavations at the Unfinished Step

Pyramid at Saqqara and at pyramids at Meidum and Lisht have uncovered the ramps used for reaching the lower portions of those structures. They prove that ramps were used by the ancient Egyptians in building pyramids as scholars had long surmised.[35] When a pyramid was finished, its ramps were demolished and the material used in building them removed. It is only an accident that traces of the ramps have survived at a few sites.

Herodotus, the fifth-century-B.C. Greek historian, was told that 400,000 men (employed in three month shifts of 100,000 men each) labored year-round for twenty years to build the Great Pyramid.[36] However, while as many as 100,000 men *might* have been used at a time, there was probably only *one* shift—the three month inundation period. During the three months of the year when the fertile land of Egypt was covered by the flood waters of the Nile, virtually the entire population was at the disposal of a pyramid builder. Most of the work on the pyramids was almost certainly done by the Egyptian peasants themselves, not by hordes of slaves. Using the large number of men available during the flood season and organizing them properly, the Egyptians should have been able to finish the Great Pyramid in less than the twenty years mentioned by Herodotus.[37]

Of course, some work did continue year-round. Slaves and criminals were kept busy continually quarrying stone. And craftsmen and masons worked all year at the pyramid itself finishing stones, preparing ramps, carving inscriptions, etc. Barracks found near the Pyramid of Khafre at Giza housed about four thousand men, probably the number of full-time workers at the site.[38]

The most amazing aspect of pyramid construction is not the movement of the stones (which only took a great amount of brute force), but the planning and organization that was necessary. Someone had to decide how many men were needed for each task; others had to be ready to secure these men when the flood season released them from their farming jobs and take them to their new occupations; still others had to store food to feed the multitude of workers at the various sites (quarries, docks, boats, and pyramid). The time needed for each job also had to be calculated and the activities of various groups synchronized for maximum efficiency. As the Old Kingdom pharaohs gained greater and greater control over all aspects of Egyptian life and their bureaucracies grew larger and more efficient, their pyramids became larger and larger. This trend reached its height with the Great Pyramid in Dynasty IV. After Khufu, the pyramids declined in size, although Khafre was almost able to match his father's (or grandfather's) achievement. Probably the bureaucracy became too large for the pharaoh to control, and the efficiency of Khufu's staff could not be duplicated. In later periods, the stone was still there in Egypt's hills, the workers were still available, but without the master planners and an efficient bureaucracy to carry out the plans, another Great Pyramid was impossible.

The Egyptians did not have any mysterious powers or lost secret methods enabling them to build the Great Pyramid. Theoretically the Great Pyramid could be duplicated today either by using the methods that the ancient Egyptians used or in less time by utilizing modern technology and mechanical aids. But no individual, corporation, or nation would be willing to spend the vast amounts of money and labor necessary to erect such a huge pile of stone. The pyramids stand as a testimony to the power of the Old Kingdom pharaohs, and to the willingness of the Egyptians to dedicate a large portion of their productivity to assuring an afterlife for their divine rulers.

Pyramids in Mesopotamia and the New World

In the mid-nineteenth century, pyramidal structures similar to the step pyramids of Egypt were discovered in Mesopotamia and in the Americas. Many popular theories from that time to the present have linked these various pyramids together. Some have claimed that the New World monuments are evidence that Egyptians and/or Mesopotamians visited the Americas in ancient times.[39] Others have seen the various pyramids as descendants of the original architecture of a lost parent-civilization, Atlantis or Mu.[40] But differences in date, function, and the way the structures were built have convinced anthropologists and ancient historians that there is no connection between Egyptian, Mesopotamian, and New World pyramids.

The Mesopotamian pyramidlike structures are called "ziggurats." The origin of the ziggurat can be traced back to c. 3500 B.C. when the low platforms on which temples were built began to be raised high above ground level.[40] At one southern Mesopotamian city, Uruk, earlier temples were covered by a new platform fifty feet high. The temple on top of this huge structure was similar in size and plan to earlier temples—it was just the size of the platform raising it heavenward that was a new departure.[42] Ziggurats attained their classic multistepped form during the Third Dynasty of Ur (c. 2100–2000 B.C.), and they continued to be built until the end of the Neo-Babylonian Period (c. 540 B.C.).

Thus, while their development began almost a millennium before the first pyramid was erected in Egypt, Mesopotamian ziggurats did not attain their pyramidlike form until some 550 years after the creation of Djoser's Step Pyramid. There is a possibility that the multistage form of the classic ziggurat was influenced by the step pyramids of Egypt, but the time lag between the two developments makes this unlikely. By the time Mesopotamian architects began adding multiple levels to their temple platforms, the Egyptian step pyramids had evolved into smooth-sided true pyramids. The Mesopotamians would have been copying ancient monuments, rather than the ones being built in twenty-second- or twenty-first-century-B.C. Egypt. Even the Great Pyramid was more than 450 years old when the ziggurat at Ur (one of the first ziggurats to have a stepped form) was built. Despite evidence that there were trade contacts between these two ancient Near Eastern civilizations, the pyramids of Egypt and Mesoptamia seem to have been developed independently.

Ziggurats were the most impressive features of ancient Mesopotamian cities. They were virtually solid mud-brick structures with one or more staircases on one side leading to the top. The ziggurat at Ur, built c. 2100 B.C., had a base of 200 × 150 feet and probably rose in three stages (or four if one counts the temple on top) to a height of over 100 feet. The later sixty-century-B.C. ziggurat at Babylon (the likely inspiration for the biblical story of the Tower of Babel) was 300 feet square at its base and probably 200 to 300 feet high with seven stories.[43] By Egyptian standards, however, such pyramids were not particularly large. Djoser's Step Pyramid was 411 × 358 feet at its base and 204 feet high. The Great Pyramid's base was 756 feet square and it was about 481 feet high.[44] At least twelve Egyptian pyramids were probably bigger than the largest of the Mesopotamian temple towers.

If Mesoptamian ziggurats did draw some inspiration from the earlier step pyramids of Egypt, it was only in outer appearance. Their functions were quite different. Egyptian pyramids were tombs for divine rulers. But the Mesopotamian pyramids were never used for burials. Even while they grew larger and higher and the number of their stages increased, ziggurats remained simply platforms for the small temples or shrines at their tops.

Scholars have proposed a number of theories to explain the development of ziggurats. Some have argued that they were artificial mountains erected by people originally from the highlands who were accustomed to worshipping their gods on mountaintops. However, this theory ignores the fact that not all Mesopotamian temples were built atop ziggurats. And Mesopotamian mythology shows no signs of a highland origin. Others have seen the ziggurat as a way to elevate and emphasize the shrine of the most important of a city-state's gods. But the most convincing theory is that these towers were intended to lift their shrines to a midpoint between earth and heaven. At the base of each ziggurat was a temple where daily religious rites were conducted. But on special occasions men could ascend to the shrines atop the ziggurats and meet their gods halfway.[45]

New World pyramids looked more like ziggurats than like Egyptian pyramids. They were step pyramids with flat tops and staircases or ramps on one or more sides. Also, like ziggurats, small temples or shrines were built on their summits. Such pyramids were a common element in the successive cultures of Middle America—Olmec, Maya, Zapotec, Toltec, and Aztec. Similar temple pyramids were built by the pre-Columbian people of Peru. And pyramid-shaped temple mounds made of beaten earth were erected in the Mississippi and Ohio valleys of North America.

It was once thought that New World pyramids were only platforms for temples. But in 1952, Alberto Ruz Lhuillier discovered the first evidence of burials in a Meso-American temple pyramid. Ruz had become intrigued by a large stone in the floor of the Temple of Inscriptions at Palenque. This stone showed signs that a number of holes had been drilled around its edges and then carefully plugged. Ruz had the stone raised on the hunch that these strange holes once had been finger holes for moving the slab. Beneath the flagstone was a staircase filled with rubble. It took three seasons of excavation to clear the stairs, which led deep into the pyramid on which the temple stood. But finally the excavators uncovered a cryptlike box containing the skeletons of six youths who had' died at about seventeen or eighteen years of age. Beyond these burials, a large stone in the north wall of the corridor was found to conceal a triangular doorway leading into a vaulted chamber. Within this room was a large carved slab (the one with von Däniken's "astronaut" on it) covering a sarcophagus containing the bones and jade burial offerings of an esteemed king or priest. The sarcophagus and its carved lid were too large to have been carried down the stairs to the chamber, so the burial must have been planned from the beginning. As in Egypt, the chamber with its sarcophagus had been built into the pyramid as the monument was being erected.[46]

Other burials have since been found within Meso-American pyramids,[47] indicating that these New World structures combined the functions of Mesopotamian ziggurats and Egyptian pyramids. But the theory that Mesopotamians and Egyptians brought their concepts of the pyramid to the New World still founders on problems of chronology and building techniques.

Adobe and stone platforms and temples were built in Peru at a fairly early date, c. 2500–1800 B.C. These ancient structures belong to the Pre-ceramic Period IV in that area, a time when pottery had not yet come into use.[48] The classic pyramid form developed gradually out of these early platforms. By about 900 B.C., a stone-faced, triple-terraced pyramid with a temple on top was constructed at Kuntur Wasi in the northern highlands.[49] Peruvian pyramids were bases for temples or palaces; they do not seem to have been used for burials.

Archaeological excavations have shown that Meso-American pyramids also evolved from low platforms over a period of time. The earliest known example of this development occurred in the Olmec culture, which appeared about 1200 B.C. By around 1000–800 B.C., the Olmecs were building ceremonial centers complete with pyramids at San Lorenzo and La Venta in the Mexican states of Veracruz and Tabasco. One of their early pyramids was a cone-shaped clay structure some 420 × 240 feet at its base and about 103 feet high.[50]

Recently, evidence of a similar development among the Maya has been unearthed. At Cuello in Belize, as early as c. 2200 B.C., an early Maya group constructed low platforms upon which to build timber-frame, thatched-roof temples or civic buildings. In about 400 B.C., these low, plastered platforms and their temples were covered by a massive platform about 200 feet square and 12 feet high. Still later, c. A.D. 200–300, in- dividual pyramids were constructed elevating their temples as much as thirty feet above the level of the large platform.[51] At other Maya sites, ceremonial centers containing pyramids also appeared between c. 300 B.C. and A.D. 300, an era known as the Late Formative (or Late Pre-classic) Period.[52]

But these early Meso-American pyramids were made of earth and rubble covered with clay or plaster. The impressive stone structures that tourists travel to Mexico City, Yucatan, and Guatemala to see belong to the Classic Period (c. A.D. 300–900) or later. Even these later monuments were built with a core of earth and rubble and only an outer coating of limestone blocks. This building technique is quite different from those used to erect pyramids in Egypt or ziggurats in Mesopotamia.

The era between 2500 and 1800 B.C., the time when temple platforms first appeared in Peru, was a period when true smooth-sided pyramids were being constructed in Egypt and when the ziggurat was reaching its classic form in Mesopotamia. If travelers from either of those Near Eastern lands were responsible for introducing pyramid construction into Peru, why don't the pyramids from that area appear fully developed from the start? And why would the Peruvians learn terrace-building from the newcomers, but not pick up the more practical knowledge of pottery- making?

The Egyptians stopped erecting pyramids around 1500 B.C., long before the appearance of the fully developed step-pyramid form in the Americas. Any Egyptian seafarers who traveled to the New World after 1500 B.C. would have taught the natives to bury their dead rulers in chamber tombs, not pyramids. So, the Meso-American practice of bury- ing some dead leaders inside pyramids must have developed independently.

On the other hand, Mesopotamians continued to erect ziggurats until c. 550 B.C. Thus, the Assyrian and Babylonian ziggurats do overlap in time with the earliest New World pyramids. But in addition to the differences in construction techniques between New World pyramids and Mesopotamian ziggurats, evidence that American pyramids evolved from earlier temple platforms and the absence of any other Mesopotamian culture traits in the Americas makes it very unlikely that Mesopotamians brought the idea of pyramid-building to the New World.

The earthen temple mounds of North America are even less likely to be due to arrivals of Egyptians, Mesopotamians, Phoenicians, Israelites, or any other Old World people. These flat-topped earthen pyramids appeared in the Mississippi Valley at a relatively late date, c. A.D. 700, and they were still being used in some areas when the European explorers arrived in the sixteenth and seventeenth centuries. They probably derive in some way from the pyramids of Mexico.[53] In any case, they are far too late to be credited to any of the ancient Near Eastern pyramid-building groups. (Likewise, pyramid temples of Southeast Asia are too late, c. A.D. 850, to be derived from Egypt or Mesopotamia or to be ancestral to the New World pyramids.)

The idea of ancient Egyptians or Mesopotamians crossing the ocean and teaching the natives they found in the New World to build pyramids is very romantic, but it is not supported by the evidence. The archaeological record indicates that the pyramid form appeared at different times in various parts of both the New and the Old Worlds, each time with signs of development from earlier constructions in the same area. It is thus extremely probable that these developments were independent of one another. Those who find such a coincidence hard to believe should consider L. Sprague de Camp's observation that, for anyone attempting to erect a very high ediface without the use of structural steel or the true arch and vault, the pyramid form is a natural choice for the sake of stability.[54] Children playing with blocks usually discover this fact without adult help. Why, then, is it so surprising that people in different parts of the world and at different times figured out that monuments could be built as much as several hundred feet high if the pyramid form were used?

Pyramid Power and Egyptian Mummies

Today, many claim that pyramids, especialy the Great Pyramid or models with the same proportions, are sources of tremendous energy.[55] Belief in "pyramid energy" or "pyramid power" seems to have begun in the 1930s when a traveler named Antoine Bovis visited the Great Pyramid. He noticed that the garbage in the King's chamber did not smell the way most such refuse does. Among the piles of litter were the bodies of some kittens which had become mummified. When he returned home he constructed a two-and-a-half-foot high model of the pyramid and placed the body of a dead cat inside. Instead of putreyfing, the body dehydrated into a mummy.[56]

Bovis's story inspired a Czech radio engineer named Karel Drbal to experiment with model pyramids. Drbal claimed that pyramids not only mummified dead bodies and preserved perishable foods, but also sharpened razor blades. A dull razor blade placed in the pyramid model at the level of the King's Chamber supposedly regained its sharp edge. Drbal found that a razor blade stored in a pyramid between uses could be used for more than a hundred shaves.[57] He patented his pyramid model and now sells them world-wide.

Pyramids, whether closed in or just framework, are supposed to make plants grow faster, cause crystals to grow in unusual shapes, cure various ailments, and amplify the power of prayer. It is also claimed that placing a small pyramid under one's bed at night or meditating within a larger model focuses cosmic energy, relieving worry and tension, improving mental acuity, increasing sex drives, and producing an almost euphoric feeling of well-being.[58]

However, such claims are difficult to verify. Few, if any, researchers have been able to duplicate the findings of Bovis or Drbal. The horticultural department of the University of Guelph in Canada has shown that pyramids have no effect on the growth of plants. Other scientifically controlled experiments with dead animals, razor blades, and other objects have produced contradictory results even though all variables remained the same. Advocates of pyramid power admit this inconsistency, but they do not let it trouble them. Neutral observers cannot be so nonchalant. A basic rule of science is that experimental results must be consistent and repeatable before a claim can made.[59]

Most of the "miraculous" cures credited to pyramid power are also unverifiable. Many of them can be explained in natural terms, and were probably due solely to belief in pyramid power. One "cure" often cited is that of a woman who had an eleven-year-old, wartlike condition on her finger. She put the afflicted area under a pyramid for fifteen minutes twice in one day and the wart disappeared. However, it has been demonstrated that warts can be caused and cured by hypnotic suggestion. It was probably the woman's faith in the pyramid that effected the cure, not some concentrated cosmic power.[60]

Believers in pyramid energy often support their contentions by citing scientific experiments conducted within Khafre's pyramid at Giza in 1968. A team of American and Egyptian scientists led by Nobel Prize-winning physicist Dr. Luis Alvarez placed a cosmic ray detector in the pyramid's only known chamber. Since cosmic rays travel at different rates of speed through stone and air, it was hoped that readings from this instrument would indicate whether or not there were any undiscovered chambers or passages in the pyramid. But when some of the readings from the detector were fed into a computer for analysis, the computer could not make sense of them. This problem prompted an Egyptian to speculate to reporters that the pyramid might itself be producing rays which were confusing the scientific instruments. Newspapers all over the world picked up the story, and it is mentioned in practically all the books on pyramid power. Typical of the generally erroneous reporting of this incident is the following:[61]

> Dr. Alvarez never discovered exactly what the trouble was. He eventually gave up, because the cosmic ray counter continued to go awry whenever he tried to use it inside the pyramid. He has wondered ever since whether something sealed inside that mountainous stone structure is still at work emitting (or attracting?) some sort of rays or waves.

In fact, the reasons for the problematic readings from the cosmic ray detector *were* discovered. The narrow passage into the pyramid chamber necessitated the use of two small spark chambers rather than one large one. Where the two chambers joined, no readings were being taken, a factor which had not been taken into consideration when the computer program to interpret the data was made. It was also discovered that the neon in the spark chambers had been contaminated. When the chambers were flushed with fresh neon they recovered their substantially uniform sensitivity and produced the kinds of readings that had been expected.[62] After analyzing the data in a variety of ways, the team of scientists found that no unknown pyramid chambers or other features were discernible.[63] Dr. Alvarez uncovered no evidence of mysterious pyramid forces, but his conclusions have been ignored by supporters of pyramid power who prefer to believe the earlier erroneous news reports.

Reports that pyramids cause corpses to mummify have led to some speculation that ancient Egyptian bodies have lasted through the centuries because they were originally placed in pyramids. Another popular belief (usually held by those who see the pyramids as repositories of esoteric wisdom) is that the Egyptians had secret embalming methods that have been lost. Both views are wrong.

The excellent state of preservation of many Egyptian mummies owes nothing to "pyramid power" or mysterious secret techniques. It is due in part to Egyptian embalming procedures (which today can be reconstructed in detail) and probably in part to the Egyptian climate. Embalming or mummification was not practiced by the Egyptians from earliest times. Prehistoric burials were made in shallow graves dug into the sandy desert near the Nile, with no attempt being made to preserve the bodies. Yet some of the corpses in these predynastic cemeteries are better preserved than later mummies. The hot, dry desert sand dehydrated the bodies, removing the moisture before they could putrefy. The skin became like tanned leather.[64]

Perhaps when new graves were being dug, one or more of these naturally mummified bodies was uncovered, leading the Egyptians to attempt artificial means of preservation in the belief that if the body could be made to survive, the soul would live on also. The poor continued to place their dead in shallow graves covered with sand and stones, but during the First Dynasty kings and nobles began to be buried in underground chambers lined with brick or stone. Above these burial chambers were mastabas, rectangular "houses for eternity," which would contain objects for use by the dead.[65] The bodies themselves were simply wrapped in cloth and placed in wooden coffins. But these attempts to protect the corpses backfired. In the relatively cool underground chambers, the bodies did not dry out and become mummified as they had in the desert sand. They rotted until only bones remained.[66]

This experience led to the development of embalming at the end of the Third or beginning of the Fourth Dynasty, c. 2600 B.C. The Egyptians discovered that natron, a naturally occurring salt found in the area of Cairo, absorbed moisture and so could dry out bodies as the desert sands had earlier. Natron is also mildly antiseptic, a quality that helped it ward off putrefaction. After much trial and error, the embalmers perfected the method of mummification which would be used with only slight variations for over twenty-five hundred years of Egyptian history.[67]

When a body was delivered to the mortuary, it was washed with a natron solution and the face was given a thin coat of hot resin to protect it. Before the Eighteenth Dynasty, this was all that was done to the head at this point in the proceedings, but from Dynasty XVIII onward, the brain was removed. After breaking into the skull through the sinus cavity, a wire could be inserted and stirred around to cut the brain into pieces. These fragments were then removed with a spoon-shaped instrument. Next, the entrails and contents of the chest were taken out through a incision made in the left side of the abdomen. The abdomen and chest cavity were rinsed with spices and palm wine and packed with rags, straw, wood shavings, or other temporary stuffing. The body and the internal organs were then covered for forty days with heaps of dry natron.[68]

After the prescribed time had elapsed, the internal organs were dressed with scented oil and resin, wrapped in linen, and placed in special jars for burial with the body. The body itself was washed and dried, restuffed with resin-soaked linen or sawdust, rubbed with a lotion of juniper oil, beeswax, spice, and natron, and covered with a thin layer of molten resin. This process toughened the skin and made it waterproof. Next, the wrapping began. Each finger and toe was bandaged separately, then each limb. As the wrapping proceeded, various amulets and bits of jewelry were placed among the bandages. Finally, the whole body was covered by one or more shrouds bound in place by linen strips. The dead person was then ready to be returned to relatives for burial, the entire mummification process having taken some seventy days.[69]

Many, though not all, mummies prepared this way have lasted through the ages. Those that were completely dehydrated and thoroughly covered with resin or bitumen would have survived almost anywhere, but others were preserved as much by Egypt's relatively dry climate as by the embalming procedures. As soon as some mummies are unwrapped, they begin decomposing again.

The embalming methods developed by the Egyptians demonstrate the intelligence and perseverance displayed by those ancient people in their quest for eternal life. But like the pyramids, mummies are no less amazing and wonderful as products of human ingenuity and skill than they would be if they were due to some sort of cosmic energy, space-travelers, or supernatural forces.

VI
CHAPTER

Early Voyagers to the Americas

Other than the American Indians, who first discovered the New World? For generations the answer was simple—Christopher Columbus. Schoolchildren were taught how the brave sailor set forth from Spain in 1492 with three small ships. He was trying to reach the East Indies by sailing west, but instead he landed in the Caribbean. Then, a few decades ago, the picture became clouded somewhat by recognition that the Vikings had beaten Columbus to America by almost five centuries. Textbooks now credit Leif Eriksson with being the first explorer to set foot in the New World. But *was* he the first?

Israelites, Phoenicians, Egyptians, Babylonians, Greeks, Romans, Scythians, Celts, Danes, Arabs, Mongols, Chinese, Koreans, and Japanese—all have been touted as early explorers and settlers of the Americas. Popular books purporting to provide evidence supporting the claims of one or more of these groups appear almost every year. But the debate over pre-Columbian trips to the New World is not really new. It is the continuation of a conflict that has been going on almost since the time of Columbus himself.

Atlanteans, Lost Tribes, and the Mound-Builders

When the Spaniards first landed on the Yucatan Peninsula in 1517, they discovered plumed Mayan warriors protecting cities that had massive stone pyramids and palaces, colorful wall paintings, and elaborate sculptures. Later other Indian civilizations were found in Mexico (1519) and Peru (1527). Driven by a lust for adventure, gold, and power, as well as a desire to spread the True Faith among the heathen, the conquistadors overwhelmed the native empires, establishing Spanish control over Mayan, Aztec, and Inca lands. The Indians were enslaved and often transplanted from their villages to the estates of the new Spanish land-

131

owners. Ancient cities and temples were abandoned.[1]

With the conquistadors came Franciscan and Dominican missionaries who, in their zeal to convert the red men, often did everything in their power to eliminate the last vestiges of the native cultures and traditions. The Indians were forbidden to practice their former religions—altars and statues of the ancient gods were smashed, and harsh penalties were imposed on those caught venerating pagan images. The Maya, the only American people to independently develop writing, saw their books publicly burned because in the opinion of the priests they "contained nothing in which there was not to be seen superstition and lies of the devil."[2] The records of centuries of civilization—astronomical observations and calculations, religious myths and ceremonials, literature, perhaps even historical records—were lost forever. Vegetation gradually covered the stone monuments, and even the Indians forgot the locations and former functions of their once teeming cities. A number of Mayan centers, especially those in the Petén region (in what is now Guatemala), had been abandoned centuries before the arrival of the Spaniards, but their continuity with northern Yucatan's cities would have been apparent if the campaign against native traditions had not been so thorough.

A few priests and soldiers attempted to describe the native customs, religions, and historical traditions that were rapidly being destroyed. Their accounts were usually sent back to Spain for the enlightenment of the Royal court, but there they were deposited in the archives and "lost" for hundreds of years. The origins of the stone cities in the jungles were soon forgotten by Spaniards and Indians alike. When Diego Garcia de Palacio stumbled upon the ruins of Copán in 1576 he was unable to determine what people had once lived there. Palacio's report was also buried in the archives (it was not published until 1840), so that knowledge of the very existence of great pre-Columbian cities in America gradually faded.

Two centuries passed before remains of New World civilizations were rediscovered. In the late eighteenth century, Spanish officials in Guatemala heard reports that strange ruins had been seen in the jungle. They dispatched Antonio del Rio, a captain in the Spanish army, to investigate the stories. Del Rio and an artist named Ricardo Almendáriz spent months hacking their way through extremely dense jungle undergrowth before they came upon a number of stone buildings almost completely hidden under a growth of trees and other vegetation. They had found the ruins of Palenque.[3]

During the early part of the nineteenth century, other explorers investigated evidence of pre-Hispanic civilization in the Americas. The famous German naturalist Alexander von Humboldt toured the Spanish colonies in the New World, noting archaeological remains in Peru and Mexico.[4] And in Central America, a number of adventurers and artists revealed ruins belonging to the vanished Mayan culture: Dupaix and Castañeda described Palenque, Galindo visited Palenque and Copán, and Waldeck produced drawings of ruins at Copán, Palenque, Uxmal, and Chichén Itźa.[5] But credit for making most educated Americans and Europeans aware that a great civilization had once flourished in the jungles of Central America belongs to John Lloyd Stephens and his artist-friend, Frederick Catherwood. Stephens's accounts of the two explorers' adventures while investigating the remains of cities at Copán, Palenque, Uxmal, and Chichén Itźa, illustrated with Catherwood's superb engravings of the ruins, became best-sellers when they appeared in 1841 and 1843.[6]

The first Spanish reports of cities and civilizations in the New World had led some sixteenth-century scholars to theorize that the newly discovered cultures were remnants of the lost civilization of Atlantis. When the American sites were rediscovered in the early nineteenth century, this theory was revived and quickly grew in popularity. Many individuals saw the similarity between American pyramids and those of Egypt and Mesopotamia as evidence that both New and Old World civilization had developed from one source—Atlantis (see chapter 2).

Meanwhile, early European explorers and settlers of North America had found their own mysterious archaeological remains. They discovered no stone cities like those in Mexico, Central America, and Peru, but there were a number of large earthen mounds which obviously had been erected by human hands. These "tumuli" or "barrows," as they were called, were found from the east coast to the Mississippi Valley. Some of the mounds were semi-conical in form; others were shaped like truncated pyramids; still others had the forms of animals or birds. Many had large trees growing atop them, proclaiming their great age. They ranged in size from small hillocks seven or eight feet high to truly immense monuments. The 78-foot-high mound near Miamisburg, Ohio, contains 311,353 cubic feet of earth, and the Cahokia Mound in Illinois is over 100 feet high, 710 feet wide, and 1,080 feet long (its base is almost 200,000 square feet larger than that of the Great Pyramid of Giza, Egypt). What had been the purpose of these strange monuments, and what people had constructed them?

The first person to scientifically investigate these questions was Thomas Jefferson, who excavated a small mound in Virginia sometime prior to 1781. He cut a trench through the center of the mound down to virgin soil. After studying the mound's stratigraphy (the various layers of earth, stones and bones of which it was composed), Jefferson concluded that it had not been constructed all at one time. The mound had grown as a result of periodic burials on the spot over an unknown number of years. He attributed this mound and others like it to American Indians.[7]

But there were other views about mound origins that were quite different from those of the future president. In 1783, after receiving some information about the huge Ohio mounds, Ezra Stiles, then president of Yale College, argued that the mounds as well as the civilizations of Mexico and Peru were the work of Canaanites who had been driven out of Palestine by Joshua. Benjamin Franklin, a friend of Stiles, was a bit more cautious. His suggestion, accepted also by Noah Webster in 1787, was that the Ohio earthworks had been erected by the Spanish explorer De Soto during his wanderings. Another work published in 1787 claimed that the mounds were built by Danes who eventually migrated to Mexico where they became known as "Toltecs."[8]

One of the most popular theories credited American antiquities to the "Lost Tribes of Israel." After King Solomon's death (c. 922 B.C.) the Hebrew people had split into two nations—Israel, located in the north of Palestine and comprising ten of the twelve Hebrew tribes, and Judah, the southern kingdom, which had only two tribes. When the kingdom of Israel fell to the Assyrians in the eighth century B.C., the upper classes were carried off into captivity, settled in other Assyrian territories, and lost to history. They thus became the "ten lost tribes" of later historical speculation. While some sixteenth-century scholars accepted the New World cultures as offshoots of Atlantis as has been mentioned, others declared them to be the products of the "lost tribes," which had arrived in America either by migrating across Asia and the Bering Strait or by crossing the Atlantic in Phoenician ships.[9]

Most of the early Lost Tribes advocates (including such well-known figures as Roger Williams, founder of Rhode Island, and William Penn, founder of Pennsylvania) believed the Indians themselves to be descendants of the Israelites. For example, James Adair, who lived among Indian tribes for forty years before writing *The History of the American Indians* in 1775, saw Jewish parallels to virtually every Indian custom or ceremony and derived numerous Indian words from Hebrew.[10] But a number of other late eighteenth- and early nineteenth-century theorists placed the Mound-Builders in a separate category from the Indians. While the Mound-Builders might have been descendants of the Lost Tribes, these writers felt sure that the Indians weren't. The gigantic earthworks of the Ohio and Mississippi valleys must have required extensive planning and the organized expenditure of untold hours of labor. Were "savages" capable of such effort? Many people agreed with the Reverend Thaddeus M. Harris's arguments that they were not. In an 1805 book, Harris concluded that it was impossible for the relatively small and poorly organized North American Indian tribes to construct the mounds noted in Ohio.[11] Thus, the idea of a "lost race" of Mound-Builders—variously identified as Israelites, Danes, Phoenicians, Egyptians, or other Old World peoples—became widely accepted. A variation of the Lost Tribes of Israel theory, which used migrations of various groups of pre-Hebrew and

Israelite people to explain the many different cultures in the New World, even became part of Mormon church doctrine.[12]

There were some, though, who agreed with Jefferson and rejected the idea of a vanished race of Mound-Builders. Dr. James H. McCulloh dug into a few mounds in Ohio in 1812 and noted that the skeletons he found were no different from those of Indians. His conclusions were supported in 1839 by Dr. Samuel G. Morton of Philadelphia. Morton, often called "the father of American physical anthropology," systematically studied hundreds of skulls of all races and discovered that an individual's racial identity could almost always be determined on the basis of ten skull measurements—longitudinal diameter, facial angle, horizontal periphery, and so forth. When he compared the measurements of Mound-Builder crania with those of modern Indians, he found no significant differences. The people buried in the mounds were of the same race as the modern North American Indians, as well as the native peoples of Mexico and Peru. On the other hand, this Indian race was distinct from any of those which occupied the Old World.[13]

Another important figure in the debate over the mounds was Albert Gallatin, Secretary of the Treasury under Thomas Jefferson and founder of the American Ethnological Society. In 1836, he published a book on North American Indians in which he rejected the theory of a separate race of Mound-Builders. Gallatin noted similarities between the flat-topped rectangular mounds of the southern United States and the temple pyramids of Mexico, but unlike Ezra Stiles and others, he did not conclude that Aztecs or Toltecs had migrated south from Ohio. Instead (like modern scholars), he posited a gradual diffusion of agriculture and pyramid-temple architecture northwards from Mexico to the United States.[14]

Despite the evidence cited by scholars like Morton and Gallatin, the belief that the Mound-Builders had been Indians remained a minority opinion. Theories about the mysterious disappearance of an unknown people were far more appealing to the public. When, in 1833, a writer named Josiah Priest published a work supporting the vanished Mound-Builder hypothesis, it sold over twenty-two thousand copies in only thirty months, making it a runaway best-seller in that day.

There were probably some deep-seated psychological reasons why the myth of the Mound-Builder race caught the national fancy and held it for so long, as Robert Silverberg has noted:[15]

> The dream of a lost prehistoric race in the American heartland was profoundly satisfying; and if the vanished ones had been giants, or white men, or Israelites, or Danes, or Toltecs, or giant white Jewish Toltec Vikings, so much the better. The people of the United States were then engaged in

undeclared war against the Indians who blocked their path to expansion, transporting, imprisoning, or simply massacring them; and as this century-long campaign of genocide proceeded, it may have been expedient to conjure up a previous race whom the Indians had displaced in the same way. Conscience might ache a bit over the uprooting of the Indians, but not if it could be shown that the Indians, far from being long-established settlers in the land, were themselves mere intruders who had wantonly shattered the glorious Mound Builder civilization of old.

Whatever the reason for their acceptance, myths about lost Mound-Builders remained popular until the 1930s and are still accepted by some people today.

One of the most important contributions to the solution of the mystery of the Mound-Builders was made in the late 1840s by two amateur archaeologists from Chillicothe, Ohio. Ephraim George Squier, editor of a Chillicothe newspaper, and Dr. Edwin H. Davis, a physician, were brought together by their deep interest in antiquities—particularly in the remains of the Mound-Builders. For more than two years, Squier and Davis traveled throughout the valleys of the Ohio and Mississippi rivers surveying and mapping mound sites. They dug test shafts into more than two hundred mounds, collected artifacts, noted evidence of stratification, and hypothesized about the original purposes of the mounds. Their book, *Ancient Monuments of the Mississippi Valley* (1848), is regarded as a classic in North American archaeology, and it laid the foundations for a systematic approach to the riddles of the mounds.

Squier and Davis worked out a classification system for the different types of mounds they observed. They distinguished mounds from earth-work enclosures, and within the mound classification they recognized the differences between conical burial mounds like the one Thomas Jefferson had excavated, temple mounds (flat-topped, pyramidlike structures that served as platforms for temples or chieftains' houses), and effigy mounds constructed in the forms of bears, snakes, birds, turtles, and other animals (including men). They noted that some mounds stood in isolation while others had been built in groups surrounded by earthen embankments. Long causeways or raised earthwork avenues often linked mound groups or enclosures to one another. While Squier and Davis believed that most of the mounds had been built by a vanished non-Indian race of people, the differences in form, contents, and uses of the mounds led them to correctly conclude that at least some of the mounds had been erected either by different peoples or at different times. However, their attempts to identify the peoples responsible for the mounds were far off the mark.[16]

Order and system finally became an integral part of the study of

American antiquities in the last decades of the nineteenth century. In 1879, the Smithsonian Institution established the Bureau of American Ethnology to scientifically investigate problems relating to the Mound-Builders. The archaeological division of the Bureau undertook a program of professional archaeological exploration, mapping, and excavation in the 1880s. These efforts were supplemented by the work of archaeologists from Harvard's Peabody Museum, the New York State Museum, the American Museum of Natural History, and other institutions.[17] At the same time, Alfred Maudslay began the scientific study of Mayan sites, and, in 1892, F. Max Uhle introduced careful, stratigraphical excavation methods into Peruvian archaeology.[18] As a result of such profesional study and continued advances in archaeological methodology, American archaeological sites gradually are giving up their secrets.

It is now known that the North American mound-building cultures developed agriculture and truncated pyramid-shaped temple mounds later than the Meso-American and South American civilizations did. Thus, theories of Mound-Builders migrating from Ohio to Mexico have come to be regarded as impossible. It is also clear that instead of one Mound-Builder group, there was a succession of cultures that constructed mounds. Archaeologists have named these cultures Adena (c. 1000–300 B.C.), Hopewell (c. 300 B.C.–A.D. 700), and Mississippian (c. A.D. 700–1700). They were created by Indians who were farmers and traders, who developed complex organizational structures for their societies, and who produced beautifully carved stone pipes, copper plaques and ornaments, engraved shells, and other skillfully made artifacts.[19] Agriculture, it turns out, was once widespread in North America—the nomadic tribes living in tepees and hunting buffalo (Sioux, Cheyenne, Comanche, etc.) were actually a fairly late development. Their way of life became dominant on the Great Plains only after Europeans arrived in the New World, bringing with them the horse. Yet it is the "savage" nomads most people picture when they think of "Indians," rather than the settled agriculturalists who produced the great mounds of North America.

Archaeology seems to have disposed of the Mound-Builder myth at last. Today few, other than Barry Fell, seek to credit a lost race with construction of the mighty earthworks of the Ohio and Mississippi valleys.[20] Generally, the mounds have ceased to play a prominent role in popular speculations about Atlantis or pre-Columbian visitors to the New World. On the other hand, many still see Meso-American and South American pyramids and other cultural elements as evidence of outside influences in the Americas. Theories deriving these monuments from Atlantis, Egypt, Mesopotamia, or Phoenicia continue to flourish (see chapters 2 and 5) despite strong archaeological evidence to the contrary.

Visitors from the Ancient Near East

After Atlantis, the favorite source for hypothetical voyagers to the Americas has been Egypt. Many books have argued that similarities between New World civilizations and ancient Egyptian culture prove Egyptian influence. And Thor Heyerdahl has even sailed a papyrus boat across the Atlantic to demonstrate how the Egyptians could have reached America.

The two most able champions of links between Egypt and the New World are G. Elliot Smith and R. A. Jairazbhoy. Smith, a noted brain anatomist, became convinced that civilization originated in Egypt, then spread to other parts of the world. In *The Migrations of Early Culture* (1915) and a series of other works,[21] he traced the use of pyramids and the practice of mummification of the dead from Egypt through Asia to the Americas. He also noted Egyptian features such as lotus friezes, elephants, and feathered headdresses in American art. Egyptian culture supposedly reached the New World during the Egyptian Twenty-first Dynasty, c. 1100–950 B.C.

However, most of the parallels Smith cited do not stand up under close scrutiny. For example, the elephants he noted in Mayan reliefs at Copán are almost certainly macaws. These long-nosed figures do look elephantlike, but their artistic development can be traced back through a series of stylized forms to clearly birdlike representations.[22] Smith failed to notice that his "elephants" had nostrils in the upper portions of their "trunks" near their eyes or that their eyes are surrounded by what appear to be scales (this is actually the conventional Mayan depiction of short feathers). Such features certainly are not found on Old World elephants!

The problems of connecting New World pyramids with those of Egypt were detailed in the previous chapter. As was stated there, dates and construction methods of New and Old World pyramids do not coincide, and the American structures did not appear suddenly in their classic forms; they evolved over a period of time.

Smith's attempt to trace the diffusion of Egyptian mummification practices to Indochina, India, Polynesia, and America also has been shown to be wrong. Roland B. Dixon, a noted anthropologist, examined every known occurrence of mummification from around the world, carefully noting all details associated with this custom in each culture practicing it. There was no evidence that Egyptians had taught other peoples some secret technique or process by which bodies could be preserved forever. Dixon found significant analogies with Egyptian procedure in only one culture—a primitive people on the islands of the Torres Straits between New Guinea and Australia, an area far removed from likely lines of cultural diffusion from Egypt or any other Western culture.[23]

R. A. Jairazbhoy has based his claims for an Egyptian presence in the Americas on cultural similarities between the Olmec culture of Mexico and ancient Near Eastern civilizations. His book, *Ancient Egyptians and Chinese in America* (1974), points out that a number of features of Near Eastern civilizations, such as the phallic cult, the use of incense burners, the practice of wrestling, and the presence of dwarfs at the royal courts— in addition to stepped pyramids—are found among the Olmecs, creators of the earliest Middle American civilization known. He regards the huge Olmec stone heads with wide noses and thick, heavy lips as portraits of African Negroes, while other sculptured figures with beards are supposed to represent Caucasian Semites. Numerous parallels between Egyptian and Mexican beliefs and iconography are also presented. Egyptians are supposed to have brought these various Near Eastern and African elements to the New World about the time of the Egyptian pharaoh Rameses III (c. 1198–1166 B.C.).

Many of the "parallels" Jairazbhoy mentions (such as wrestling, dwarfs at court, use of incense burners, etc.) are so general and commonplace that they prove nothing. His religious parallels are usually more specific, but in many cases he compares Egyptian practices with Mexican beliefs or rituals described by Spanish writers of the sixteenth century. He cannot relate these religious elements to the Olmecs. While some sixteenth-century Aztec and Maya customs undoubtedly derive from earlier cultures, many significant changes occurred in Mexican religion between the time of the Olmecs in the twelfth century B.C. and the arrival of the Spaniards in A.D. 1519.[24] Thus, instead of parallelling Egyptian and Olmec customs from c. 1150 B.C., Jairazbhoy actually compares the religion of Twentieth Dynasty Egypt with that of a number of different Mexican cultures which rose and fell over a span of more than twenty-five hundred years.

Alleged portraits of Negroes and Caucasians have often been used as evidence of Old World voyages to America. The artistic representations are usually supplemented by accounts of Indian legends about white gods such as Quetzalcoatl and Viracocha.[25] Quetzalcoatl was the legendary founder of civilization who was transformed into the Morning Star, according to Toltec and Aztec mythology. He is often described as having a flowing beard. The early Spaniards publicized a variant of the tradition in which the god had a white skin and was expected to return in human form. Viracocha was a Peruvian creator-god who also was bearded and white according to several Spanish writers.

But as with the other supposed evidence for Egyptians in America, the Negroid heads and bearded gods become much less persuasive when examined carefully. The large Olmec stone heads combine Negroid wide, flat noses, and sensuous lips with slit eyes and high cheekbones, characteristics of Mongoloid people. The American Indians are basically of Mongoloid descent, and individuals with the features portrayed on the monolithic heads still can be found in the Tabasco region of Mexico where the Olmec civilization arose. When the Spaniards first arrived in the New World they observed Negroid features among some Indians. The gene pool of the people who became the American Indians probably contained these Negroid elements before they migrated from Asia into the Americas, for some Negroid characteristics still occur among many Mongoloid groups in Asia.[26] It is virtually impossible to accurately determine an individual's race on the basis of only one or two features, especially noses or lips.

It also should be noted that on some small jade Olmec figurines, the supposedly Negroid features result from combining human and animal elements. These figurines depict "were-jaguars," half-child and half-jaguar creatures. The wide, flat noses and downturned mouths are among the feline elements in the statuettes.[27]

Models for the bearded "Caucasian" figures also could have been found among the native American population. Mongoloid peoples, including American Indians, are generally less hairy than Caucasians, but they can and do grow beards, especially in old age. Beards and long mustaches have long been the mark of sages and old men in China. And an eyewitness report of the first meeting between Cortez and Montezuma describes the Aztec ruler as having a thin, light, well-arranged beard.[28] Beards on Mexican and Peruvian gods probably were symbols of old age and authority.

Paintings of bearded Mexican gods which have survived usually show them with red-brown skins. A few are black and one is even blue. So much for the theory that bearded gods must represent Caucasians! The idea that Quetzalcoatl had a white skin may have arisen among Montezuma and his advisors to explain the landing of white, bearded strangers from the east. The Spaniards then made use of this interpretation of the Quetzalcoatl legend for their own purposes. But Quetzalcoatl was not generally regarded as a white-skinned deity. In fact, when he appeared in codices in human form rather than as a plumed serpent, Quetzalcoatl's face is entirely black or black with vertical yellow stripes. The legends also reveal no expectation that he would one day return to earth—he returned constantly as the Morning Star.[29]

Viracocha (also known as Kon-Tiki) was a Peruvian sun-god who, like Quetzalcoatl, was bearded. He was thought to have created various groups of men from figures of stone and clay and to have given them the elements of civilization. Then he departed, walking across the waves of the sea into the west. An alternative account states that he was consumed by fire on the coast. But while the native legends often pictured Viracocha dressed in a white cloak or robe, they seldom described him as white-skinned. And they contained no prediction that he would return to earth in human form. The Spanish conqueror Pizarro, seeking to duplicate the success Cortez had had in Mexico, claimed that he and his men were Viracocha and his sons returning from the West. His modified version of the Peruvian myth was repeated by many Spanish chroniclers, but this propaganda ploy did not prove as useful in Peru as the Quetzalcoatl legend had been for Cortez in Mexico.[30]

The white-god concept was almost certainly a late addition to traditional Indian beliefs. The Indians accepted such alterations of their myths first as an explanation for the arrival of the Spaniards and of the strange beasts (horses) and powerful weapons they possessed. Later, when questioned about Quetzalcoatl or Viracocha by Spanish priests or chroniclers, the natives probably went along with the white-god versions in order to flatter or placate their conquerors. A number of European features in these "native" myths (a robed god walking the countryside healing the sick, or opposition to human sacrifice, for instance) become apparent when they are compared with the rest of the mythology of the Mexican and Peruvian peoples. The absence of the "returning white-skinned god" motif in the few surviving pre-conquest painted images and native-language accounts of Quetzalcoatl and Viracocha makes it very unlikely that Mexican and Peruvian Indians were awaiting the return of bearded white gods who had taught them civilization long ago.

While some individuals use such unsatisfactory evidence to argue for an Egyptian presence in America, others have used most of the same material to support theories of Phoenician voyages across the Atlantic. The Egyptians, after all, were not a seafaring people. Their ships were built for use on the Nile, not for withstanding the pounding of ocean waves. Thor Heyerdahl's voyage across the Atlantic in the payprus boat, *Ra II,* proved it could be done. However, the fact that the *Ra I* sank in mid-ocean is indicative of the difficulties involved.[31] On the other hand, the Phoenicians who lived in what is now Lebanon and coastal Syria were gifted seamen. They dominated Mediterranean trade routes in the eleventh to sixth centuries B.C., and ancient writers mention that they frequently sailed as far as the Tin Island (Britain). A Phoenician expedition in the employ of the Egyptian pharaoh Necho II even circumnavigated Africa in about 600–595 B.C. They are, thus, far better candidates for an Atlantic crossing than are the Egyptians.

Since Phoenicians were in close contact with Egyptians, Mesopotamians, and other Near Eastern peoples, they could have transmitted elements from those groups to the New World. In this way theorists can claim that Negroid and Semitic portrait heads, Mesopotamian zigguratlike temples, Egyptian sun-worship, Hittite pointed-toe shoes, and other features of various Near Eastern cultures noted in America all resulted from visits by Phoenician middlemen.[32]

We have already seen that pyramids, bearded portraits, white-god legends, etc., are not proof of visitors from the Old World. They are, thus, no better evidence for Phoenician voyagers than for Egyptians, Mesopotamians, Greeks or any others. But supporters of the Phoenician hypothesis claim to have documentary evidence that their theory is correct. In 1872, a copy of an inscription supposedly found at Pouso Alto near the Pairaba in Brazil was sent to the president of the Institute of History and Geography in Rio de Janeiro. The text turned out to be a Phoenician account of a sixth-century-B.C. voyage from the port of Ezion-geber on the Gulf of Aqaba (an arm of the Red Sea) to the coast of Brazil. According to the inscription, ten ships manned by sailors from Sidon set out down the Red Sea to sail around Africa and enter the Mediterranean through the Strait of Gibraltar. But off the west coast of Africa, a storm separated one ship from the others and blew it across the Atlantic. Twelve men and three women survived to land in the New World.

Portions of the text were sent to Ernest Renan, one of the nineteenth century's leading authorities on Canaanite linguistics, for his opinion. Renan declared that he was confident the inscription was a forgery. And Dr. Ladislau Netto, director of the National Museum in Rio and the first to support the text's authenticity, eventually came to agree with Renan's assessment. So scholars gradually forgot about the Paraiba inscription. But in 1968, after studying a copy of the inscription found at a rummage sale, Cyrus Gordon, a specialist in Northwest Semitic languages, proclaimed its authenticity.

Renan's negative assessment was based in part on several linguistic "mistakes" that he noted in the text. However, Gordon argues that the inscription contains linguistic features which had not been attested in Phoenician in 1872. A forger could not have made a nineteenth-century fake that contained accurate grammatical forms discovered only in the 1930s or later. Instead of branding it a forgery, the strange features of the text prove its authenticity, according to Gordon.[33]

However, the case against the authenticity of the Paraiba inscription consists of more than just a few unusual linguistic features. First, there is the problem that no scholar has ever seen the actual stone on which the inscription was supposedly carved, and the place where it was supposedly found has not been located. There are a number of places named Pouso Alto in Brazil, and there are two Paraibas (one a river, the other a province). After much effort in 1873–74, Netto was unable to determine the place where the stone had been found or to locate the person who had sent the copy of the text to the Institute of History and Geography. This does not prove forgery, but it is a very unusual and suspicious circumstance.

Once Netto's suspicions were aroused, he wrote letters to the five

men in Brazil capable of concocting a forged Phoenician text. He compared their handwritten replies with the letter announcing the discovery
and found one of the answers was in the same handwriting as the 1872
letter. He then wrote another letter to the suspect. The handwriting in the
reply further confirmed Netto's suspicion. The museum director did not
announce the man's name because he was socially prominent and a noted
scholar, but this test convinced Netto that the inscription was a forgery.[34]
While Netto was not a handwriting expert, his conclusions are very convincing in the light of more recent evidence against the text.

For one thing, there is the script in which the text is written. Styles
of writing change over the centuries. Experts in paleography (the study of
ancient letter forms) can usually date a manuscript or inscription on the
basis of the way the letters are shaped, the way they slant, the thickness of
the strokes, and their position above or below a guide line (either imaginary or real). According to Frank Moore Cross, the leading expert on
Semitic writing, the facsimile copy of the Paraiba inscription combines
letter forms ranging from the ninth through the first centuries B.C. Such a
wide range of writing styles should not occur in a single inscription. Few
Phoenician inscriptions were known in the 1870s, and even fewer were
accurately dated. Most of the ones known at that time were fairly late
(fourth to first centuries B.C.). Thus, a forger could not know that when
he selected examples of various letters from Phoenician script charts he
was choosing styles separated by hundreds of years.[35]

The spelling of the words in the text also betray it as a forgery.
Most ancient Semitic languages, including Phoenician, were written without vowels. Eventually a few consonants came to be used to indicate long
vowels. For example, *yod* (*y*) would show that long *i* was to be read or
waw (*w*) would mark a long *o* or *u*. Consistent use of consonants as
vowel markers did not occur in Phoenician inscriptions until the third
century B.C. But the supposedly sixth-century-B.C. Paraiba inscription is
full of these rudimentary vowel signs. Furthermore, the text mixes
together Phoenician and Hebrew spellings from a variety of different
periods.[36]

Hebrew and Phoenician grammatical elements from various eras
also are combined in the Paraiba inscription. The forger was presumably
better acquainted with Hebrew than Phoenician, causing him to utilize
grammatical forms which persisted in Hebrew but disappeared from
Phoenician by the tenth century B.C.[37]

Gordon's contention that the Paraiba inscription includes recently
discovered linguistic elements that a nineteenth-century forger could not
have anticipated is simply wrong, according to Cross. "Everything in the
inscription was available to the forger in nineteenth century handbooks or
from uninspired guesses based on these easily available sources," Cross

states.[38] Each of the examples Gordon cites can be explained in terms of the knowledge available in 1872.[39]

Cyrus Gordon had one more card to play, however. He claimed that the inscription contained a cryptogram validating its date and indicating that the person who inscribed the text was an Israelite in Phoenician employ.[40] This would explain some of the mixtures of Hebrew and Phoenician elements in the inscription. The presence of such cryptograms in ancient texts was unknown in the 1870s, Gordon claimed, so it would not have been put there by a forger. If the cryptogram is genuine, the text must be also.

Gordon does not explain away all of the discrepancies enumerated by Cross. His attempt to deal with the variety of letter types is particularly unconvincing.[41] Furthermore, the existence of a cryptogram in the Paraiba text is extremely questionable. The method Gordon used to discover the secret message is very subjective. By applying these techniques to the Kensington stele, a Viking inscription long regarded as a fake (see p. 162), Gordon and others discovered a cryptogram validating its medieval date. But another individual used the same method to find a cryptogram in the stele naming the Kensington residents who found the stone and the year it was discovered (1898). There is obviously something wrong with a methodology which can produce such widely divergent results.[42]

Even more devastating to his argument was Gordon's discovery of a similar cryptogram in the Vinland Map, thought to have been made in the 1440s and based on earlier Viking charts.[43] In 1974, it was discovered that the ink used on the map contained anatase, a compound first used in ink in 1917. This fact, as well as the presence of other suspicious features, prompted Yale University, the owner of the map, to declare that it was a twentieth-century forgery.[44] If Gordon's method can produce an ancient-medieval type cryptogram in a modern forgery, it certainly is not a reliable guide to the authenticity of a text.

The evidence that the Paraiba inscription is a forgery remains overwhelming. It must be rejected as proof of a Phoenician presence in the New World. So while it is *possible* that a Phoenician ship at some time crossed the Atlantic to land somewhere in the Americas, there is no persuasive evidence that any actually did so. The supposed Near Eastern elements in New World cultures are probably all the result of independent American development.

Old World Megaliths, Inscriptions, and Coins

Many writers in the past believed that the Old World features they discerned in American cultures could have originated from the landing of a single ship or fleet—Egyptian, Phoenician, Greek, or whatever—which found the New World by accident. But today, Cyrus Gordon, Barry Fell, and others claim that there was almost continuous contact between New and Old World cultures over a period of more than two thousand years. In addition to Egyptians, Phoenicians, and Israelites, groups of Celts, Libyans, Greeks, Romans, and Arabs are supposed to have left traces of their visits in the Americas.

Among the remains credited to these early explorers and settlers are a number of stone structures found in New England. Few people paid much attention to these monuments before the appearance of Barry Fell's best-seller, *America B.C.: Ancient Settlers in the New World* (1976). Fell, an emeritus professor of invertebrate zoology at Harvard University, became impressed by similarities between the stone-slab chambers of Mystery Hill in North Salem, New Hampshire, and the megalithic monuments of Europe. He learned that structures of the same type also were found in Connecticut, New York, Massachusetts, and Vermont. Like William Goodwin before him,[45] Fell decided that Celtic peoples had erected these stone "temples" and "astronomical observatories" in the New World.[46]

The New England monuments include large free-standing stones, dolmens (large stones atop three or more smaller ones), circles of stones, and slab-roofed chambers.[47] The standing stones and roofed chambers are often oriented in significant astronomical directions—due east (sunrise at the vernal and autumnal equinoxes), a declination plus or minus $23\frac{1}{2}°$ on the eastern horizon (sunrise at the summer or winter solstices), or due south (direction of maximum elevation of any celestial body being used to calculate latitude by means of an astrolabe).[48] Fell claims that similar megalithic monuments in Europe were used (and in many cases built) by the Celts.[49] He and his followers believe that the American examples, supposedly erected as early as the second millennium B.C., were associated with various festivals of the Celtic year and were dedicated to Celtic deities, especially the sun-god Bel.[50]

As proof of their Celtic origin, Fell cites Ogam (or Ogham) inscriptions found inside or on the lintels of these New England monuments. Ogam is an old British and Irish alphabet which uses combinations of straight lines to represent various letters (see Figure 13). According to Barry Fell, the American Ogam inscriptions are in a variety of the script which originated in Spain and Portugal (Iberia). Due to influence from Phoenician colonists in Spain, this Iberian Ogam contains only consonants with no vowels. The inscriptions are supposedly written in Goidelic, an old Celtic language (the ancestor of Gaelic), but they contain a number of Semitic grammatical features and loanwords.[51]

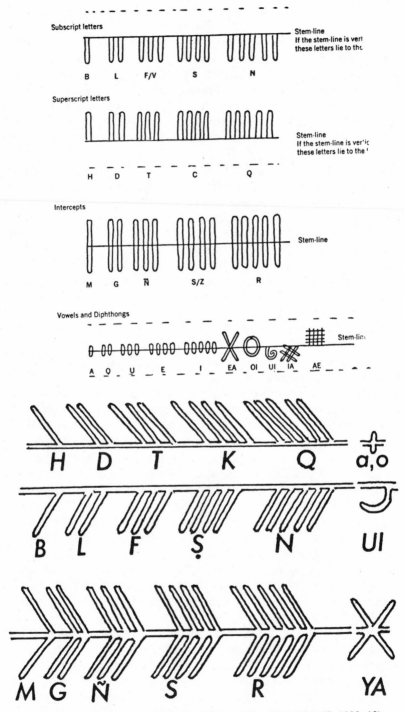

FIGURE 13: Forms of the Ogam alphabet (after Fell 1976: 47; 1982: 12)

Fell also noted inscriptions in Phoenician in some of the stone structures.[52] Presumably Phoenician merchants visited and traded with their Celtic friends in the New World as they did in the Old, or perhaps Phoenicians established colonies with most of the population drawn from Iberian Celts and Basques.[53] The Phoenician individuals in this mixture of peoples from Spain and Portugal also supposedly left their mark on the American Indians—a Pima Indian chant is interpreted as an ancient Semitic (Phoenician) hymn.[54]

Libyans from North Africa also left inscriptions in America, according to Fell. The Zuni language, as well as that of the Polynesians, he claims to be Libyan with some Anatolian and Asian elements.[55] Other inscriptions supposedly proclaim a Greek and an Arab presence in the New World,[56] while (it is claimed) Egyptians left their calling card in the form of influence on the Micmac Indian script and language.[57]

Professional archaeologists and linguists have disputed all of these claims, but they have had little influence on Fell's hardcore following. Many of the "megalithic stone structures" were investigated in 1978 and 1979 by a Vermont state archaeologist and by a team from the University of Massachusetts. They found "no evidence for ancient voyager origins and considerable evidence for historic construction as chimney supports, spring houses, and root cellars."[58] While Fell claims that the American stone chambers are temples, the evidence indicates that most of the European megalithic chambers were used as tombs, though some may have served also as temples.[59] However, burials are not found in the American stone structures. Furthermore, specialists in European archaeology point out that the megaliths of western Europe had no connection with the Celts. The popular association of the Druids (Celtic priests) with megalithic structures, especially Stonehenge, arose out of seventeenth- and eighteenth-century speculation about the builders of these monuments.[60] The megalith-builders flourished between c. 4000 and 2000 B.C., more than a millennium before the Celts moved into France, Spain, Portugal, Britain, and Ireland.[61] The Celts may have reused some of these monuments, but while they constructed many earthwork ramparts and a few stone-wall fortifications, the Celts built no megalithic structures of their own.[62] So Iberian Celtic or Phoenician travelers to America in the second millennium B.C. or later would not have brought with them the habit or the knowledge of building megalithic stone "temples" and "astronomical observatories."

Fell's inscriptional and linguistic evidence has even less to recommend it. Ogam writing was developed in the British Isles (probably in South Wales) no earlier than the fourth century A.D. by someone who had studied Latin and was aware of the linguistic theories of the Latin grammarians.[63] There is no valid evidence supporting Fell's claims that a form of this script was used to write Celtic words in ancient Spain and Portugal[64] and Old Norse inscriptions in Scandinavia.[65] The only authentic Ogam inscriptions known come from the British Isles.[66]

Ogam is such a simple writing system that once one omits vowels and allows the writing to be read in any direction, "inscriptions" can be found almost anywhere. Fell produced an Egyptian-Libyan text from a copy of a Pitcairn Island rock carving published in 1870. But when the original carving was checked recently, the copy Fell had used was seen to be in error and his decipherment would not work on the original. On another occasion, a sketch of some rock markings that Fell deciphered as a Phoenician Ogam inscription turned out to represent nothing more than a set of cracks produced by nature.[67] The four strokes which Fell reads as B-BL (Celtic *Bi Bel,* "dedicated to bel") could also be read as HT, TH, B(or V)F, FB(or V), LL, S(or Z), MGM, GBH, and more.[68] Words to fit almost any of these combinations of consonants could be found after rummaging through the vocabularies of Gaelic, Basque, Phoenician, Norse, and Libyan! In fact, since the B-BL inscription was on a lintel stone, it could just as plausibly be read L-BB (Arabic *li-Bâb,* "belonging to the door or entrance").

Similar objections can be raised against Fell's decipherment of supposed American inscriptions in Tifinag (a Berber North African alphabet consisting for the most part of dots, circles, straight lines, and crosses) and Kufic Arabic. The random lines, dots, and circles that Fell turns into words are not very convincing. His claims are especially questionable when some of the "letters" are written incorrectly or in an uncharacteristic form. Also, Arabic letters that should connect with the following ones do not always do so in these American inscriptions, while letters that should not connect sometimes do. There is space here for only a few examples. In Fell's Arabic-Greek bilingual text from Nevada,[69] the Arabic letters *jim* (j or g), *'alif* ('), and *ha'* (h) have uncharacteristic shapes, and in the first word there are too many "squiggles" or "pointed waves" to represent only the *ya'* (y) and *ba'* (b) that Fell reads. In another "Arabic" text,[70] the letters are not joined as they should be, and the form of *ya'* (y), which should be used only at the end of a word, is used in the middle of two of the words and at the beginning of another. Fell accepts such problems with these "inscriptions" because the writers presumably were only semi-literate.

But if one allows for this kind of freedom in the writing, many of Fell's "Arabic" inscriptions could be made to produce letters and words quite different from those he finds. For instance, an inscription that Fell reads FLQ (*fulk* [sic], "felluca"—a kind of boat)[71] could also be read MLM, MLF, MLQ, FLM, etc. Another "Arabic" text has the words arranged in haphazard fashion with uncharacteristic forms for the letters equivalent to "h," "l," and "d."[72] Yet Fell interprets this "semi-literate" text as an instruction in Arabic on how to find the area of a circle!

There are additional problems with many of Fell's readings. Some of the words he finds exist in *modern* Gaelic, Norse, and Arabic, but did not exist (at least not in the same form) in the ancient and medieval versions of those languages. And there are numerous mistakes. Fell interprets a California petroglyph as *Yasus ben Maria,* (which he claims is "Jesus was the son of Mary" written in Arabic (see Figure 14).[73] However, in Arabic "Jesus" is written with the equivalents of 'YSY = *'Isâ*, not YSS = *Yasus* as Fell claims. And the Arabic word for "son" is *'ibn;* Fell's *ben* is Hebrew. Finally, "Mary" is not written with only the equivalents of MR—it should be MRYM *(Maryam)*. In the three-word "inscription," every word is incorrect! Another inscription, supposedly in Greek,[74] has the wrong form for nearly every letter. Particularly troublesome are the *omikron* (o) which looks more like *upsilon* (u), and the *tau* (t), which is written like a lower case Roman or English *t* rather than like the Greek letter. In this text the letters ZT are read as the word *zete* written without vowels—a practice not found in Greek. Even if one allows this questionable interpretation to stand, the text cannot be twisted to mean "Look out for snakes" as Fell translates it. *Zēteō* means "to seek; to inquire into; to desire, to wish for," almost the exact opposite of Fell's "look out [for], beware of; avoid." (Also, the imperative of this verb should be *zētei*, not *zete,* but since the vowels are not written in the inscription, this is Fell's mistake, not that of the "text.") Still another alleged Greek inscription is deciphered as a land title claim cut by an individual who spelled his name EMILI[A]NU[S].[75] Fell thinks this Emilianus was a Christian of the Byzantine era from North Africa. But Emilianus is a Roman name, not Greek, and it should be written AEMILIANUS. Why didn't Aemilianus write his inscription in Latin? If he knew enough Greek to carve a title claim in this language, he also should have known that Latin names ending in *-us* are written with an *-os* ending in Greek. The Greek spelling of this name should have been AIMILIANOS, not the EMILI[ ]NU of Fell's "inscription."

Fell's case is also weakened by the fact that very few of these alleged inscriptions were uncovered by objective, professional archaeological excavation. Some of the carvings he accepts as genuine are definitely forgeries. For example, the Davenport Calendar stele, which according to Fell contians a trilingual inscription in Egyptian hieroglyphs, Iberian–Punic, and Libyan,[76] has been shown to be a nineteenth-century forgery.[77] Yet Fell provides no refutation of Marshall McKusick's convincing arguments in *The Davenport Conspiracy.* Although he was aware of the case against the stele before *America B.C.* was published, Fell does not even warn his readers that the authenticity of this text has been ques-

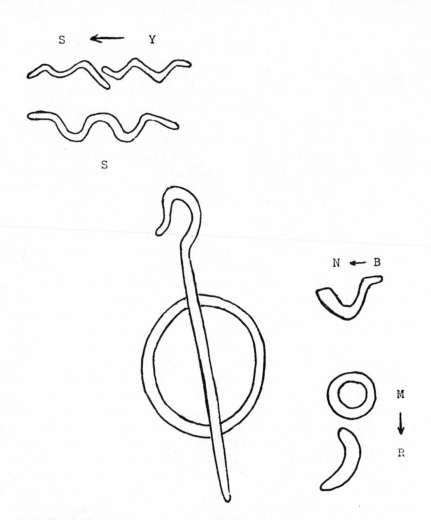

A. California Petroglyph, which Fell reads *Yasus ben Maria,* "Jesus [was the] son of Mary" (after Fell 1980: 173).

B. The correct way to write "Jesus, son of Mary" in Arabic (*'Isâ 'ibn Maryam)*

FIGURE 14. One of Fell's "Arabic" Inscriptions

tioned. This is the antithesis of genuine scholarship![78]

A number of Fell's supposed American inscriptions are nothing more than accidental scrapes or plough marks. Others were certainly carved by humans (probably by American Indians), but seem to be random designs or decorations rather than writing. Still others are certainly recent fabrications (Fell has not had any of the carvings tested scientifically to verify that the incised lines are, in fact, old). But whatever they are, these "inscriptions" are not convincing evidence of Old World traders and colonists in America.

Alleged traces of Old World tongues in American Indian languages are also imaginary. Fell's analysis of a Pima Indian chant as Semitic is based on an arbitrary division of the words, misinterpretation of some of the phonetic symbols in the original publication, and a lack of understanding of either Pima or Semitic grammar. The chant makes perfectly good sense in the Pima language, which is unrelated to Phoenician or any other Semitic tongue. Fell's claim that the language of the Zuni Indians of New Mexico derives from ancient Libyan is likewise in error due to his faulty knowledge of both Zuni and Libyan.[79]

Furthermore, neither Micmac writing nor language is related to ancient Egyptian, as Fell asserts. The Micmac script was developed by Roman Catholic missionaries as a mnemonic device to aid the Indians in remembering their Christian prayers. It has a totally different structure from the ancient Egyptian hieroglyphic writing system. And there are no demonstrable Egyptian loanwords in the Micmac language.[80]

Fell plays the "word-list" game that was so popular in the nineteenth century. This method of comparing and relating languages was abandoned by competent linguists long ago. It takes more than superificial similarities in the sound and meaning of a few words to prove a connection between two languages. But Fell continues to rely on this outmoded methodology. The only one of his alleged Old World loan-words in Indian languages that is genuine is the Algonquian word *pados,* "boat." However, it was not borrowed from Gaelic *bata* as Fell claims; it is a relatively recent borrowing form French *bateau* (which in turn was borrowed from Old English *bāt,* as was Gaelic *bata*). Fell's linguistic arguments are absoluely worthless as evidence for pre-Columbian contacts between the Old World and the New.[81]

The remaining evidence for Israelite, Phoenician, Greek, Roman, Libyan, and Arab voyages to the New World consists of Old World artifacts found at a number of places in both North and South America.[82] However, except for the "bronze" tools and weapons uncovered in North American mounds, such objects are not found in stratified archaeological deposits. Actually, the "Mound-Builder" implements are copper, not bronze as Fell asserts.[83] They are native products and not European imports. The remaining artifacts consist primarily of coins and small pottery objects. While a few of these artifacts seem to be forgeries, most of them are undoubtedly authentic. Unfortunately, though, the vast majority of them were found on or just beneath the surface by people digging in their gardens, walking on a beach, ploughing, etc. Ancient coins, lamps, and small jars long have been favorite tourist souvenirs of visits to the Holy Land, Rome, or other ancient sites. And modern coin collectors and travelers sometimes lose or discard ancient coins or lamps just as ancient Israelites or Romans are supposed to have done. So the presence of a few such objects in fields, backyards, or beaches in the Americas is not really proof that ancient voyagers left them there.

The most significant discovery of Old World coins in the New World occurred in Venezuela. A hoard of several hundred Roman coins ranging in date from the reign of Augustus (27 B.C. to A.D. 14) to about A.D. 350 were found packed in a jar and buried in the sand of the shore. Constance Irwin argued that since there were many duplicates, the coins could not be a numismatist's collection. She theorized that they were probably "a Roman trader's ready cash, carefully buried in the sand by their owner or washed ashore after a shipwreck."[84] However, the discovery in the hoard of two eighth-century-A.D. Arab coins caused Cyrus Gordon to modify Irwin's theory slightly. Gordon believes the coins were a Moor's ready cash.[85]

The circumstances surrounding this discovery have never been published, so many details remain sketchy (for instance, the jar in which the coins were found has not been described or illustrated). But the likelihood that this collection was the ready cash of an ancient or medieval trader is extremely low. None of the hundreds of hoards of Roman coins found in various parts of Europe cover a range of dates as wide as the Venezuelan collection. Roman coins simply did not remain in use for centuries after they were minted.[86] If all of the coins in the Venezuelan hoard had belonged to the same era, say the Julio-Claudian Dynasty of Rome (27 B.C.-A.D. 68), the assemblage would be better evidence for an ancient voyage to the New World. Instead, the fact that it includes examples from every period between Augustus and A.D. 350 with two eighth-century Arab coins for good measure is a strong indication that this hoard belonged to a modern-day coin collector. And despite Irwin's argument to the contrary, duplicates are almost always found in such collections.[87]

There has been a vast amount of careful archaeological excavation in the Americas over the past century.. If Old World explorers, traders, and colonists had been coming to this hemisphere for more than two thousand years, why hasn't one of their trading posts or settlements been discovered? As we shall soon see, a Viking installation in Newfoundland *has* been found and excavated. So, when evidence exists, it can be located and uncovered. If the New England stone chambers were built by Celts, why hasn't abundant confirmation of this turned up in excavations? Why hasn't one Phoenician house complete with pottery sherds and other artifacts been found in America when many have been discovered at Phoenician outposts in Spain and North Africa? Why isn't there even one New World example of a Greek or Roman temple or Moslem mosque? Why does the evidence for Egyptian, Phoenician, Israelite, Greek, Roman, Celtic, Libyan, or Arab visitors to America consist solely of material without a firm archaeological context—questionable inscriptions scratched on rocks, coins found in gardens or on beaches, vague resemblances between some Old World and New World art and architecture, alleged Old World loan-words in Indian languages?

Cyrus Gordon, Barry Fell, and their followers do not answer such questions. They do not point out that in the hundreds of modern professional archaeological excavations of pre-Columbian American sites, not a single unquestionably Old World artifact has been found except at the Viking settlement in Newfoundland. Marshall McKusick sums up perfectly the approach that characterizes books like *Before Columbus* or *America B.C.*: "It is as if scientific archaeology had vanished from the scene, or had never existed, and we had no more knowledge of the past than the early nineteenth century antiquarians."[88] The reader should not be fooled by the volume of purported evidence Gordon and Fell gather to support their thesis. Examine it carefully and it will become clear that no matter how many times one multiples zero, the result will still be zero!

Voyagers from Southeast Asia?

Most popular theorists have concentrated their attention on possible parallels between American cultures and those of Europe and the Near East. But in recent years an increasing amount of study has been devoted to similarities between the New World and Southeast Asia. And the leading proponents of transpacific voyages from China, India, Cambodia, and Indonesia are professional anthropologists and orientalists, rather than amateur theorists.

The parallels in art and architecture between the two areas are indeed striking. The elaborately decorated stepped pyramids of Borobudur in Java and Ankor in Cambodia are far more like those at Tikal and other Maya sites than are Egyptian or Mesopotamian pyramids. Cylindrical tripod vessels with conical lids found at Teotihuacán in Central

Mexico are very similar to bronze and pottery tripod jars of the Han Dynasty in China. A stone interlace design typical of the Tajin style of Gulf Coast Mexico is almost identical to a pattern used in the Late Chou period in China. Dragon/serpent motifs play a prominent role in the art of both areas. Also, the Mexican game Patolli was played on a cross-shaped board like that of the Hindu game Pachesi, and the rules of both games were much the same. Finally, in India, a part fish, part crocodile, part elephant sea-monster called the "Makara" was often represented with a human being emerging from its mouth. The Mayans also depicted hybrid creatures with humans coming out of their mouths.[89]

These and other similarities led the late Robert Heine-Geldern, an Austrian orientalist, and Gordon Ekholm, an American archaeologist, to argue for prolonged contact between the Far East and the Americas (principally Mexico). The Asiatic influences supposedly appeared as early as the Olmec culture of the early first millennium B.C. and continued through the late Maya period at Chichén Itza around the end of the first millennium A.D.[90]

Chinese historians of the first century B.C. recorded legends of magical islands in the Eastern Ocean (the Pacific) that contained palaces made of silver and gold and a drug that conferred immortality. An expedition led by Hsü Fu set out in 219 B.C. to find these blessed isles. Three thousand young men and maidens were taken along, as well as artisans of every sort and the seeds of five grains. But the sailing vessels and their occupants never returned to China.[91] Later Chinese writers mention a land named Fusang which was somewhere east of Japan. A Buddhist monk named Hui-Shen returned to China in A.D. 499 with a tale that he had spent forty years in Fusang, which was more than 6,600 miles further east than Japan. Hui-Shen said that in Fusang gold and silver were not considered valuable. There were large trees that provided a pear-like fruit. The inhabitants also ate the young shoots of these trees, just as the Chinese ate bamboo shoots. The bark of Fusang trees was used to make a rough cloth and a kind of writing paper. The inhabitants of this wonderful land possessed no weapons, lived in unfortified wooden houses, and were totally peaceful. They used copper, but did not know of iron.[92]

Some believe that these stories record early Chinese voyages to America. The Kuroshio Current (also known as the Japan Current) flows across the North Pacific from west to east. It would help propel oriental ships eastward to the New World. A vessel sailing from China could follow this current along a route that would take it to Japan, along the Kurile island chain to the Kamchatka Peninsula, across a short stretch of open water to the Aleutians, and then down the west coast of America. Such a voyage could be made without venturing out of sight of land for more than a few hours. If that is the route Hui-Shen followed, the 20,000 *li* (c. 6,000 miles) mentioned in his account would have taken him to the vicinity of Acapulco in Mexico.[93]

Until recently, the only direct evidence favoring such Chinese voyages was a cache of ancient Chinese coins and a bronze fan with Chinese characters on it found at Cassiar, British Columbia, in 1882. This find, it is claimed, indicates that Chinese vessels reached the shores of America by at least 1200 B.C., supposedly the date of most of the coins.[94] However, this date must be an error (perhaps A.D. 1200 is meant), since the Chinese did not have coinage as early as the thirteenth and twelfth centuries B.C. In the last few years another find has buoyed the hopes of those who believe in ancient Chinese voyages to the New World. About a quarter mile off the Palos Verdes Peninsula south of Los Angeles, two divers found a cluster of some twenty or more worked stones, most with holes drilled through them. After seeing photographs and drawings of these stones, a Chinese maritime historian announced in 1980 that they were anchors of a type used for thousands of years in China. And two anthropologists from the University of San Diego have declared that the stone anchors are evidence of a large Asiatic vessel that probably was shipwrecked several hundred years ago.[95]

Widespread cultivation of maize ("corn") in Asia is also seen by some as evidence of pre-Columbian contacts across the Pacific. Maize is native to the New World, but by the early part of the sixteenth century it was well established in many parts of Asia. And some of the Asian varieties of maize are mutants derived from a strain of the plant grown in the Philippines. It is argued that maize must have been introduced into Asia in pre-Columbian times in order to account for its sixteenth-century distribution and for the development of new Asiatic varieties.[96]

However, chronology produces problems for those supporting Southeast Asian contacts with America just as it does for champions of Near Eastern or European voyages. The cylindrical tripod vessels of Teotihuacán might possibly be derived from those of the Han Dynasty of China, since the early Teotihuacán Period (c. A.D. 1–300) overlaps the dates for the Late Han era (A.D. 24–220). But the Tajin designs that are compared to those of the Chou Period in China are almost five hundred years later than the end of the Chou Dynasty in 256 B.C. And the c. A.D. 1200 water-lily friezes from Chichén Itźa are almost a thousand years later than the lotus friezes in India from which they supposedly derive. In an attempt to bridge such gaps in time, Ekholm and Heine-Geldern have argued that these designs and motifs once used on Asian stone reliefs were perpetuated for hundreds of years in wood carvings before appearing in American stone sculpture. However, this explanation is not very satisfying. Date glyphs on Mayan art works indicate that contemporaneous carvings in wood and stone were done in the same style. There is no support for a wood-carving style persisting for hundreds of years before being imitated in stone.[97]

On the other hand, the Mayan pyramids at Tikal are hundreds of years *earlier* than the examples in Cambodia and Java to which they are likened. In this instance, architectural influences would have had to travel from America to Asia rather than the other way around. Unless proponents of Far Eastern contacts with the New World can produce more evidence of close similarities between roughly contemporaneous artifacts on both sides of the Pacific, it must be concluded that the alleged parrallels are more apparent than real.

It should also be noted that in A.D. 285 the Chinese naturalist Chang Hua wrote that he knew of no one who had crossed the vast Eastern Ocean.[98] How can such a direct statement from a knowledgeable Chinese scholar be reconciled with theories of frequent contacts between China and America starting as early as 1200 or 1000 B.C.? This passage especially calls into question claims for Han Dynasty influence on the Teotihuacán culture of Mexico. The Han Dynasty ended only sixty-five years before Chang Hua wrote, so information from that era still should have been available to him. This seems to be the case, for Chang Hua knew of contacts between China and the Roman Empire during the Han Period. But he was unaware of any voyages to America. This is fairly persuasive evidence that no roundtrip Chinese transpacific voyages had yet occurred by the end of the third century A.D.

Then was Hui-Shen the first to reach America c. A.D. 459? Some elements of his description of Fusang, especially the cloth and writing material made of bark and the use of copper but not iron, suggest features of Meso-American Indian cultures. And the distance to Mexico is given correctly. However, other portions of this account definitely do not favor the Fusang = America hypothesis. The great trees he saw have been identified with redwoods[99] and century plants,[100] but neither has an edible pear-like fruit. Hui-Shen claimed that the people of Fusang had no military weapons. However, though the Classic cultures of Middle America may not have been as warlike as later groups such as the Aztecs, they did possess and use weapons.[101] Hui-Shen's story also describes carts drawn by horses, cattle, and tame deer when neither wheeled vehicles nor domesticated beasts of burden existed in the New World. And he tells of fantastic hair-covered amazons who lived beyond Fusang. Their children were born after only six or seven months of pregnancy, the infants walked within 100 days after birth, and were fully grown in three or four years![102]

Later Chinese mapmakers placed Fusang just off the northeast coast of Asia. Obviously they did not accept the great distance to Fusang given in Hui-Shen's account. Either they felt he was guilty of gross exaggeration, or the number given in the texts which have survived is the result of a scribal error. Supporting the mapmakers' view that Fusang was near the Asian mainland is the fact that in Hui-Shen's story the titles borne by officials of this land are derived from Korean. The island of Sakhalin, northeast of Japan, is a far better candidate for the land of Fusang than is any portion of America.[103]

The direct evidence for Chinese visits to America—the coins and the stone anchors—is also unreliable. The coins and bronze fan were not found in a pre-Columbian archaeological deposit. And like the Venezuelan Roman coins, details of the find are lacking. The entire assemblage does not seem to have been published.[104] As has been mentioned, such finds could have gotten to the New World by many means other than ancient sailors. The stone anchors are even less likely to be evidence of ancient Chinese voyages. These stones are carved from shale containing a high content of the mineral cristobalite. This composition is characteristic of Monterey shale, one of the most common types of coastal rock in southern California. The shapes of the stones give no indication of their date, since the same styles continued in use for hundreds of years down to the present century. And there are too many stones over too wide an area to be the result of a single shipwreck. They probably indicate an area where boats were frequently anchored. Since nineteenth-century Chinese fishermen in California built junks as they had in the Old World and used traditional types of stone anchors on them, these stone artifacts at Palos Verdes probably were produced by relatively recent Chinese immigrants to the New World. They represent anchors, mooring stones, and net weights associated with the nineteenth-century California fishing industry.[105]

There remains to be considered the argument based on the widespread cultivation of maize in Asia. One of the major supports of this argument, the presence of a peculiar variety of maize in Asia that was unknown or extremely rare in America, must be dealt with by botanists. Is the claim correct? If so, was it impossible for such distinctive varieties of maize to have been developed within only one generation after Columbus's discovery of America? If the botanists show that this feat was indeed impossible, then we would finally have genuine evidence of pre-Columbian contact between the Old World and the New. A decision on this argument must await their further study.

However, other attempts to demonstrate the existence of pre-Columbian maize in the Old World have failed. They largely depend upon the questionable assumption that vernacular names for maize after the time of Columbus also referred to maize *before* 1492. The error of such an assumption can be demonstrated by looking at the English word *corn*. This term comes from an Anglo-Saxon word that referred to the seed of any of the cereal grasses, and it can still be so used. In colloquial usage, however, it has come to be applied to the principal cereal crop of each of the various areas where English is spoken. Thus, in Scotland and Ireland, "corn" refers to oats, in England to wheat, and in the United States and Australia to maize. In the same way, the words for maize in Portuguese, Italian, and other Old World languages did not necessarily mean maize in pre-Columbian times.

It has also been shown that maize was not introduced into the Far East directly across the Pacific. It was Arabs who brought maize to Southeast Asia from the Near East.[106] The Arabs in turn probably got it from the Spaniards.[107] Maize spread rapidly along Arab trade routes, reaching the Philippines before Magellan arrived in 1521. So if the presence of maize in Turkey and parts of Asia *can* be shown to predate Columbus, the evidence of its spread from the Mediterranean to Asia will provide support for *transatlantic* voyages to the New World, not trans-pacific ones. But at present, there is no firm evidence that maize or any other New World plant was cultivated in the Old World before 1492.

It is also noteworthy that no Old World staples like rice or wheat were grown in the Americas before Columbus arrived. Could Asians have visited the New World for hundreds of years and not introduced the natives to rice? Heine-Geldern answers this question by pointing out that cultural borrowing is a very selective process. Old World crops would have had difficulty making headway against the firmly established tradition and religious associations of maize-growing in America.[108]

Despite the arguments of Heine-Geldern and Ekholm to the contrary, it is difficult to believe that over centuries of contact American cultures would copy Asian art motifs or building styles, but not borrow rice and wheat or the plow or iron tools and weapons. The Indians of Teotihuacán are supposed to have copied Chinese tripod pottery, but not the pottery wheel on which it was made. In the small villages of the New World traditional ways of doing things might have continued even after centuries of contact with outsiders (as they have to this day in parts of the Americas). But in the major centers of civilization where the artistic styles were supposedly being copied, wouldn't some of these other foreign elements have had some impact as well? The natives adopted European weapons whenever they could get them after 1492. Why would they have spurned iron knives or axes before that date? The absence of Old World crops as well as implements like the plow and potter's wheel in America seems to make sense only if contacts were extremely sporadic (and unimportant) or nonexistent. While no one can deny the possibility that one or more Asian ships might have reached America, the evidence does not seem to support theories of continuous, long-term transpacific contact.

Viking Explorations and Settlements

In the eighth and early ninth centuries A.D., plundering groups of Vikings set forth from Scandinavia to ravage European coastal areas. The destruction, chaos, and sense of insecurity these raids produced had a lasting impact on western society. But in the latter half of the ninth and into the tenth centuries, the Northmen also became settlers and traders, occupying some of the territories their predecessors had pillaged. Vikings settled in portions of England, Ireland, and France. A Swedish tribe penetrated southward into Russia, establishing a kingdom centered on Kiev. Some explorers and traders from this group followed the Volga River to the Caspian, and a few journeyed as far as Baghdad.

When a Viking who had been blown off course found Iceland in 861, this island also became a haven for land-hungry Norse colonists. The small band of Celtic monks who had previously lived there fled home to Ireland, leaving Iceland to the newcomers. Within only two generations, the population grew to about sixty thousand. Icelandic poets composed and preserved sagas celebrating the discovery of their island, detailing the backgrounds of the great families that had settled there, and recounting the deeds of a few heroic figures. Among these tales were accounts of the discovery of Greenland and Vinland.

According to the poets, Erik Thorwaldson (better known as Erik the Red) was exiled from Iceland in 981 for killing two men. He sailed to the west, eventually finding a large island, which he named Greenland. After spending three years exploring the new land's coast, Erik returned to Iceland with news of his discovery. Twenty-five ships bearing some five hundred colonists and their livestock set out for Greenland, but only fourteen vessels succeeded in reaching the new land. Nevertheless, two colonies were established, and both grew despite harsh climatic conditions.[109]

Not long after Erik the Red and his first fleet of settlers had embarked for Greenland, a young man named Bjarni Herjolfsson returned to Iceland from Norway. He learned that his father had sailed to the new land with Erik, so he set out in pursuit. However, a storm drove his ship off course. After sailing steadily westward for a number of days, land was finally sighted. The coast had small, wooded hills, but there were no signs of the mountains and glaciers which were supposed to be features of Greenland. Since the storm had pushed him south of his initial course, Bjarni turned north or northeastward and sailed for two more days before he found another forested coastline, this one flat. Realizing that this too was not the landfall he sought, Bjarni pushed on. He came to a rocky land which had glaciers, but the mountains of Greenland were not present. Finally, he turned back toward the east, and on his return trip found Greenland. Bjarni had almost certainly seen America and sailed along its coast, but he had not landed.[110]

Word of Bjarni's discoveries spread through Greenland. Six years later, in 992, Erik the Red's son, Leif, decided to learn more about the lands Bjarni had sighted. He purchased a ship, secured a crew, and set off to follow in reverse Bjarni's route. The first land he came to was barren and glacier-covered (probably the southern part of Baffin Island in the Canadian Arctic). Leif named it "Helluland" (Stone Land) because, except for glaciers, it seemed to be one large flat rock. The Vikings sailed on until they came to the flat, wooded country Bjarni had described. This area (probably part of Labrador) Leif called "Markland" (Forest Land). Finally, after two more days' sailing they came to the place where Bjarni had made his first landfall. Here Leif Eriksson and his crew decided to spend the winter. The winter's period of daylight was longer than in Greenland, grass and trees were abundant, large salmon were plentiful, and there were even wild grapes (though some have suggested that these might really have been currants or some other kind of berries). Leif named this territory "Vinland" (Wineland), presumably because of the vines and grapes. Its exact location has been hotly debated, but Vinland was probably in Newfoundland or Nova Scotia. In the early spring, the explorers loaded their ship and left the New World.[111]

Thorvald, Leif's brother, thought that Vinland should be more thoroughly explored, so with thirty men he returned to the place where Leif had wintered. He found Leif's camp and made it his base of operations. For two years Thorvald and his men explored the coastal regions of Vinland. Then disaster struck. While examining an area north of the base camp Thorvald and some of his Vikings came upon a party of Indians. Eight were killed, but one escaped to spread the alarm to his fellow tribesmen. Soon the Norsemen were under attack by hundreds of natives in many small, skin-covered boats. The assault was beaten off, but Thorvald was wounded by an arrow and died. After burying their leader, the members of this exploratory party rejoined their companions at the Vinland camp, and as soon as winter was over, the entire crew sailed home to Greenland.[112]

Two later expeditions sailed to Vinland with plans to colonize the area, but both ended in failure. Thorfinn Karlsefni led a party of 160 migrants, including a few women, to the new land. They built huts near a river and a lake somewhere south of the place where Leif and Thorvald had encamped, and there they lived for about two and a half years. At first they managed to trade peacefully with the natives, but eventually hostilities broke out. The Indian attacks persuaded Thorfinn and his colonists to return to Greenland.[113]

The last known Viking expedition to attempt to settle in America supposedly was led by Freydis, an illegitimate daughter of Erik the Red. However, quarrels among the settlers doomed this colonization effort. After some of the colonists were murdered by Freydis and her husband, the enterprise was abandoned.[114]

The Icelandic oral sagas were not written down until the fourteenth century, and for a long time they were regarded as legends with little historical value. But in the 1920s· the Greenland glaciers retreated a bit and portions of Erik the Red's western settlement were revealed. It had been abandoned in the fourteenth century, presumably because the climate had worsened and ice sheets had advanced toward it. By the beginning of the sixteenth century, all Norse settlement in Greenland had come to an end, leading to the later skepticism about Viking colonies there. Since the stories of the discovery and settlement of Greenland were evidently true, maybe the accounts about Vinland were also reliable. Scholars began treating the sagas with more respect.

Various possible locations for Vinland were proposed and debated without positive result. Some placed Leif's encampment at Bass River or Falmouth on Cape Cod, Massachusetts, while others located it as far south as Chesapeake Bay.[115] Helge Ingstad, a scholar who was convinced of the accuracy of the sagas, thought that Vinland was located further to the north. He interpreted Vinland to mean "Meadow Land," but even if the name meant "Wineland," in earlier times the climate had been warmer, and grapes had grown in latitudes now beyond their northernmost range. A sixteenth-century explorer had even seen wild grapes in Newfoundland. So in 1960, Ingstad began examining the eastern seaboard north of Rhode Island for the various topographical features mentioned in the poems. He had no success until he came to the north coast of Newfoundland. There, at a spot known as L'Anse aux Meadows, he found a cape projecting to the north, and a wide green plain behind which were low wooded hills. The site matched the descriptions of Vinland given by Bjarni and Leif. Between 1961 and 1968, excavation uncovered a number of houses with fireplaces, boat houses, and a smithy containing scraps of copper and iron. A bronze ring-headed pin, stone lamp, bone needle, and spindle-whorl, all unqeustionably Norse, were found in the ruins. And radiocarbon dating indicated that the settlement belonged to the end of the tenth century A.D., the period when the sagas claim Leif, Thorvald, and Karlsefni undertook their expeditions. Vinland had been found.[116].

It is not absolutely certain which Viking settlement the Newfoundland remains represent. Perhaps· these buildings belonged to Thorfinn Karlsefni's colony or to an unknown Norse expedition. But the likelihood is that at L'Anse aux Meadows archaeology has uncovered the camp where Leif Eriksson wintered in the New World and where Thorvald and his men lived for three years. In any case, the excavations have proved that Vikings *did* discover and briefly settle in America some five hundred years before Columbus.

The Icelandic sagas give no detailed descriptions of Norse expeditions to Vinland after the failure of the colonization efforts of Karlsefni and Freydis. But they do mention occasional visits to the New World, and the use of American larch trees in some late construction in Greenland may indicate that contact with Vinland was maintained for centuries. Some writers have argued that Vikings continued to explore and settle America into the fourteenth century. The primary supports for this contention are a stone tower in Rhode Island, Viking artifacts from Minnesota, and Norse inscriptions found in Oklahoma, Minnesota, and Maine.

A twenty-five-foot high stone tower in Newport, Rhode Island, has often been credited to pre-Columbian Viking settlers. It is usually compared to the central rotundas of twelfth- and thirteenth-century Norse churches built when Byzantine influence was strong in Scandinavia.[117]But archaeologists claim that the tower was built by English colonists in the seventeenth century, probably as a mill. Excavations turned up several colonial artifacts in the foundation trenches beneath the tower, and a piece of a clay pipe was found under the corner of one of the supporting columns.[118] Holand argues that colonial treasure hunters had beaten archaeologists to the site, disturbing the stratigraphy and depositing the seventeenth-century objects found under the tower.[119] However, where earlier digging had occurred, evidence of the fact was noted by the archaeologists. The colonial artifacts were in undisturbed portions of the foundation trench, not in treasure hunters' pits.[120] The fact remains that seventeenth-century artifacts *were* found associated with the building, and Norse objects were not. In addition, it should be mentioned that in 1677 the owner of the land on which the tower stands referred to the structure in his will as "my stone-built windmill." The Newport stone tower is certainly not evidence of Norse settlement in Rhode Island.

Mooring stones, iron axes, halberds, and a few other iron objects found in Minnesota are supposed to indicate that a Viking expedition reached the southern end of Hudson's Bay in Canada, then traveled overland to the Great Lakes region.[121] However, the large boulders with holes drilled through them cannot be dated, and it is not known whether or not they were used for mooring boats, Viking or otherwise. And the iron artifacts were not found in pre-Columbian archaeological contexts. They were not scientifically excavated from house remains like the materials at L'Anse aux Meadows or from early Indian sites. They were found lying in fields or under rocks. Often the details of the supposed discoveries are not available. This fact makes them unsuitable as valid archaeological evidence. The type of object most commonly found is an iron halberd, and these "weapons" are certainly not Norse. Even supporters of the Viking origin of these halberds admit that no examples like those found in Minnesota are known in Scandinavia, and that the American halberds are too small and light to have been useful as real weapons.[122] They are actually tobacco cutters distributed in the 1890s by the American Tobacco Company to advertise its "Battle Axe" brand chewing tobacco.

The various American inscriptions written in medieval Norse letters called "runes" are also almost certainly spurious. The most famous of these inscriptions is the stele or rune stone supposedly found buried under tree roots near Kensington, Minnesota in 1898. When translated, the text told of thirty Vikings from Vinland who undertook an expedition to the west in 1362. Scandinavian scholars immediately declared the stele a forgery. But in 1907, Hjalmar Holand acquired it, and for the next fifty years vigorously defended its authenticity.[123] To Holand's arguments more recent supporters have added the claim that its text contains a cryptogram validating its date.[124] However, it has already been mentioned above that the method used to find the enclosed date—Sunday, April 24, 1362—can also be used to reveal the date 1898 and the names of the stone's finders. And runic experts still repudiate the inscription. It is written in a mixture of modern Norwegian, Swedish, Danish, and English with some inconsistent archaic features thrown in to give it a semblance of authenticity. This forgery was probably inspired by the Chicago World's Fair of 1893 which featured a replica of a Viking ship which had just sailed the Atlantic from Norway to America.[125]

The meanings of runic inscriptions from Oklahoma[126] and Spirit Pond, Maine[127] are very uncertain. But they seem to have been written by someone more familiar with the Kensington Stone than with medieval Norse runes. One of the stones from Spirit Pond has a map of Maine's coast on its back. However, the map shows the present coastline, not that of a few centuries ago, which was quite different. In another case, a modern Swedish word occurs rather than its Old Norse equivalent, and runic numbers are misused to write a date.[128] There simply are no authentic Norse runic inscriptions in the New World.

It is now certain that Northmen visited America long before Columbus. But it is not known how long such contacts continued or how much of the New World the Vikings explored. The only definite evidence of their presence is the short-lived settlement at L'Anse aux Meadows from about A.D. 1000. This is not really so surprising, for the colony in Greenland was itself too precarious to do much to exploit the discoveries of Bjarni and Leif. The Vikings had neither the technology nor the numbers to assure triumph over the American Indian tribes they had to displace. While the Greenland Northmen may have kept up some contact with Vinland and Markland after the eleventh century, their voyages had virtually no effect on either America or Europe.

The Origin of New World Civilizations

Many of the theories considered in this chapter are trying to answer one basic question: "Where did civilization in the Americas come from?" No matter who is supposed to be responsible—Lost Tribes of Israel, Egyptians, Phoenicians, Chinese, or others—the common idea is that the elements of civilization were brought to the New World by voyagers from the Old. In some quarters, obviously, there is still strong resistance to the idea that American Indians could have created highly developed, civilized societies without outside help. However, by providing a chronology for the various developments leading to civilization in the New World, archaeology has undermined the case for most of the popular theories.

It is now known that domestication of plants and animals began almost as early in America as in the Old World. Around 6000–5000 B.C. the avocado pear and a kind of squash started to be cultivated in Mexico. Gradually, other plants were domesticated as well. By 3500 B.C. beans, chili peppers, and maize had joined the squash and avocado as staples of the Mexican diet. Some five hundred years later cotton was being cultivated and used to weave cloth. And in Peru the situation was much the same. By 5000 B.C., there are signs that the guinea pig and llama had been domesticated. Soon afterward, positive evidence of the cultivation of gourds, squash, and cotton appears.[129]

These developments are much too early to be credited to Old World influences. In 6000–5000 B.C. Near Eastern cultures were just perfecting their own agricultural systems. Towns were just beginning to develop. The civilizations of Sumeria and Egypt were still some two thousand years in the future. China and Europe had not yet experienced the advent of agriculture. And boats capable of making ocean crossings were as yet unknown. The evidence strongly suggests that agriculture and the domestication of animals was independently invented in both the Old World and the New. In fact, there is increasing evidence that this invention occurred independently *more* than once in each hemisphere.[130]

In Peru and Meso-America, archaeologists have traced the slow development from incipient cultivation to village agriculture, then village ceremonial centers, and finally, major temple centers with monumental architecture and other elements of true civilization.[131] In none of the critical formative stages are there signs that new, fully developed institutions, technology, and architectural styles have been introduced from outside.[132] It was once thought that one important development—pottery-making in South America—might have been introduced by a shipload of Japanese who arrived c. 3000 B.C. A number of Ecuadorian vessels from that time resemble Japanese pottery of the same era. And the cultures of the two areas were at about the same level of complexity (both groups were coastal fishers, shellfishers, and food collectors), which would explain why only one feature—pottery—was borrowed by the South Americans. This case, therefore, has the best chance of representing a genuine example of transpacific contact between the Old World and the New. But there are also significant differences between the Ecuadorian and Japanese assemblages. Also the South American material is not duplicated at any single Japanese complex—a number of sites from different parts of Japan (all dating to c. 3000 B.C.) have to be used to reconstruct the hypothetical prototype for the Ecuadorian culture.[133] More importantly, in recent years, still earlier types of pottery have been found in Ecuador. So while the argument about the borrowing of specific pottery types from Japan may continue, it is now clear that the *idea* of pottery-making did not come to America from Japan.[134]

The continuity and evolution observed in crucial American cultural traditions is strong evidence for local development. And when it is combined with the lack of viable evidence of Old World contacts during formative periods, the independence of America's civilizations becomes virtually unassailable. Carroll L. Riley's conclusions of a decade and a half ago are still valid:[135]

It is clear that no significant amount of the native American civilization came from the Old World. Proponents of schemes that have American Indians dependent on the Old World for their complex societies simply ignore the implications of time, space, and common sense. It is possible that a few items, pottery types, certain art motifs, one or two food plants, were so transported, but there is, as yet, no definite proof even for any of these. It is then reasonable to believe that, in the Old World and the New, very similar civilizations grew up independently.

The possibility and even the probability of pre-Columbian voyages across both the Atlantic and the Pacific cannot be denied. Prevailing winds and currents would help carry ships to America whether or not their captains intended to go there. Surely, in the past three or four thousand years a few Old World vessels must have reached the New World. But it is clear that frequent, customary voyages of the type postulated by Gordon, Fell, and others did not take place. Whatever ships did come to America have left no discernible trace. Their arrival had little or no effect on the development of the indigenous American cultures or on the Old World societies from which they came. So there is no reason to change elementary school history books—the *real* discovery of America took place in 1492.

VII
CHAPTER

Popular Theories and the "Establishment"

In the preceding chapters we have reviewed the evidence for a number of popular theories and enumerated the reasons why these theories are rejected by scientists, archaeologists, anthropologists, and ancient historians. But despite this professional opposition, such ideas remain extremely popular. The books of Velikovsky, von Däniken, et al. have sold millions of copies, and continue to sell quite well. Why? What makes such questionable theories so persuasive? Perhaps identifying characteristic elements which link these hypotheses to one another will help us answer this question.

Common Features of Popular Theories

The popular theories of the past that have been considered here present different answers to questions about man's early history. Nevertheless, they do have a number of common features.

1. *The nature of their evidence.* The careful reader will have noted the appearance of the same kinds of "evidence" in chapter after chapter, as well as the same significant omissions. Popular theories reject or ignore the results of modern archaeology, which in many cases is our only objective source of information on man's early history. Especially challenged are the scientific dating methods (such as radiocarbon dating) that have provided a chronology for prehistoric periods. Archaeological chronology cannot be reconciled with the kinds of cultural and historical comparisons desired by believers in a universal Flood, Atlantis, a second millennium near-collision between Earth and Venus, astronaut visitors in antiquity, strange pyramid forces, or pre-Columbian voyagers to America. So archaeological chronology must be dispensed with.

In place of professionally gathered archaeological evidence, a variety of

167

other material is used, such as generalized cultural comparisons, bogus inscriptions, and subjective impressions. But popular theorists' favorite type of evidence seems to be their special interpretations of ancient myths and legends. Interestingly, the same myths are often used to support different reconstructions of the past. Flood myths from around the world are cited by different authors as proof of the historicity of the Genesis Deluge, the destruction of Atlantis, or the catastrophes caused by the close approach of the planet Venus. Von Däniken claims that American Indian stories about Viracocha and Quetzalcoatl, legendary civilization-bringers who eventually went to the heavens, show that astronauts were present in early times. But others use these same myths (though emphasizing the bearded and white-skinned nature of these "gods") to prove that Phoenicians, Greeks, or other Old World people came to America thousands of years ago. As has been stressed more than once above, such interpretations of myths are quite subjective and usually ignore the cultural contexts in which the various accounts arose. Furthermore, the belief of most popular theorists that myths are simply distorted remembrances of historical events is contradicted by modern research into the nature and origins of mythology.

Michael Carroll, a sociologist and a student of myth, has commented that the evidence presented in support of popular theories "is so impressionistic that it serves a function analogous to the inkblots on a Rorschach test, namely, such evidence serves as an ambiguous stimulus onto which the subject can project what he wants to see."[1] This is another way of saying what we have noted before, that many people believe in popular theories not *because* of the evidence, but *despite* its ambiguous and questionable nature.

2. *Easy answers to hard questions.* A second common feature of popular theories is their ability to provide relatively simple explanations for extremely complex events and difficult questions. One issue almost all of them deal with in one way or another is the origin of civilization. Did man develop civilization on his own or did he receive it from some outside source? Did all civilizations have a common origin? Flood advocates believe all civilization can be traced back to the descendants of the family that survived the Deluge. Others claim Atlantis or spacemen as the source of all civilization. Believers in pyramidology can use pyramid measurements and supposed mysterious pyramid powers as arguments for the existence of an early super-civilization (such as Atlantis or Mu), ancient astronauts, or divine revelation as the source of human knowledge. And by deriving New World civilization from that of the Old World, advocates of early pre-Columbian voyages to America simplify the problem and allow for a common origin of all civilization. Velikovsky's theory is the only one which does not deal with the beginnings of civiliza-

tion. However, his disparagement of geology and evolution[2] and his un-critical acceptance of the Bible as a reliable historical source allows many of his followers to adopt the biblical answer to this problem.

Some of the popular theories go beyond questions about civiliza-tion's origins and concern themselves with issues normally reserved for religion: Where did man come from, and is there some superior being or supernatural power present in the universe? Believers in the Flood, ancient astronauts, and pyramid mysteries differ in the ways they answer these questions, but they generally believe in some power outside of the earth. By tracing our origins to a nonearthly source, such theories also hold out the hope that our future problems might be solved by the same entity—whether it be the traditional God, a superior race of spacemen, or a mysterious cosmic force.

3. *Anti-establishment rhetoric.* Finally, authors of popular theories consistently attack the scholarly "establishment" which they know will reject their ideas. They claim that professional scholars are so blindly committed to a prevailing dogmatic view that they cannot recognize the validity of new concepts. For example, statements such as the following can be found in the prefaces of books defending all of the theories re-viewed above:

> Dull ears and dimmed eyes will deny this evidence, and the dimmer the vision, the louder and more insistent will be the voices of protestation. This book was not written for those who swear by the *verba magistri*—the holiness of their school wisdom; and they may debate it without reading it as well.[3]

> It took courage to write this book, and it will take courage to read it. Because its theories and proofs do not fit into the mosaic of traditional archaeology, constructed so laboriously and firmly cemented down, scholars will call it nonsense and put it on the Index of those books which are better left unmentioned."[4]

Sometimes such remarks about the lack of scholarly objectivity can be quite vicious, but on occasion they are made in a somewhat lighthearted and humorous way:

> All the lights in the House of the High Priests of American Anthropology are out, all the doors and windows are shut and securely fastened (they do not sleep with their windows open for fear that a new idea might fly in); we have rung the bell of Reason, we have banged on the door with Logic, we have thrown the gravel of Evidence against their windows; but the only sign of life in the house is an occasional snore of Dogma.[5]

It is paradoxical that authors who complain so much about scholarly blindness and ignorance almost always point with pride to any support they receive from members of "the establishment." Harold Gladwin, author of the quotation immediately above, saw no contradiction in having one of the "High Priests of American Anthropology," Dr. E. A. Hooten (then professor of anthropology at Harvard University and curator of physical anthropology at the Peabody Museum) write the preface to Gladwin's *Men Out of Asia.* Barry Fell includes in his books many photographs of scholars who supposedly agree with his theories.[6] Authors of similar works also quote statements by leading scholars showing real or (more commonly) fancied approval of their ideas.[7] The popular theorists' ridicule and scorn of the "dogmatic" scholarly "establishment" seems to be a psychological defense against rejection by authorities whose approval they desperately would like to have.

When, as predicted, most scholars *do* reject the revolutionary theories (and the insufficient evidence behind them), their authors usually declare that they have been persecuted, and proclaim themselves martyrs for truth. Galileo and Einstein frequently are cited as examples of theorists whose ideas were also attacked by their conventional-thinking contemporaries. The parallel, of course, is very inexact. Though regarded as radical by some authorities of the time, the theories of Galileo and Einstein were accepted fairly quickly by their scientific colleagues. For the evidence was on their side. However, it is precisely the faulty nature of their evidence that causes popular theories to be opposed by professional scholars. Moreover, while popular theories are not usually included in university textbooks, they are well represented on the shelves of almost any bookstore, and television specials as well as movies favorably present their claims to the public. This is certainly unlike any censorship or persecution of the past.

There are other similarities between the works of most popular theorists—for example, a sensationalistic writing style that discusses evidence as if presenting an exposé of a scholarly "cover-up." Another is the tendency to argue that a given concept is *possible,* then treat this idea as if it were not only possible, but also *probable.* In popular works it is also commonplace to find authors stressing evidence that experts have not yet been able to adequately explain, then leaping to the logically false conclusion that such evidence is *unexplainable* under conventional theories. But the essential characteristics of popular theories seem to be the three already described: they distain scientific, objective evidence and methodology in favor of impressionistic, subjective evidence and arguments, particularly interpretations of myths and legends; they often provide simple, compact answers to complex and difficult questions, especially those related to origins; and they take a persecuted "underdog," anti-establishment stance.

Why Are These Theories Popular?

Undoubtedly people are drawn to popular theories for different reasons. Some individuals accept such ideas simply because they cannot objectively assess the arguments and evidence presented. The claims of Velikovsky, von Däniken, Fell, and others often appear to laymen to be accurate and well-documented. Those who know little about archaeology, linguistics, and other scholarly disciplines have difficulty recognizing the erroneous nature of supposedly "factual" statements by popular theorists. When told that pyramids appeared simultaneously in many areas of the world, that some American Indian tribes speak a Semitic language, or that the Easter Island statues could not have been carved with stone tools, the average person does not recognize immediately that these assertions are false. It is for such people who are genuinely seeking knowledge about the past that this book has been written.

But the strong emotional attachment many people have for various popular theories must have a different explanation. No matter how many books like this one are written, no matter how much scientific evidence to the contrary is presented, many individuals will still believe in a worldwide Flood or Atlantis or ancient spacemen. These are people who *want* to believe, regardless of the evidence. For such individuals it would seem that the unscientific, quasi-religious, anti-establishment nature of the theories is what is important.

In some ways, popular theories function the way myths do in primitive cultures.[8] They resolve psychological dilemmas and provide answers for the unknown or unknowable. When science developed in the West, myth was generally abandoned as a way of explaining the physical world. Religion limited itself to questions of meaning, purpose, ethics, and metaphysics while recognizing the validity of scientific study of the material universe. But the objective methods of modern scholarship cannot provide immediate, simple explanations for all phenomena. Those who have a low tolerance for the psychological discomfort caused by unresolved issues become prime candidates for the new mythologies (some of which, of course, are continuations of very old mythologies). Often popular theories can provide the "answers" that traditional scholarship cannot. Or, where answers have been given, popular theories can often provide ones that are more psychologically satisfying. Of course, from childhood almost everyone in Western society has been taught that he or she should make decisions based on logic and reason, so some "evidence" must supoprt these theories. But the evidence favoring a given popular hypothesis need be only strong enough to provide a rational pretext for those who already want to believe.

The mythlike nature of popular theories may account for their frequent use of traditional myths as evidence. Of course, the old myths are reinterpreted—they are not usually taken literally. But they are treated as reliable sources of historical information, as important as (and sometimes more important than) the objective evidence of science and archaeology. Perhaps subconsciously those who develop popular theories recognize their kinship with the myth-makers of the past.

The anti-establishment and even anti-intellectual rhetoric that usually accompanies popular theories also helps account for their acceptance in some quarters. Anti-scientific movements ranging from traditional biblical fundamentalism and its recent offspring, scientific creationism, to astrology and mystical Eastern religions are currently quite popular. A number of people seem to feel that science and reason have failed them. The "knowledge explosion" has not solved the world's problems and produced utopia. So, many individuals react favorably to attacks on science and traditional scholarship. The longstanding Western tendency to sympathize with an underdog also helps create a supportive emotional response for theories whose authors claim to be persecuted by a blind, dogmatic community of scholars.

Desire to be part of a community that possesses special knowledge may be bound up with this anti-establishment facet of popular theories. Organizations whose members share secret rituals, arcane knowledge, and mystical symbols have long been popular. They supply a sense of "belonging," of community identity, that many of their members cannot find elsewhere. In the same way, those who accept popular theories become part of a special community. They see themselves as believers in the Truth that dogmatic scholars won't accept. For such individuals, rejection of their favorite theory by the scholarly establishment is not a problem to be overcome, it is a mark of honor to be borne proudly. It proves that they are part of a small elect persecuted because of their superior insight. Being part of such a community of believers who share a rejected Truth appeals to many, especially when the "persecution" doesn't involve threats to life, limb, or property.

There is no way to determine how many followers of popular theories are simply laymen unaware of the theories' errors as opposed to those who believe because of subconscious, semi-religious feelings. But only the first group can be reached by reason. There will always be some fervent believers in Atlantis, ancient astronauts, or cosmic catastrophism no matter how effectively scholars present the case against them.

The Communication Gap Between Scholars and the Public

As knowledge within each of the scholarly disciplines has grown, an increasing degree of specialization has been required. There is more than a little truth to the claim that modern Ph.D.'s know "more and more about less and less." Specialization has made it difficult for researchers to communicate effectively with their colleagues in other disciplines, let alone with the general public. A communications problem has developed between professional scholars and laymen, a rift which seems to widen year by year.

In 1962, Robert Wauchope noted that professionals considered popular theorists a danger "only to the extent that their extremely popular writings persuade so many intellectually unwary people that research is simply a process of manipulating facts, intuition, and imagination in approximately equal parts."[9] But over the past twenty years, we academics have done little to make the public less "intellectually unwary" than they were before. During that period many science, archaeology, and ancient history books have been written for interested laymen, but few of these grapple with the issues raised by popular theorists. Most professionals seem to feel that discussing a popular theory would make it seem more worthy of serious consideration than it really is. However, the relative silence of scholars is at least partially responsible for the widespread followings these theories attract.

On the other hand, professionals rightly object that, if they tried to answer all of the contentions of popular authors, there would be little or no time left for more productive research. The poor scholarship and faulty research exhibited by most popular writers are easily perceived by those normally engaged in scholarly pursuits. So why should professional scholars spend time and effort dealing with what are clearly erroneous ideas? Surely society benefits more from ongoing conventional research.

Unfortunately, in the public's mind, the reluctance of professional scholars to discuss popular theories lends credence to charges of establishment dogmatism. Of course, if most people read the heated and sometimes acrimonious exchanges of views that appear in scholarly journals, they would realize how groundless the idea of a scholarly conspiracy really is. New interpretations of evidence are always being presented in every field of scholarship. These ideas are criticized, debated, tested, refined, and modified. If they withstand this testing process and are shown to explain the evidence better than previous theories, they become generally accepted. Just a few decades ago the idea of continental drift was a geological theory with few adherents. But new research on the ocean floor and space-age technology for precisely pinpointing locations on the earth's surface showed that the continents *are* moving. Today the concept of plate tectonics, a modern revised version of the continental drift theory, is accepted by almost all geologists.[10] When the evidence supports a new idea, scholars adopt it—they have no "dogma" which can stand in the way. Popular theories are rejected not because they contain ideas that are too radically different from old explanations, but because (as we have seen) the evidence simply does not support them.

Recently the problem of communicating scholarly theories and methods to laymen has taken on a new urgency. In a number of states efforts are underway to pass laws requiring the teaching of "scientific creationism" as well as evolution in science courses in public schools. To many people, these proposals seem to be a fair way to give students a choice between alternative theories of origins. Suddenly scientists are finding it necessary to explain to the general public (and its representatives in various legislative bodies) what science is and how its conclusions are reached. For, evolution and creationism are not really comparable—labeling both "theories" makes them sound more alike than they actually are. The evolution of species is a scientific concept supported by vast amounts of evidence from a variety of fields, including genetics, comparative anatomy, and geology. On the other hand, creationism (the belief that the world and all of its species of living things were created individually less than ten thousand years ago) is a religious belief that is not scientific at all. It attempts to make the physical evidence conform to ideas derived from the biblical book of Genesis. Of course, those who wish to accept creationism in place of evolution are free to do so, but it is not science! Scientists argue that to present both theories equally in a *science* class would give students a false conception of the scientific method and of the nature of scientific evidence.

Anthropologists, archaeologists, and historians should learn from this controversy over the teaching of scientific theories, for the average person doesn't really understand our methodology either. Laymen think of the past in terms of "facts." By digging in the ground or rummaging through old documents, scholars discover these "facts." But few people understand the details of *how* this process works. So when a von Däniken or a Barry Fell comes along announcing the discovery of new and different "facts" about the past based on his own study of ancient myths, strange inscriptions, or archaeological monuments, it is difficult for the average person to judge the validity of the claims.

Professional scholars may not have the time or the inclination to extensively discuss every popular theory that appears. But if they spent a little more time making their methodology understandable, maybe the public would be able to recognize the problems with popular theories without professional help. What is needed are more works written without scholarly jargon that not only describe what is known about the past, but also tell *how* we know it. We need more authors who can communicate scholarly problems to laymen and explain the ways various proposed solutions have been developed. We need more television series like "Nova" and "Odyssey" to show what archaeology is really like, countering the false impression people get from sources such as *Raiders of the Lost Ark*. Perhaps with concerted effort we can narrow the communcation gap between scholars and the general public and make people less intellectually unwary than they have been heretofore. If so, popular theories may become much less popular in the future.

Notes

Chapter 1: The Deluge

1. E.g., Waltz 1974; Gaskill 1975.
2. Hacker 1984.
3. Graves 1960: I, 138-40.
4. Graves 1960: I, 141; de Camp 1970: 236.
5. *Timaeus* 22c-e.
6. *City of God,* XVIII, 8-9.
7. Haber 1959: 1.
8. Daniel 1962: 24-25.
9. Gillispie 1959: 3.
10. Wendt 1955: 6-7.
11. Wendt 1955: 8-9.
12. Gillispie 1959: 42; Haber 1959: 43-44, 105-12.
13. Haber 1959: 115-19.
14. Haber 1959: 119-30.
15. Gillispie 1959: 43-44; Haber 1959: 160-61.
16. Wendt 1955: 144-57; Gillispie 1959: 98-120; Haber 1959: 195-204.
17. Daniel 1962: 44.
18. Gillispie 1959: 46-49; Haber 1959: 164-69.
19. Gillispie 1959: 121-48; Haber 1959: 215-19.
20. Wendt 1955: 194-95; Haber 1959: 210-11.
21. Wendt 1955: 97-99, 166-71; Daniel 1962: 49-53.
22. Wendt 1955: 202-06.
23. Daniel 1962: 53-56.
24. Daniel 1962: 54.
25. Wendt 1955: 235-59; Haber 1959: 265-72.
26. S. Lloyd 1980: 146.
27. Speiser 1955: 93-95.
28. S. Lloyd 1980: 147.
29. Kramer 1955: 42-44; 1961: 97-98; Speiser 1955: 72-73; Tigay 1982.
30. Genesis 21:33; 22:14; 24:3, ;7; 26:22, 25; 27:27; 28:16, 21; 32:10.
31. Pfeiffer 1948: 134-41; Speiser 1964: XX-LII; Bermant and Weitzman 1979: 45-54.

177

32. Marks 1962: 279; Speiser 1964: 47-56.

33. Marks 1962: 280-83; Speiser 1964: 54-56; *The New American Bible* 1970: 11.

34. Schofield 1967: 319.

35. Shanks 1976: 42; Bermant and Weitzman 1979: 164.

36. Macqueen 1975: 145.

37. E.g., Patten 1966: 164-65; Filby 1970: 37-58; Balsiger and Sellier 1976: 23-24; LaHaye and Morris 1976: 231-41.

38. Filby 1970: 49.

39. Vitaliano 1973: 152-53.

40. Vitaliano 1973: 163-64.

41. Vitaliano 1973: 144 (italics in the original).

42. Vitaliano 1973: 142-78.

43. Filby 1970: 51-52.

44. Filby 1970: 52-53.

45. J. Wilson 1955: 3-4, 10-11; Clark 1960: 35-43, 103-06, 181-83.

46. Muck 1978: 217-19.

47. Woolley 1965: 26-36.

48. Bright 1942.

49. E.g., Velikovsky 1950: 24-26; 1955: 1-9; Whitcomb and Morris 1961: 288-91; Patten 1966: 104-09; Filby 1970: 21-25.

50. Herz 1903; Vitaliano 1973: 281.

51. Vitaliano 1973: 280.

52. Whitcomb and Morris 1961: 116-30; Balsiger and Sellier 1976: 40-49.

53. Filby 1970: 9.

54. Whitcomb and Morris 1961: 334-91; Patten 1966: 135-36, 303; Filby 1970: 13-18.

55. Renfrew 1979: 48-51.

56. Renfrew 1979: 69-83.

57. Whitcomb and Morris 1961: 370-78; Filby 1970: 13-14; Balsiger and Sellier 1976: 189-90.

58. Renfrew 1979: 74.

59. See the chart in Renfrew 1979: 75.

60. Kenyon 1957: 74.

61. Mellaart 1967: 52.

62. Whitcomb and Morris 1961: 344-46.

63. Gaskill 1975; Balsiger and Sellier 1976; LaHaye and Morris 1976.

64. Montgomery 1974: 325-27; Balsiger and Sellier 1976: 74-81; LaHaye and Morris 1976: 15-27, 62-98.

65. Josephus, *Antiquities of the Jews,* Book xx, iii, 2; Bailey 1978: 25, 33-34.

66. Bailey 1978: 24-29, 31, 102-104.

67. Bailey 1978: 22-24, 29-31.

68. H. Hübschmann, quoted in Bailey 1978: 99-107.

69. LaHaye and Morris 1976: 28-41.

70. Cummings 1972: 188-203; Noorbergen 1974: 106-07; Balsiger and Sellier 1976: 89-91; LaHaye and Morris 1976: 43-49.

71. Bryce 1896: 280-81; see also Balsiger and Sellier 1976: 91-94; LaHaye and Morris 1976: 50-55.

72. Noorbergen 1974: 107-08; Balsiger and Sellier 1976: 94-95; LaHaye and Morris 1976: 56-63.

73. Bailey 1978: 52.

74. Cummings 1972: 118-33; Montgomery 1974: 110-12; Noorbergen 1974: 96-102; Balsiger and Sellier 1976: 95-97; LaHaye and Morris 1976: 64-67.

75. Montgomery 1974: 113; Noorbergen 1974: 164-71; Balsiger and Sellier 1976: 68-72; LaHaye and Morris 1976: 68-72.

76. Cummings 1972: 109-14; Montgomery 1974: 119-25; Noorbergen 1974: 82-96; Balsiger and Sellier 1976: 102-09; LaHaye and Morris 1976: 73-92.

77. Montgomery 1974: 125-28; Balsiger and Sellier 1976: 153-55; LaHaye and Morris 1976 98-101.

78. Cummings 1972: 160-61; Balsiger and Sellier 1976: 155-59; LaHaye and Morris 1976: 102-114.

79. Balsiger and Sellier 1976: 159-60; LaHaye and Morris 1976: 115-25.

80. Bailey 1978: 56.

81. Cummings 1972: 213-23; Montgomery 1974: 128-31; Balsiger and Sellier 1976: 160-61; LaHaye and Morris 1976: 135-37.

82. Navarra 1974; see also Cummings 1972: 177-87; Balsiger and Sellier 1976: 167-90; LaHaye and Morris 1976: 126-34.

83. Montgomery 1974: 316-17, 350-55; Balsiger and Sellier 1976: 164-65, 192-201, photographs following 106; LaHaye and Morris 1976: 176-78, 190, 203-07.

84. Balsiger and Sellier 1976: 195-97; Bailey 1978: 61, 88.

85. See the discussion in Bailey 1978: 47-58.

86. Bailey 1978: 68.

87. Balsiger and Sellier 1976: 190; LaHaye and Morris 1976: 132.

88. Bailey 1978: 72-73.

89. Bailey 1978: 75-80.

90. Bailey 1978: 94-98.

91. LaHaye and Morris 1976: 205-09; Bailey 1978: 87-88.

92. LaHaye and Morris 1976: 177; Bailey 1978: 60.

93. Balsiger and Sellier 1976: 164; Bailey 1978: 61.

Chapter 2: Atlantis, the Sunken Continent

1. *Timaeus* 20e-25e; translation in Cornford 1937: 13-19.

2. *Republic,* Books V-VII.

3. *Critias* 108e-112e.

4. *Critias* 113c-115c.

5. *Critias* 115c-119b.

6. *Critias* 119c-121c.

7. Strabo, *Geography* 2.102; see de Camp 1970: 299.

8. Proclus, *Commentary on Plato's Timaeus* 24a; de Camp 1970: 309.

9. De Camp 1970: 10-20; Ramage 1978: 23-27.

10. Wauchope 1962: 30-31; de Camp 1970: 28-29.

11. De Camp 1970: 31-32.

12. De Camp 1970: 36-37.

13. See, e.g., Tompkins 1976: 110-17, especialy the last paragraph on p. 117, and Muck 1978: 192.

14. Wauchope 1962: 7-21; Tompkins 1976: 165-75.

15. Le Plongeon 1896: Chapter 14.

16. Le Plongeon 1896: Chapter 15.

17. De Camp 1970: 54-58.

18. Churchward 1926, 1931, 1934, 1938.

19. Donnelly 1882: Chapter 1.

20. Donnelly 1882: Chapters 4-5.

21. Donnelly 1882: Chapter 6.

22. Donnelly 1882: Chapters 7-10.

23. Donnelly 1882: Chapters 11-23.

24. Braghine 1940: 188.

25. Braghine 1940: 187-88; Muck 1978: 133-34.

26. Berlitz 1975: 148-49, 153-56.

27. Menard 1969; Vitaliano 1973: 225.

28. Vitaliano 1978: 139.

29. De Camp 1970: 161-62; Vitaliano 1973: 225-28; 1978: 140.

30. Spence 1924: 27-28; Braghine 1940: 78-79; Muck 1978: 151-52.

31. De Camp 1970: 164; Vitaliano 1973: 223-24; 1978: 141-42.

32. Galanopoulas and Bacon 1969: 55-57.

33. De Camp 1970: 165-73; Galanopoulos and Bacon 1969; 89-92; Vitaliano 1978: 139.

34. Wright 1978: 162-67.

35. Wright 1978: 167-74.

36. E.g., Carli 1788, Donnelly 1883, Hörbiger 1913, Braghine 1940; Velikovsky 1950, and Muck 1978.

37. For further examples of problems with supposed cultural connections between the Old and New Worlds see de Camp 1970: 41-43, 99-102.

38. Ramage 1978: 34-36.

39. De Camp 1970: 103-44; Vitaliano 1978: 1940-41.

40. Spence 1924: 14-15.

41. Spence 1924: 57-82.

42. Spence 1924: 42-43, 113-14.

43. De Camp 1970: 314-18.

44. Harrison 1971; Berlitz 1976: 191-95; Zink 1978.

45. Marinatos 1939, 1972; Galanopoulos and Bacon 1969; Luce 1969, 1976, 1978; Mavor 1969; Page 1970; Forsyth 1980: 115-68.

46. Hood 1971: 56-60.

47. K. Frost 1913.

48. Marinatos 1939.

49. Luce 1969: 84-86, 90-93; Platon 1971: 227-78; Vitaliano 1973: 207-08.

50. Luce 1969: 74-82; Vitaliano 1973: 184-87.

51. Marinatos 1968.

52. Luce 1969: 63-65; Vitaliano 1973: 204-05. However, recent C^{14} dates for

material from Thera have been inconsistent, reducing the value of this piece of evidence.

53. Pichler and Friedrich 1980.
54. Luce 1969: 69-74.
55. Velikovsky 1950: 147; Galanopoulos and Bacon 1969: 133-34, 170.
56. Forsyth 1980: 159-60.
57. Luce 1969: 44-45.
58. Luce 1969: 145-72.
59. Vitaliano 1973: 190-91, 203-04; 1978: 151-53; Blong 1980; McCoy 1980.
60. Vitaliano 1973: 194-95, 203; 1978: 147-49.
61. Pichler 1980.
62. Pichler 1980; 324.
63. Vitaliano 1973: 191-94; 1978: 149-51.
64. Fears 1978: 132.
65. Starr 1954; Buck 1962; Fears 1978: 125-30.
66. Fredericks 1978: 83-84.
67. Hood 1970; Vitaliano 1973: 189-90; 1978: 154-55.
68. Luce 1976: Forsyth 1980: 131-42.
69. Vitaliano 1973: 206-07.
70. Platon 1971: 290-91.
71. Hood 1971: 55.
72. Vitaliano 1973: 208; Vitaliano and Vitaliano 1980.
73. J. Wilson 1955: 242.
74. Luce 1978: 53.
75. *Republic* 382d, translation by P. Shorey in Hamilton and Cairns 1961: 629.
76. Stewart 1960: 220.
77. Forsyth 1980: 76-77.
78. *Gorgias* 523a, translation by W. Woodhead in Hamilton and Cairns 1961: 303.
79. *Republic* 621c, translation by Shorey in Hamilton and Cairns 1961: 844.
80. *Phaedrus* 247c, translation by R. Hackforth in Hamilton and Cairns 1961: 494.
81. *Meno* 81a-b, translation by W. K. C. Guthrie in Hamilton and Cairns 1961: 364.
82. *Statesman* 268d-272b.
83. *Statesman* 271b, translation by J. Skemp in Hamilton and Cairns 1961: 1036.
84. *Laws* 713a-714b.
85. *Timaeus* 19c, Cornford 1937: 11.
86. Cornford 1937: 7.
87. De Camp 1970: 246-47.
88. Cornford 1937: 8.
89. Cornford 1937: 7-8.
90. Stewart 1960: 192; Fredericks 1978: 89-90, 93.
91. Thucydides, *Peloponnesian War* III, 89; translation from Warner 1954: 213.
92. Taylor 1928: 56; de Camp 1970: 227; Luce 1978: 73.
93. Bunbury 1883; de Camp 1970: 215-26; Ramage 1978: 20-22.

94. *Periplous* 112; de Camp 1970: 294-95.
95. *Meteorologica* II, i, 354a; de Camp 1970: 293.
96. Bunbury 1883: 398.
97. Stewart 1960: 417-18.
98. Forsyth 1980: 169-76.
99. Forsyth 1980: 174-76.
100. *History* I, 98 and 178.
101. Luce 1978: 71.
102. Harden 1962: 30-32, 130-31.
103. Bérard 1929; de Camp 1970: 188-89.
104. Luce 1978: 72.

Chapter 3: Cosmic Catastrophism

1. Carli 1788; Donnelly 1883; Hörbiger 1913; Braghine 1940; Muck 1978.
2. Whiston 1696; Patten 1966; Filby 1970.
3. Velikovsky 1950 and 1952.
4. Velikovsky 1952: v. Unless another author is specified, references in this chapter are to the works of Immanuel Velikovsky.
5. 1950: 172-75.
6. 1950: 48-58.
7. 1950: 58-76.
8. 1950: 76-90.
9. 1950: 91-104, 183-87.
10. 1950: 126-138.
11. 1950: 39-46, 141-206.
12. 1950: 207-371.
13. W. Alvarez, et al., 1980 and 1984.
14. *The New York Times* 1984.
15. Sagan 1977: 62-63, 94-99.
16. Sagan 1977: 63.
17. 1977b: 31, 33-34; Juergens 1977: 85-87.
18. 1950: 40-44, 385-86; 1977b: 34-36.
19. Sagan 1977: 64.
20. Morrison 1977: 153-54.
21. Morrison 1977: 154-55; Sagan 1977: 73-78; Owen 1982: Tables II and IVb. In 1977b: 42-47, Velikovsky disputes Sagan's claim that the atmosphere of Venus doesn't contain hydrocarbons, but he doesn't address the problem of the differences between the atmospheres of Jupiter and Venus.
22. Morrison 1977: 151; Mulholland 1977: 113-14; Sagan 1977: 85-86.
23. Mulholland 1977: 113.
24. Mulholland 1977: 113-14.
25. 1950: 279-80.
26. Mulholland 1977: 111.

27. 1950: 187.
28. Sagan 1977: 70-71.
29. Sagan 1977: 69-70.
30. 1977b: 40-42, especially the last sentence of this section.
31. Morrison 1977; Mulholland 1977; Sagan 1977; Pettengill, Campbell and Masursky 1980.
32. For example, see Velikovsky 1977b; Juergens 1977; Greenberg and Sizemore 1978.
33. Sagan 1977: 91-92.
34. Braghine 1940: 104-38.
35. E.g., see 1950: 43, 49, 55, 58-59, etc.
36. 1950: 253-54, 269.
37. Davies 1979: 177.
38. Davies 1979: 177.
39. Davies 1973: 8.
40. Simoni 1965: 473.
41. 1950: 261-64, 275, 281.
42. Kramer 1955: 58-59; 1963: 134; Speiser 1955: 103-04, 180.
43. 1950: 253-54.
44. Simoni 1965: 464-65; Davies 1973: 18, 306.
45. 1950: 253.
46. 1950: 168-73.
47. 1950: 170.
48. Graves 1960: I, 29; Grimal 1965b: 103.
49. 1950: 170 and 251.
50. *City of God,* Book VII, Chapter 16, quoted by Velikovsky in 1950: 170.
51. 1950: 172-75.
52. 1950: 81-85.
53. 1950: 173.
54. 1950: 85, 172.
55. Sagan 1977: 55.
56. 1977b: 26.
57. Graves 1960: I, 44-47, 133-35; Grimal 1965b: 103, 108-09, 130.
58. Sagan 1977: 54.
59. 1950: 246-53.
60. See, e.g., Grimal 1965a, especially pages 13-14; Fredericks 1978: 81-82, 85-88.
61. 1950: 264-65, 305-06, 310.
62. Sagan 1977: 50-51.
63. Psalms 29:4-8.
64. Psalms 46:6.
65. 1950: 86-87.
66. Psalms 93:1; 96:10.
67. Psalms 78:69.
68. Psalms 119:90.
69. Alvarez, Kauffman, Surlyk, Alvarez, Asaro, and Michel 1984.
70. See Velikovsky 1955.

71. 1955: 221-232.
72. 1955: 255-59.
73. Sagan 1977: 53.
74. Sagan 1977: 53.
75. 1950: 315-16.
76. 1950: 320-24.
77. Mulholland 1977: 107-08.
78. 1950: 139-40, 216; 1955: 188-99.
79. MacKie 1978: 56-65.
80. See Velikovsky 1973a.
81. See the chart in Renfrew 1971: 66-67.
82. 1952: 12-47.
83. 1952: 48-53.
84. E.g., Van Seters 1964.
85. J. Wilson 1955: 441-44.
86. 1952: 25-26.
87. J. Wilson 1955: 441.
88. 1952: 55-94.
89. 1952: 98-101.
90. 1952: 103-41.
91. 1952: 223-340.
92. 1978: 84-139.
93. 1977: 3-162.
94. Knudtzon 1908-15; Albright 1955: 483-90; Oppenheim 1967: 113-34.
95. Knudtzon 1908-15: letters no. 144 and 147.
96. Knudtzon 1908-15: letters 1-16; Oppenheim 1955: 273.
97. 1952: 233-37, 321-33.
98. I Kings 22:43; II Chronicles 19:4.
99. 1952: 235.
100. II Kings 8:7-15; Luckenbill 1926: Vol. 1, section 681; Oppenheim 1955: 280.
101. 1952: 235 and 294.
102. 1952: 231-33.
103. Luckenbill; 1926: Vol. I, section 302; Oppenheim 1955: 275.
104. Luckenbill 1926: Vol. I, sections 479 and 578; Oppenheim 1955: 276, 280.
105. Oppenheim 1955: 279.
106. 1952: 230-31.
107. Oppenheim 1955: 284.
108. 1952: 270-76.
109. Labat 1959: 219, sign no. 252.
110. Greenberg 1955.
111. Greenberg 1955: 19.
112. Stiebing 1973.
113. 1952: 307, 328-32; 1978: 242, note 14.
114. Stiebing 1973: 11-12, especially note 17; Bimson 1978b: 16.
115. See Velikovsky 1973 and 1974 for attempted rebuttals. However, the arguments presented there miss the point as is noted in Stiebing 1974 and Bimson 1978b: 16.

116. Courville 1971: Vol. 2, 196; Bimson 1978a and 1978b.
117. Ackroyd 1967: 343-44; Avigad 1978: 1041.
118. Bimson 1978b: 21-22.
119. Bimson 1978b: 22.
120. Bimson 1978b: 22.
121. Yadin 1975: 252, 259-64; 1976: 485.
122. Yadin 1975: 252.
123. Albright 1955; 320-21.
124. Glueck 1967: 447-48; Tushingham 1975: 332.
125. Numbers 21:1; 33-40; Joshua 12:14.
126. Aharoni 1975: 75-89.
127. Aharoni 1975: 167-68.
128. Stubbings 1951.
129. Boardman 1964: 178-84, 187-89.
130. Woolley 1953: 172-73, Plates 19b and 20b; Boardman 1964; 61-70; Pritchard 1975: 67-70, 94-96.
131. See Bimson 1978b: 23.

Chapter 4: The Search for Ancient Astronauts

1. Story 1976: 14.
2. See, for example, Tomas 1971; Bergier 1974; Blumrich 1974; Drake 1974; Landsburg 1974 and 1975; Sitchin 1976; or Chatelain 1977.
3. Von Däniken 1977: 252-92. Hereafter, unless another author is specified, all references in this chapter are to works by Erich von Däniken.
4. 1968: 35-37.
5. 1968: 40-41.
6. 1980: 11-25.
7. 1968: 37-39; Blumrich 1974; Landsburg 1974: 134-43.
8. 1968: 42-43, 67; 1973b: 38-51.
9. 1968: 45-50.
10. 1968: 55; 1973b: 60-61, 77-80.
11. 1980: 145-50.
12. 1968: 56-60.
13. 1980: 36-51.
14. Hapgood 1966; von Däniken 1968: 14-16; 1973b: 132-36, figures 163-65.
15. 1968: 15.
16. 1968: 16-17 and photos in the center of the book; 1973b: figures 264-67.
17. 1968: 17-18; 1973b: figures 260-263.
18. 1968: 63-64.
19. 1973a: 4-7.
20. 1973a: 6.
21. 1973a: 8-10.
22. 1973a: 20-21.

23. 1973a: 21-26; 1973b: 144-57, figures 173-209.
24. 1973a: 10.
25. 1968: 19-22, 74-79, 90-91.
26. 1968: 27-28.
27. 1968: 104-06; 1973b: 129-32, figures 159-61.
28. 1968: 31 and illustration in central photo section; 1973b: 62, figure 57.
29. 1968: 31-33; 1973b: 59-67.
30. 1968: 100-01; 1973b: 85-93, figures 97a-99a.
31. 1968: 100-01.
32. 1968: 36-37.
33. C. Wilson 1972: 54-55; Story 1976: 16-17.
34. 1968: 40-41; 1973: 46.
35. 1968: 40.
36. Exodus 25:10-15; 37:1-5.
37. C. Wilson 1972: 36-38; 1975: 156-57.
38. 168: 40.
39. See Deuteronomy 31:9; Joshua 4:10-11, 16-18; 6:12; 8:33, etc.
40. C. Wilson 1972: 38-40.
41. 1980: 17-25.
42. Exodus 16-19, 36-37.
43. C. Wilson 1972: 59; Story 1974: 17-19.
44. 1968: 37-38.
45. C. Wilson 1972: 59-60.
46. 1968: 42, italics added.
47. Ferris 1974: 56, italics added; see also von Däniken 1973: 38.
48. 1968: 41-42.
49. Russell 1964: 59-60; Rost 1976: 151-54.
50. Russell 1964: 51-53; Rost 1976: 133-40.
51. G. Lloyd 1973: 53-74.
52. See C. Wilson 1972: 48-51 and Scarborough 1974-75: 22-23.
53. 1968: 45-46.
54. Speiser 1955: 75.
55. 1968: 49.
56. 1968: 62.
57. 1968: 48; see Speiser 1955: 90.
58. Kramer 1955: 47-48.
59. 1968: 62-63.
60. 1968: 56; 1970: 129.
61. Radhakrishnan and Moore 1957: 99; C. Wilson 1972: 62-63.
62. Basham 1954: 38-39.
63. Basham 1954: 27-28; Wheeler 1966: 78-79; Allchin 1968: 143, 154-55.
64. See 1970: 28.
65. E.g., 1968: 46, 56-59, 62-63, 66, 92-93, 104; 1970: 127-33; 1973b: 3-17.
66. 1968: 58-60.
67. 1968: 62.
68. 1968: 65.
69. Ferris 1974: 57.

70. Story 1976: 5.
71. Hapgood 1966: 1.
72. Hapgood 1966: 2.
73. Hapgood 1966: 39-41.
74. Hapgood 1966: 75.
75. Hapgood 1966: 193-206.
76. 1968: 15.
77. Story 1976: 5-6, 32-33.
78. 1968: 14-15; see also 1973: 32-36.
79. See Hapgood 1966: 60-77 for such comparisons.
80. 1973b: figure 163.
81. Hapgood 1966: 38-39, figure 18.
82. C. Wilson 1972: 76-77; Scarborough 1974-75: 21; Story 1976: 29-31.
83. Hapgood 1966: 223.
84. Ferris 1974: 60, 64.
85. 1977: 289.
86. McIntyre 1975: 724; Isbell 1978: 146, 148-49.
87. 1968: 17.
88. 1970: 103-06.
89. 1973b: 196.
90. 1973b: 33-38.
91. McIntyre 1975: 718; Story 1976: 40.
92. 1968: the fourth page of the photo section.
93. C. Wilson 1975: 111.
94. See 1973: 196, top right-hand corner.
95. Kosok and Reiche 1949.
96. Story 1976: 38-39.
97. Story 1976: 37-38.
98. Isbell 1978; 147-49.
99. McIntyre 1975: 725.
100. Isbell 1978: 143-50.
101. 1977: 291.
102. C. Wilson 1975: 113-14.
103. *Encounter* 1973: 12; Story 1976: 80.
104. *Encounter* 1973: 8, 12; Story 1976: 80.
105. *Encounter* 1973: 12; Story 1976: 80.
106. *Encounter* 1973: 9-10; Ferris 1974: 58.
107. Ferris 1974: 58.
108. Ferris 1974: 58.
109. *Encounter* 1973: 12.
110. 1977: 261-62; Story 1976: 81.
111. *Encounter* 1973: 12.
112. 1977: 264; Story 1976: 82.
113. 1977: 263.
114. 1968: the ninth page of the photo section.
115. 1973: 86-88.
116. Stuart 1977: 83.

117. Ferris 1974: 52.
118. Story 1976: 68.
119. Story 1976: 68-72.
120. Robertson 1974.
121. Schele 1974; Story 1976: 75.
122. Story 1976: 75-76; Stuart 1977: 75; Gallenkamp 1981: 108-109.
123. Ferris 1974: 52.
124. Mathews and Schele 1974; Stuart 1977:77; Gallenkamp 1981: 115.
125. 1968: 31-32; 1973b: 61-63.
126. See 1973b: Figure 52; Lhote 1959: Plate C.
127. See Lhote 1959: Plates 22, 24, and 44.
128. Lhote 1959: 194-95.
129. 1968: 33.
130. 1973b: Figures 53-54, 57.
131. 1968: fourteenth page of the photo section; 1970: 67, Plates 7, 26; 1973b: Figures 52, 62, 64, 246, 253, 257.
132. 1970: Plate 5; 1973b: Figures 99, 273-74.
133. 1973b: Figures 154-55.
134. 1968: 91.
135. 1968: 91.
136. Story 1976: 51.
137. Heyerdahl 1958: 133-38; Story 1976: 48-50.
138. Heyerdahl 1958: 149-50; Story 1976: 50-51.
139. 1968: 91.
140. Story 1976: 50.
141. Heyerdahl 1958: 142-48; Story 1976: 51-60.
142. Heyerdahl 1958: 375.
143. Heyerdahl 1958: 373-75.
144. Willey 1971: 86, 158-59.
145. 1968: 21-22.
146. 1968: 22-23 and the sixth and seventh pages of the photo section.
147. Von Hagen 1961: 148.
148. Von Hagen 1961: 145-49.
149. 1968: 63.
150. See Baines and Malek 1980: 72.
151. Story 1976: 90-91.
152. 1968: 27.
153. Story 1976: 96.
154. 1968: 27-28.
155. 1968: 73.
156. Basham 1954: 220; Moffett 1976: 102-03; Story 1976: 88-89.
157. Ferris 1974: 64.
158. 1968: 104-06.
159. Price 1959.
160. G. Lloyd 1973: 53-58, 69.
161. Brumbaugh 1966.

Chapter 5: Mysteries of the Pyramids

1. Dr. Gunther Rosenberg, founder and past president of the European Occult Research Society, as quoted in W. Smith 1975: 6.
2. Cottrell 1956: 47-48, 58.
3. Cottrell 1956: 88; Pochon 1978: 95-96.
4. Smyth 1877: 13.
5. Smyth 1877: 29-30.
6. Smyth 1877: 512-13.
7. Petrie 1883.
8. Cottrell 1956: 167.
9. Fakhry 1969: 117-20; Edwards 1976: 119-30.
10. E.g., Edgar 1924; Davidson 1932.
11. W. Smith 1975: 90.
12. Von Däniken 1968, 76-77; Landsburg 1974: 111-12; W. Smith 1975: 14-15, 58-68.
13. Smyth 1877: 458-64; von Däniken 1968: 79-80; Tompkins 1971: 218-19.
14. Fakhry 1969: 101.
15. Von Däniken 1968: 79.
16. Edwards 1976: 126-27.
17. Fakhry 1969: 20-21.
18. Fakhry 1969: 38-40; Edwards 1976: 53-60.
19. Fakhry 1969: 41-70; Edwards 1976: 79-92.
20. Fakhry 1969: 71-97; Edwards 1976: 96-115.
21. Fakhry 1969: 125-236; Edwards 1976: 151-253.
22. J. Wilson 1951: 83-84.
23. Edwards 1976: 288.
24. Edwards 1976: 290-91.
25. Frankfort 1946: 19-20.
26. Edwards 1976: 116, 265.
27. Edwards 1976: 255-56.
28. Cottrell 1956: 235; Edwards 1976: 255.
29. De Camp 1963: 34-35; Edwards 1976: 259-61.
30. Von Däniken 1968: 75-79; W. Smith 1975: 6-10.
31. De Camp 1963: 33-34. Edwards 1976: 262-64.
32. Edwards 1976: 262.
33. Fakhry 1969: 12; Edwards 1976: 265-66.
34. De Camp 1963: 34.
35. Fakhry 1969: 13-14; Edwards 1976: 270-74.
36. *Histories,* II, 124.
37. De Camp 1963: 32; Edwards 1976: 282-84.
38. De Camp 1963: 32-33; Edwards 1976: 283.
39. E.g., G. Smith 1929; Irwin 1963: 48-60; Heyerdahl 1971: 9-16, 24-31, 337-41.
40. E.g., Donnelly 1882: 111-12; Pochan 1978: 272-79.
41. Roux 1980: 78-79, 157.
42. Mallowan 1965: 39-41; Roux 1980: 79.
43. Roux 1980: 156, 363.

44. Edwards 1976: 55, 118.
45. Roux 1980: 156, 363.
46. Ruz Lhuillier 1953; Stuart 1977: 74-78; Gallenkamp 1981: 105-15.
47. Gallenkamp 1981: 76.
48. Willey 1971: 97-101.
49. Willey 1971: 122.
50. Willey 1966: 97-99; Coe 1968: 61, 64-65, 70.
51. Hammond 1982.
52. Gallenkamp 1981: 76-78.
53. Willey 1966: 292-311.
54. De Camp 1963: 56.
55. W. Smith 1975: 207-16.
56. Landsburg 1974: 100; Moffett 1976: 3.
57. Landsburg 1974: 100-01; W. Smith 1975: 211-12.
58. W. Smith 1975: 215.
59. Moffett 1976: 8, 11.
60. Moffett 1976: 167-69.
61. Landsburg 1974: 100.
62. L. Alvarez 1970: 834-36.
63. L. Alvarez 1970: 835.
64. Hamilton-Paterson and Andrews 1978: 33-34; Hoffman 1979: 110.
65. Hoffman 1979: 270-72.
66. Hamilton-Paterson and Andrews 1978: 35.
67. Hamilton-Paterson and Andrews 1978: 37-39.
68. Hamilton-Paterson and Andrews 1978: 44-48.
69. Hamilton-Paterson and Andrews 1978: 48-53.

Chapter 6: Early Voyagers to the Americas

1. Von Hagen 1961: 204-08; Gallenkamp 1981: 17-24.
2. Diego de Landa, as quoted in Gallenkamp 1981: 26.
3. Brunhouse 1973: 5-14.
4. Willey and Sabloff 1974: 34-35.
5. Brunhouse 1973: 17-83.
6. Brunhouse 1973: 84-109; Gallenkamp 1981: 35-54.
7. Silverberg 1968: 42-47; Stiebing 1981.
8. Silverberg 1968: 26-32.
9. Wauchope 1962: 53; Silverberg 1968: 51-52.
10. Wauchope 1962: 57.
11. Silverberg 1968: 48-49.
12. Wauchope 1962: 59-68.
13. Silverberg 1968: 58, 106-08.
14. Silverberg 1968: 79-82.
15. Silverberg 1968: 57-58.

16. Silverberg 1968: 110-32; Willey and Sabloff 1974: 43-46.
17. Silverberg 1968: 171-221.
18. Willey and Sabloff 1974: 74-78; Gallenkamp 1981: 63-64.
19. Willey 1966: 268-311; Silverberg 1968: 222-337.
20. Fell 1976: 21, 164-68; 1982: 263-264.
21. E.g., G. Smith 1923; 1924; 1929.
22. Wauchope 1962: 24-25.
23. Wauchope 1962: 23-24; Davies 1979: 159-60.
24. Davies 1979: 161-62.
25. See, for example, Gladwin 1947: 197-211; Irwin 1963; 35-38, 260-62.
26. Davies 1979: 89-92.
27. Davies 1979: 89, 92-93.
28. Davies 1979: 130.
29. Davies 1979: 131-34.
30. Davies 1979: 135-37.
31. See Heyerdahl 1971.
32. E.g., Irwin 1963: 139-57, 196-242; Gibson 1974: 46-109.
33. Gordon 1968.
34. Gordon 1974: 25-26.
35. Cross 1968: 454-60; 1979: 41.
36. Cross 1968: 448; 1979: 42.
37. Cross 1968: 442-44; 1979: 42.
38. Cross 1979: 42.
39. Cross 1968: 453; 1979: 43.
40. Gordon 1974: 79-92.
41. Gordon 1974: 72.
42. McKusick 1979: 53.
43. Gordon 1974: 93-106.
44. McKusick 1979: 53.
45. Goodwin 1946.
46. Fell 1976: 81-92.
47. Fell 1976: 131-55.
48. Fell 1976: 135.
49. Fell 1976: 129-31.
50. Fell 1976: 139-42.
51. Fell 1976: 45-80; 1980: 208-09, 304-10.
52. Fell 1976: 56, 122, 142.
53. Fell 1976: 58, 100-01, 157-69.
54. Fell 1976: 169-73.
55. Fell 1976: 174-91.
56. Fell 1980: 95, 175, 177-78, 237-95.
57. Fell 1976: 277-85.
58. Cole 1980: B8 (italics in the original).
59. Daniel 1980: 81, 85.
60. Daniel 1962: 28-29.
61. Daniel 1977: 12-14; 1980; Renfrew 1979: 120-66.
62. Norton-Taylor 1974.

63. Jackson 1953: 151-52; Diringer 1962: 164.
64. Fell 1976: 63-80.
65. Fell 1982: 13-34.
66. Daniel 1977: 12-14; Goddard and Fitzhugh 1978: 86.
67. Davies 1979: 154.
68. Korn 1978: 743.
69. Fell 1980: 95.
70. Fell 1980: 109.
71. Fell 1980: 266-67.
72. Fell 1980: 331.
73. Fell 1980: 173.
74. Fell 1980: 95.
75. Fell 1980: 178.
76. Fell 1976: 261-68.
77. McKusick 1970.
78. Davies 1979: 155; McKusick 1980: 155.
79. Goddard and Fitzhugh 1978: 87.
80. Goddard and Fitzhugh 1978: 86.
81. Goddard and Fitzhugh 1978: 86-87; Davies 1979: 155-56.
82. See, for example, Fell 1980: 56, 59, 117-63.
83. Fell 1976: 96.
84. Irwin 1963: 258.
85. Gordon 1971: 68.
86. Buttrey 1980.
87. Epstein 1980: 6.
88. McKusick 1981: 65.
89. Davies 1979: 110-11, 114-15.
90. Ekholm 1950; 1964; Heine-Geldern 1966.
91. Davies 1979: 103-04.
92. Larson 1966: 106; Gibson 1974: 219-20; Davies 1979: 105.
93. Larson 1966: 44-45.
94. Larson 1966: 44.
95. Pierson and Moriarty 1980; Frost 1982: 24-26.
96. Phillips 1966: 300; Jeffreys 1971.
97. Davies 1979: 111.
98. Davies 1979: 103.
99. Gibson 1974: 220.
100. Larson 1966: 106.
101. See, e.g., Willey 1966: 124.
102. Larson 1966: 107.
103. F. Frost 1982: 24.
104. Epstein 1980: 11.
105. F. Frost 1982: 26-28.
106. Jeffreys 1971: 380-82.
107. Cutler and Blake 1971: 374.
108. Heine-Geldern 1966: 294.
109. Holand 1956: 19-26.

110. Holand 1956: 27-29; Tornöe 1965: 19-20.
111. Holand 1956: 33-36; Tornöe 1965: 49-51.
112. Holand 1956: 49-50; Tornöe 1965: 76-77.
113. Holand 1956: 58-64; Tornöe 1965: 85-90.
114. Holand 1956: 75-77.
115. Holand 1956: 39-47; Tornöe 1965: 52-75.
116. Ingstad 1964; 1969.
117. See, for example, Holand 1956: 207-51; Fell 1980: 362-66.
118. Godfrey 1950: 84-86; 1951.
119. Holand 1956; 231-35.
120. Godfrey 1950: 84; 1951: 124-28.
121. Holand 1956: 177-206.
122. Holand 1956: 199-200.
123. See, e.g., Holand 1956: 161-76.
124. Gordon 1974: 107-18.
125. Wahlgren 1958; Blegen 1968.
126. Fell 1980: 347-48.
127. Gordon 1974: 119-44.
128. Haugen 1972; McKusick 1979: 54.
129. Davies 1979: 53-57.
130. Davies 1979: 65.
131. Willey 1966: 78-177; 1971: 76-193, 510-11.
132. Phillips 1966: 296-314.
133. Willey 1971: 275.
134. Davies 1979: 69-70.
135. Riley 1969: 212.

Chapter 7: Popular Theories and the "Establishment"

1. Carroll 1977: 542.
2. See Velikovsky 1955.
3. Velikovsky 1955: vi.
4. von Däniken 1968: vii.
5. Gladwin 1947: 361.
6. See, for example, Fell 1980: 6-8, 39-41.
7. See Wauchope 1962: 76, 82.
8. Carroll 1977.
9. Wauchope 1962: 134.
10. See Hallam 1973.

Bibliography

Ackroyd, P. R.
 1967 "Samaria," pp. 343-54 in D. Winton Thomas, ed., *Archaeology and Old Testament Study,* London: Oxford University Press.
Aharoni, Y.
 1975 "Arad," pp. 74-89, and "Beersheba, Tel," pp. 160-68 in M. Avi-Yonah, ed., *Encyclopedia of Archaeological Excavations in the Holy Land,* Vol. 1, Englewood Cliffs, N.J.: Prentice-Hall.
Albright, W. F.
 1955 "Akkadian Letters," pp. 482-90, in J. B. Pritchard, ed., *Ancient Near Eastern Texts,* 2nd ed., Princeton, N.J.: Princeton University Press.
Allchin, Bridget and Allchin, Raymond
 1968 *The Birth of Indian Civilization: India and Pakistan Before 500 B.C.,* Baltimore: Penguin Books.
Alvarez, Luis W.
 1970 "Search For Hidden Chambers in the Pyramids," *Science,* 167: 832-39.
Alvarez, W., Alvarez, L., Asaro, F., and Michel, H.
 1980 "Extraterrestrial Cause for the Cretaceous-Tertiary Extinction," *Science,* 208:1095-1108.
Alvarez, W., Kauffman, E., Surlyk, F., Alvarez, L., Asaro, F., and Michel, H.
 1984 "Impact Theory of Mass Extinctions and the Invertebrate Fossil Record," *Science,* 223: 1135-41.
Avigad, N.
 1978 "Samaria," pp. 1032-50 in M. Avi-Yonah, ed., *Encyclopedia of Archaeological Excavations in the Holy Land,* Vol. 4, Englewood Cliffs, N.J.: Prentice-Hall.
Bailey, Lloyd R.
 1978 *Where Is Noah's Ark?,* Nashville: Abingdon.
Baines, J. and Malek, J.
 1980 *Atlas of Ancient Egypt,* New York: Facts on File Publications.
Balsiger, D. and Sellier, C. E.
 1976 *In Search of Noah's Ark,* Los Angeles: Sun Classic Books.
Basham, A. L.
 1954 *The Wonder That Was India,* New York: Grove Press.
Bérard, Victor
 1929 "L'Atlantide de Platon," *Annales de Geographie,* 38, No. 213 (May 15): 192-205.

Bergier, J.
    1974   *Extraterrestrial Visitations From Prehistoric Times to the Present,* New York: Signet Books.
Berlitz, Charles
    1975   *The Mystery of Atlantis,* rev. ed., New York: Grossett and Dunlap.
Bermant, C. and Weitzman, M.
    1979   *Ebla: A Revelation in Archaeology,* New York: Times Books.
Bimson, John
    1978a *Redating the Exodus and Conquest,* Sheffield: University of Sheffield.
    1978b "Can There Be a Revised Chronology Without a Revised Stratigraphy?" pp. 16-26, in *Ages in Chaos?* (Proceedings of the Residential Weekend Conference, Glasgow, 7-9 April 1978), *S.I.S. Review,* 6, Nos. 1-3 (1982).
Blegen, Theodore
    1968   *The Kensington Rune Stone: New Light on an Old Riddle,* St. Paul, Minn.: Minnesota Historical Society.
Blong, R. J.
    1980   "The Possible Effects of Santorini Tephra Fall on Minoan Crete," pp. 217-26, in C. Doumas, ed., *Thera and the Aegean World,* Vol. 2, London: Thera and the Aegean World.
Blumrich, J.
    1970   *The Spaceships of Ezekiel,* New York: Bantam Books.
Boardman, J.
    1964   *The Greeks Overseas,* Baltimore: Penguin Books.
Braghine, Alexander
    1940   *The Shadow of Atlantis,* New York: Dutton.
Bright, John
    1942   "Has Archaeology Found Evidence of the Flood?," *Biblical Archaeologist,* 5, No. 4 (December): 55-62.
Brumbaugh, R. S.
    1966   *Ancient Greek Gadgets and Machines,* New York: Thomas Y. Crowell.
Brunhouse, R. L.
    1973   *In Search of the Maya: The First Archaeologists,* Albuquerque, N.M.: University of New Mexico Press.
Bryce, James
    1896   *Transcaucasia and Ararat,* 4th ed., London, Macmillan.
Buck, R.
    1962   "The Minoan Thalassocracy Re-examined," *Historia,* 11: 129-37.
Bunbury, Edward H.
    1883   *History of Ancient Geography,* 2 vols., London: Murray.
Burgstahler, A. W.
    1973   "The El-Amarna Letters and the Ancient Records of Assyria and Babylonia," *Pensée,* 3, No. 3 (Fall): 13-15.
Buttrey, T. V.
    1980   Comment on J. Epstein's article, "Pre-Columbian Old World Coins . . . ," *Current Anthropology,* 21, No. 1 (Feb.): 12-13.

Carli, Count G. R. de
1788   *Lettres Americaines,* Paris: Buisson.
Carroll, Michael
1977   "Of Atlantis and Ancient Astronauts: A Structural Study of Two Modern Myths," *Journal of Popular Culture,* 11: 541-50.
Chatelain, Maurice
1977   *Our Ancestors Came From Outer Space,* London: Arthur Barker.
Churchward, James
1926   *The Lost Continent of Mu,* New York: W. E. Rudge.
1931   *The Children of Mu,* New York: Washburn.
1934   *Cosmic Forces as They Were Taught in Mu,* New York: Baker and Taylor.
1938   *The Sacred Symbols of Mu,* New York: Washburn.
Clark, R. T. Rundle
1960   *Myth and Symbol in Ancient Egypt,* New York: Grove Press.
Coe, Michael D.
1968   *America's First Civilization,* New York: American Heritage.
Cole, J. R.
1980   Review of *Saga America* by Barry Fell, *Christian Science Monitor,* 72, June 9: B-8.
Cornford, F. M.
1937   *Plato's Cosmology,* New York: Humanities Press.
Cottrell, Leonard
1956   *The Mountains of Pharaoh,* New York: Rinehart.
Courville, D. A.
1971   *The Exodus Problem and Its Ramifications,* 2 vols., Loma Linda, Calif.: Challenge Books.
Cross, Frank M.
1968   "The Phoenician Inscription from Brazil. A Nineteenth-Century Forgery," *Orientalia,* 37: 437-60.
1979   "Phoenicians in Brazil?" *Biblical Archaeology Review,* 5, No. 1 (Jan./Feb.): 36-43.
Cummings, Violet M.
1972   *Noah's Ark: Fact or Fable?,* San Diego: Creation-Science Research Center.
Cutler, H. and Blake L.
1971   "Travels of Corn and Squash," pp. 366-75, in Carroll Riley, et al., eds., *Man Across the Sea: Problems of Pre-Columbian Contacts.* Austin: University of Texas Press.
Daniel, Glyn
1962   *The Idea of Prehistory,* New York and Cleveland: World.
1977   Review of *America B.C.* by Barry Fell, *New York Times Book Review,* March 13: 8, 12-14.
1980   "Megalithic Monuments," *Scientific American,* 243, No. 1 (July): 78-90.
Davidson, D.
1932   *The Great Pyramid, Its Divine Message,* London: Williams and Norgate.

Davies, Nigel
    1973   *The Aztecs: A History*, Norman, Okla.: University of Oklahoma Press.
    1979   *Voyagers to the New World*, New York: William Morrow.
de Camp, L. Sprague
    1963   *The Ancient Engineers*, New York: Ballantine Books (hardback edition published by Doubleday).
    1970   *Lost Continents: The Atlantis Theme in History, Science, and Literature*, rev. ed., New York: Dover.
Diringer, D.
    1962   *Writing*, New York: Praeger.
Donnelly, Ignatius
    1882   *Atlantis: The Antediluvian World*, modern revised edition, 1949, New York: Harper.
    1883   *Ragnarok, the Age of Fire and Gravel*, New York: D. Appleton.
Doumas, C.
    1974   "The Minoan Eruption of the Santorini Volcano," *Antiquity*, 48: 110-15.
Drake, W. Raymond
    1974   *Gods and Spacemen of the Ancient Past*, New York: Signet Books.
Eckholm, Gordon
    1950   "Is American Indian Culture Asiatic?," *Natural History*, 59: 344-51, 382.
    1964   "Transpacific Contacts," pp. 489-510, in J. Jennings and E. Norbeck, eds., *Prehistoric Man in the New World*, Chicago: University of Chicago Press.
Edgar, Morton
    1924   *The Great Pyramid: Its Scientific Features*, Glasgow: MacLure and MacDonald.
Edwards, I. E. S.
    1976   *The Pyramids of Egypt*, 2nd rev. ed., Baltimore: Penguin Books.
Encounter
    1973   "Anatomy of a World Best-Seller: Erich von Däniken's Message From the Unknown," *Encounter*, 41, No. 2 (August): 8-17.
Epstein, Jeremiah
    1980   "Pre-Columbian Old World Coins in America: An Examination of the Evidence," *Current Anthropology*, 21, No. 1 (Feb.): 1-12.
Fakhry, Ahmed
    1969   *The Pyramids*, rev. ed., Chicago: University of Chicago Press.
Fears, J. Rufus
    1978   "Atlantis and the Minoan Thalassocracy: A Study in Modern Mythopoeism," pp. 103-34, in E. Ramage, ed., *Atlantis: Fact Or Fiction?*, Bloomington, Ind.: Indiana University Press.
Fell, Barry
    1976   *America B.C.: Ancient Settlers in the New World*, New York: Wallaby Books (hardcover edition published by Times Books).
    1980   *Saga America*, New York: Times Books.

1982   *Bronze Age America,* Boston: Little, Brown.
Ferris, Timothy
1974   *"Playboy* Interview: Erich von Däniken," *Playboy,* 21, No. 8 (August): 51-52, 56-58, 60, 64, 151.
Filby, Frederick A.
1970   *The Flood Reconsidered,* Grand Rapids, Mich.: Zondervan.
Forsyth, Phyllis Y.
1980   *Atlantis: The Making of Myth,* Montreal: McGill-Queen's University Press.
Frankfort, H. and Frankfort, H. A.
1946   "Myth and Reality," pp. 3-27, in H. Frankfort and H. A. Frankfort, et al., *The Intellectual Adventure of Ancient Man,* Chicago: University of Chicago Press.
Fredericks, S. C.
1978   "Plato's Atlantis: A Mythologist Looks at Myth," pp. 81-99, in E. Ramage, ed., *Atlantis: Fact Or Fiction?,* Bloomington, Ind.: Indiana University Press.
Frost, Frank J.
1982   "The Palos Verdes Chinese Anchor Mystery," *Archaeology,* 35, No. 1 (Jan./Feb.): 22-28.
Frost, K. T.
1913   "The *Critias* and Minoan Crete," *Journal of Hellenic Studies,* 33: 189-206.
Galanopoulos, A. G. and Bacon, E.
1969   *Atlantis: The Truth Behind the Legend,* London: Thomas Nelson.
Gallenkamp, Charles
1981   *Maya: The Riddle and Rediscovery of a Lost Civilization,* 2nd rev. ed., New York: Penguin Books.
Gaskill, G.
1975   "Have They Found Noah's Ark?" *Christian Herald,* 98, No. 8 (August); 16-18 (condensed version, "The Mystery of Noah's Ark," in *Readers' Digest* (September, 1975): 150-54.
Gibson, Frances
1974   *The Seafarers: Pre-Columbian Voyages to America,* Philadelphia: Dorrance.
Gillispie, Charles C.
1959   *Genesis and Geology: A Study in the Relations of Scientific Thought, Natural Theology, and Social Opinion in Great Britain, 1790-1850,* New York: Harper Torchbooks (originally published in 1951 by Harvard University Press).
Gladwin, Harold S.
1947   *Men Out of Asia,* New York: McGraw-Hill.
Glueck, N.
1967   "Transjordan," pp. 429-53, in D. Winton Thomas, ed., *Archaeology and Old Testament Study,* London: Oxford UniversityPress.
Goddard, I. and Fitzhugh, W.
1978   "Barry Fell Reexamined," *Biblical Archaeologist,* 41, No. 3 (September): 85-88.

Godfrey, W. S.
  1950   "Newport Tower II," *Archaeology,* 3, No. 2 (Summer): 82-86.
  1951   "Archaeology of the Old Stone Mill in Newport, Rhode Island," *American Antiquity,* 17, No. 2 (September): 120-29.
Gordon, Cyrus
  1968   "The Authenticity of the Phoenician Text from Parahyba," *Orientalia,* 37: 75-80.
  1971   *Before Columbus,* New York: Crown.
  1974   *Riddles in History,* New York: Crown.
Graves, Robert
  1960   *The Greek Myths,* 2 vols., rev. ed., Baltimore: Penguin Books.
Greenberg, L. M. and Sizemore, W. B., eds.,
  1978   *Scientists Confront Scientists Who Confront Velikovsky,* Glassboro, N.J.: Kronos Press.
Greenberg, Moshe
  1955   *The Hab/piru,* New Haven: American Oriental Society.
Grimal, Pierre
  1965a "Introduction: Man and Myth," pp. 9-15, in P. Grimal, ed., *Larousse World Mythology,* New York: Prometheus Press.
  1965b "Greece: Myth and Logic," pp. 97-175, in P. Grimal, ed., *Larousse World Mythology,* New York: Prometheus Press.
Haber, Francis C.
  1959   *The Age of the World: Moses to Darwin.* Baltimore: Johns Hopkins Press.
Hacker, Kathy
  1984   "Astronaut's Rebirth Turns Him to the Ark," *Times-Picayune/States-Item,* New Orleans, Saturday, Feb. 4, Section 5: 1, 6.
Hallam, Anthony
  1973   *A Revolution in the Earth Sciences: From Continental Drift to Plate Tectonics,* New York: Oxford University Press.
Hamilton, Edith, and Cairns, Huntington, eds.
  1961   *The Collected Dialogues of Plato,* New York: Bollingen Foundation.
Hamilton-Paterson, J., and Andrews, C.
  1978   *Mummies: Death and Life in Ancient Egypt,* New York: Penguin Books.
Hammond, Norman
  1982   "Unearthing the Oldest Known Maya," *National Geographic,* 162, No. 1 (July): 126-40.
Hapgood, Charles H.
  1966   *Maps of the Ancient Sea Kings: Evidence of Advanced Civilization in the Ice Age,* New York: Chilton Books.
Harden, Donald
  1962   *The Phoenicians,* New York: Praeger.
Harrison, W.
  1971   "Atlantis Undiscovered—Bimini, Bahamas," *Nature,* 230: 287-9.
Haugen, Einar
  1972   "The Rune Stones of Spirit Pond, Maine," *Man in the Northeast,* 4: 62-9.

Heidel, A.
1946   *The Gilgamesh Epic and Old Testament Parallels,* Chicago: University of Chicago Press.
Heine-Geldern, Robert
1966   "The Problem of Transpacific Influences in Mesoamerica," pp. 277-95, in R. Wauchope, ed., *Handbook of Middle American Indians,* Vol. 4, Austin: University of Texas Press.
Herz, O. F.
1903   "Frozen Mammoth in Siberia," *Smithosnian Institution Annual Report for 1903:* 611-25.
Heyerdahl, Thor
1958   *Aku-Aku,* New York: Rand McNally.
1971   *The Ra Expeditions,* Garden City, N.Y.: Doubleday.
Hoffman, Michael A.
1979   *Egypt Before the Pharaohs,* New York: Alfred A. Knopf.
Hood, Sinclair
1970   "The International Scientific Congress on the Volcano of Thera, 15th-23rd September 1969," *Kadmos,* 9: 98-106.
1971   *The Minoans: The Story of Bronze Age Crete,* New York: Praeger.
Hörbiger, Hans
1913   *Glazial-Kosmogonie,* Kaiserlautern: H. Kayser.
Ingstad, Helge
1964   "Vinland Ruins Prove Vikings Found the New World," *National Geographic,* 126, No. 5 (Nov.): 708-34.
1969   *Westward to Vinland,* London: Jonathan Cape.
Irwin, Constance
1963   *Fair Gods and Stone Faces,* New York: St. Martin's Press.
Isbell, William H.
1978   "The Prehistoric Ground Drawings of Peru," *Scientific American,* 239, No. 4 (October): 140-53.
Jackson, Kenneth
1953   *Language and History in Early Britain,* Cambridge, Mass.: Harvard University Press.
Jairazbhoy, R. A.
1974   *Ancient Egyptians and Chinese in America,* London: George Prior.
Jeffreys, M. D. W.
1971   "Pre-Columbian Maize in Asia," pp. 376-400, in C. Riley, et al., eds., *Man Across the Sea: Problems of Pre-Columbian Contacts,* Austin: University of Texas Press.
Juergens, Ralph E.
1977   "Sagan's 'Ten Plagues,'" 83-101, and "On Morrison: Some Preliminary Remarks," pp. 113-20, in *Kronos,* 3, No. 2.
Kenyon, Kathleen
1957   *Digging Up Jericho,* New York: Praeger.
Knudtzon, J., et al.
1908-15   *Die El-Amarna-Tafeln,* 2 vols., Leipzig: Vorderasiatische Bibliothek.

Korn, Eric
  1978 "Follow That Script" (a review of *America B.C.* by Barry Fell), *New Statesman,* 95 (June 2): 742-43.
Kosok, Paul and Reiche, Maria
  1949 "Ancient Drawings on the Desert of Peru," *Archaeology,* 2, No. 4 (December): 206-15.
Kramer, S. N.
  1955 "Sumerian Myths and Epic Tales," pp. 37-59, in J. B. Pritchard, ed., *Ancient Near Eastern Texts,* 2nd ed., Princeton, N.J.: Princeton University Press.
  1961 *Sumerian Mythology,* rev. ed., New York: Harper Torchbooks.
Labat, R.
  1959 *Manuel D'Épigraphie Akkadienne,* 3rd ed., Paris: Imprimerie Nationale.
LaHaye, T., and Morris, J. D.
  1976 *The Ark on Ararat,* Nashville: Thomas Nelson and Creation-Life Publishers.
Landsburg, Alan and Landsburg, Sally
  1974 *In Search of Ancient Mysteries,* New York: Bantam Books.
  1975 *The Outer Space Connection,* New York: Bantam Books.
Larson, Robert
  1966 "Was America the Wonderful Land of Fusang?" *American Heritage,* 17, No. 3: 42-45, 106-09.
LePlongeon, Augustus
  1896 *Queen Moo and the Egyptian Sphinx,* London: Kegan Paul.
Lhote, Henri
  1959 *The Search for the Tassili Frescoes,* trans. by A. Broderick, New York: E. P. Dutton.
Lloyd, G. E. R.
  1973 *Greek Science After Aristotle,* New York: W. W. Norton.
Lloyd, Seton
  1980 *Foundations in the Dust,* rev. ed., New York: Thames and Hudson.
Luce, John V.
  1969 *Lost Atlantis: New Light on an Old Legend* (British title: *The End of Atlantis),* New York: McGraw-Hill.
  1976 "Thera and the Destruction of Minoan Crete: A New Interpretation of the Evidence," *American Journal of Archaeology,* 80: 9-16.
  1978 "The Sources and Literary Form of Plato's Atlantis Narrative," pp. 49-75, in E. Ramage, ed., *Atlantis: Fact or Fiction?",* Bloomington, Ind.: Indiana University Press.
McCoy, F. W.
  1980 "The Upper Thera (Minoan) Ash in Deep-Sea Sediments: Distribution and Comparison With Other Ash Layers," pp. 57-58, in C. Doumas, ed., *Thera and the Aegean World,* Vol. 2, London: Thera and the Aegean World.
McIntyre, Loren
  1975 "Mystery of the Ancient Nazca Lines," *National Geographic,* 147,

No. 5 (May): 716-28.

MacKie, Euan

1978   "Radiocarbon Dating and Egyptian Chronology," pp. 56-63, in *Ages in Chaos?* (Proceedings of the Residential Weekend Conference, Glasgow, 7-9 April 1978), *S.I.S. Review,* 6, Nos. 1-3 (1982).

McKusick, Marshall

1970   *The Davenport Conspiracy,* Iowa City: University of Iowa Press.

1979   "A Cryptogram in the Phoenician Inscription from Brazil," *Biblical Archaeology Review,* 5, No. 4 (July/August): 50-54.

1980   Review of *Saga America* by Barry Fell, *Antiquity,* 54: 154-55.

1981   Review of *Saga America* by Barry Fell, *Archaeology,* 34 (January/February): 62, 65-66.

MacQueen, J. G.

1975   *The Hittites and Their Contemporaries in Asia Minor,* Boulder, Colo.: Westview Press.

Mallowan, M. E. L.

1965   *Early Mesopotamia and Iran,* New York: McGraw-Hill.

Marinatos, S.

1939   "The Volcanic Destruction of Minoan Crete," *Antiquity,* 13: 425-39.

1972   "Thera: Key to the Riddle of Minos," *National Geographic,* 141, No. 1 (January): 40-52.

Marks, J. H.

1962   "Flood (Genesis)," pp. 278-84, in *The Interpreter's Dictionary of the Bible,* Vol. 2 (E-J), Nashville: Abingdon Press.

Mathews, Peter, and Schele, Linda

1974   "Lords of Palenque—The Glyphic Evidence," pp. 63-70, in M. G. Robertson, ed., *Primera Mesa Redonda de Palenque, Part I,* Pebble Beach, California: The Robert Louis Stevenson School.

Maudslay, A. P.

1889-1902   *Biologia Centrali-Americana, Archaeology,* 4 vols., London: Dulau.

Mavor, J. W.

1969   *Voyage to Atlantis,* New York: G. P. Putnam

Mellaart, James

1967   *Çatal Hüyük: A Neolithic Town in Anatolia,* New York: McGraw-Hill.

Menard, H. W.

1969   "The Deep-Ocean Floor," *Scientific American,* 221, No. 3, (September): 126-45.

Moffett, Robert K.

1976   *Secrets of the Pyramids Revealed,* New York: Grosset and Dunlap.

Montgomery, James W.

1974   *The Quest for Noah's Ark,* 2nd ed., Minneapolis: Bethany Fellowship.

Morrison, David

1977   "Planetary Astronomy and Velikovsky's Catastrophism," pp. 145-76 in D. Goldsmith, ed., *Scientists Confront Velikovsky,* New York: W. W. Norton.

Muck, Otto
  1978   *The Secret of Atlantis*, New York: Pocket Books.
Mulholland, J. D.
  1977   "Movements of Celestial Bodies—Velikovsky's Fatal Flaw," pp. 105-15 in D. Goldsmith, ed., *Scientists Confront Velikovsky*, New York: W. W. Norton.
Navarra, Fernand
  1974   *Noah's Ark: I Touched It*, Plainfield, N.J.: Logos International.
The New American Bible
  1970   New York: Benziger.
New York Times
  1984   "Scientists Present Theory on Extinction," *Times-Picayune/States-Item*, New Orleans, February 20, 1984, Sec. 1: 3.
Newberrry, P. E.
  1893   *El Bersheh*, Part I, London: Egypt Exploration Fund.
Noorbergen, Rene
  1974   *The Ark File*, Mountain View, Calif.: Pacific Press Publishing Association.
Oppenheim, A. Leo
  1955   "Babylonian and Assyrian Historical Texts," pp. 265-317 in J. B. Pritchard, ed., *Ancient Near Eastern Texts*, 2nd ed., Princeton, N.J.: Princeton University Press.
  1967   *Letters From Mesopotamia*, Chicago: University of Chicago Press.
Owen, T.
  1982   "Planetary Atmospheres and the Search for Life," *Physics Teacher*, 20 (February): 90-96.
Page, D. L.
  1970   *The Santorini Volcano and the Destruction of Minoan Crete*, London: Society for the Promotion of Hellenic Studies.
Patten, D. W.
  1966   *The Biblical Flood and the Ice Epoch*, Seattle: Pacific Meridian.
Pettengill, G. H., Campbell, D. B., and Masursky, H.
  1980   "The Surface of Venus," *Scientific American*, 243, No. 2 (August): 45-67.
Petrie, W. M. F.
  1883   *The Pyramids and Temples of Gizeh*, London: Field and Tuer.
Pfeiffer, R. H.
  1948   *Introduction to the Old Testament*, rev. ed., New York: Harper and Row.
Phillips, Philip
  1966   "The Role of Transpacific Contacts in the Development of New World Pre-Columbian Civilizations," pp. 296-314 in R. Wauchope, ed., *Handbook of Middle American Indians*, Vol. 4, Austin: University of Texas Press.
Pichler, H.
  1980   "Discussion," pp. 324-25 in C. Doumas, ed., *Thera and the Aegean World*, Vol. 2, London: Thera and the Aegean World.

Pichler, H. and Friedrich, W. L.
   1980   "Mechanism of the Minoan Eruption of Santorini," pp. 15-30 in C.
          Doumas, ed., *Thera and the Aegean World*, Vol. 2, London: Thera
          and the Aegean World
Pierson, L. J. and Moriarty, J. R.
   1980   "Stone Anchors: Asiatic Shipwrecks off the California Coast," *Anthro-
          pological Journal of Canada*, 18: 17-23.
Platon, N.
   1971   *Zakros: The Discovery of a Lost Palace of Ancient Crete*, New York:
          Charles Scribner.
Pochan, A.
   1978   *The Mysteries of the Great Pyramids*, New York: Avon Books.
Price, Derek J.
   1959   "An Ancient Computer," *Scientific American*, 200, No. 6 (June):
          60-67.
Pritchard, J. B., et al.
   1975   *Sarepta: A Preliminary Report on the Iron Age*, Philadelphia: Uni-
          versity Museum.
Radhakrishnan, S. and Moore, C. A.
   1957   *A Source Book in Indian Philosophy*, Princeton, N.J.: Princeton
          University Press.
Ramage, Edwin S.
   1978   "Perspectives Ancient and Modern," pp. 3-45 in E. Ramage, ed.,
          Atlantis: Fact or Fiction? Bloomington, Ind.: Indiana University
          Press.
Renfrew, Colin
   1971   "Carbon 14 and the Prehistory of Europe," *Scientific American*, 225,
          No. 4 (October): 63-72.
   1979   *Before Civilization: The Radiocarbon Revolution and Prehistoric
          Europe*. Cambridge: Cambridge University Press.
Riley, Carroll L.
   1969   *The Origins of Civilization*, Carbondale, Ill.: Southern Illinois Uni-
          versity Press.
Robertson, Merle G.
   1974   "The Quadripartite Badge—A Badge of Rulership," pp. 77-93 in
          M. G. Robertson, ed., *Primera Mesa Redonda de Palenque, Part I*,
          Pebble Beach, Calif.: Robert Louis Stevenson School.
Rost, Leonard
   1976   *Judaism Outside the Hebrew Canon: An Introduction to the Docu-
          ments*, Nashville: Abingdon.
Roux, Georges
   1980   *Ancient Iraq*, 2nd ed., New York: Penguin Books.
Russell, D. S.
   1964   *The Method and Message of Jewish Apocalyptic*, Philadelphia:
          Westminster Press.
Ruz Lhuillier, Alberto
   1953   "The Mystery of the Temple of the Inscriptions," *Archaeology*, 6, No.
          1 (Spring): 3-11.

1970   *The Civilization of the Ancient Maya*, Córdoba, Mexico: Instituto Nacional de Antropologia y Historia.

Sagan, Carl
1977   "An Analysis of *Worlds in Collision*," pp. 41-104 in D. Goldsmith, ed., *Scientists Confront Velikovsky*, New York: W. W. Norton. (This article was reprinted in Chapter 7 of C. Sagan, *Broca's Brain*, New York: Random House, 1979, and in shortened form under the title "A Scientist Looks at Velikovsky's *Worlds in Collision*," in *Biblical Archaeology Review*, 6, No. 1 (January/February): 40-51.)

Scarborough, John
1974-75   "The Gods in the Image of Man: Von Däniken's New Myths," *Bulletin of the Science Fiction Writers of America*, 10, No. 3 (Winter): 20-25.

Schele, Linda
1974   "Observations on the Cross Motif at Palenque," pp. 41-61 in Merle G. Robinson, ed., *Primera Mesa Redonda de Palenque, Part I*, Pebble Beach, Calif.: Robert Louis Stevenson School.

Schofield, J. N.
1967   "Megiddo," pp. 309-29 in D. Winton Thomas, ed., *Archaeology and Old Testament Study*, London: Oxford University Press.

Shanks, H.
1976   "The Promise of Ebla," *Biblical Archaeology Review*, 2, No. 4 (December): 41-2.

Silverberg, Robert
1968   *Mound Builders of Ancient America: The Archaeology of a Myth*, Greenwich, Conn.: New York Graphic Society.

Simoni, M.
1965   "Central America: Gods of Sacrifice," pp. 459-79 in P. Grimal, ed., *Larousse World Mythology*, New York: Prometheus Press.

Sitchin, Zecharia
1976   *The Twelfth Planet*, New York: Avon Books (hardcover edition published by Stein and Day).

Smith, G. Elliot
1915   *The Migrations of Early Culture*, Manchester, England: Manchester University Press.
1923   *The Ancient Egyptians and the Origin of Civilization*, rev. ed., New York: Harper.
1924   *Elephants and Ethnologists*, New York: E. P. Dutton.
1929   *Human History*, New York: W. W. Norton.

Smith, Warren
1975   *The Secret Forces of the Pyramids*, New York: Kensington.

Smyth, Piazzi
1877   *Our Inheritance in the Great Pyramid*, 3rd ed., London: Daldy, Isbister.

Speiser, E. A.
1955   "Akkadian Myths and Epics," pp. 60-119 in J. B. Pritchard, ed., *Ancient Near Eastern Texts*, 2nd ed., Princeton, N.J.: Princeton University Press.

1964   *Genesis,* Garden City, N.Y.: Doubleday.
Spence, Lewis
1924   *The Problem of Atlantis,* New York: Brentano's.
1926   *The History of Atlantis,* London: Rider.
Starr, Chester
1954   "The Myth of the Minoan Thalassocracy," *Historia,* 3: 282-91.
Stewart, J. A.
1960   *The Myths of Plato,* 2nd ed., Carbondale, Ill.: Southern Illinois University Press.
Stiebing, W. H.
1973   "A Criticism of the Revised Chronology," *Pensée,* 3, No. 3 (Fall) 10-2.
1974   "Rejoinder to Velikovsky," *Pensée,* 4, No. 5 (Winter): 24-6.
1981   "Who First Excavated Stratigraphically?," *Biblical Archaeology Review,* 7, No. 1 (January/February): 52-53.
Story, Ronald
1976   *The Space-Gods Revealed: A Close Look at the Theories of Erich von Däniken,* New York: Harper and Row.
Stuart, George E. and Stuart, Gene S.
1977   *The Mysterious Maya,* Washington, D.C.: National Geographic Society.
Stubbings, F. H.
1951   *Mycenaean Pottery from the Levant,* Cambridge: Cambridge University Press.
Taylor, A. E.
1928   *A Commentary on Plato's Timaeus,* Oxford: Oxford University Press.
Tigay, Jeffrey H.
1982   *The Evolution of the Gilgamesh Epic,* Philadelphia: University of Pennsylvania Press.
Tomas, Andrew
1971   *We Are Not the First,* New York: Bantam Books (hardcover edition published by G. P. Putnam).
Tompkins, Peter
1971   *Secrets of the Great Pyramid,* New York: Harper and Row.
1976   *Mysteries of the Mexican Pyramids,* New York: Harper and Row.
Tornöe, J. Kr.
1965   *Norsemen Before Columbus,* London: George Allen and Unwin.
Trento, S.
1978   *The Search for Lost America: The Mysteries of the Stone Ruins,* Chicago: Contemporary Books.
Tushingham, A. D.
1975   "Dibon," pp. 330-33 in M. Avi-Yonah, ed., *Encyclopedia of Archaeological Excavations in the Holy Land,* Vol. I, Englewood Cliffs, N.J.: Prentice-Hall.
Van Seters, J.
1964   "A Date for the 'Admonitions' in the Second Intermediate Period," *Journal of Egyptian Archaeology,* 50: 13-23.

Velikovsky, I.
    1950   *Worlds in Collision,* Garden City, N.Y.: Doubleday.
    1952   *Ages in Chaos,* Garden City, N.Y.: Doubleday.
    1955   *Earth in Upheaval,* Garden City, N.Y.: Doubleday.
    1973a "The Pitfalls of Radiocarbon Dating," *Pensée,* 3, No. 2 (Spring-Summer): 12-4, 50.
    1973b "A Reply to Stiebing," *Pensée,* 4, No. 1 (Winter): 38-42.
    1974   "A Concluding Retort," *Pensée,* 4, No. 5 (Winter): 26, 49.
    1977a *Peoples of the Sea,* Garden City, N.Y.: Doubleday.
    1977b "My Challenge to Conventional Views in Science," "Afterword," and "The Ten Points of Sagan," *Kronos,* 3, No. 2: 5-48.
    1978   *Ramses II and His Time,* Garden City, N.Y.: Doubleday.
Vitaliano, Dorothy B.
    1973   *Legends of the Earth,* Bloomington, Ind.: Indiana University Press.
    1978   "Atlantis from the Geologic Point of View," pp. 137-60 in E. Ramage, ed., *Atlantis: Fact or Fictoin?* Bloomington, Ind.: Indiana University Press.
Vitaliano, D. B. and Vitaliano, C. J.
    1980   "Tephrochronological Evidence for the Time of the Bronze Age Eruption of Thera," pp. 217-19 in C. Doumas, ed., *Thera and the Aegean World,* Vol. I, London: Thera and the Aegean World.
Von Däniken, Erich
    1968   *Chariots of the Gods?* New York: Bantam Books (hardcover edition published by G. P. Putnam).
    1970   *Gods from Outer Space* (also published under the title *Return to the Stars),* New York: Bantam Books (hardcover edition published by G. P. Putnam).
    1973a *The Gold of the Gods,* New York: Bantam Books (hardcover edition published by G. P. Putnam).
    1973b *In Search of Ancient Gods,* New York: Bantam Books (hardcover edition published by G. P. Putnam).
    1977   *Von Däniken's Proof,* New York: Bantam Books (published in England under the title *According to the Evidence* by Souvenir Press).
    1980   *Signs of the Gods?* New York: Bantam Books (hardcover edition published by G. P. Putnam).
    1982   *Pathways to the Gods,* New York: G. P. Putnam.
Von Hagen, Victor W.
    1961   *Realm of the Incas,* rev. ed., New York: New American Library.
Wahlgren, Erik
    1958   *The Kensington Stele—A Mystery Solved,* Madison, Wis.: University of Wisconsin Press.
Waltz, Edward L.
    1974   "Space Age Ark-aeology," *Bible and Spade* (Autumn): 124-28.
Warner, Rex
    1954   *Thucydides: The Peloponnesian War,* Baltimore: Penguin Books.
Wauchope, Robert
    1962   *Lost Tribes and Sunken Continents: Myth and Method in the Study*

of American Indians, Chicago: University of Chicago Press.

Wendt, Herbert
1955 *In Search of Adam,* Boston: Houghton Mifflin.

Wheeler, Mortimer
1966 *Civilizations of the Indus Valley and Beyond,* New York: McGraw-Hill.

Whiston, William
1696 *A New Theory of the Earth,* London.

Whitcomb, J. C., and Morris, H. M.
1961 *The Genesis Flood,* Philadelphia: Presbyterian and Reformed Publishing Company.

Willey, Gordon R.
1966 *An Introduction to American Archaeology,* Vol. I: *North and Middle America,* Englewood Cliffs, N.J.: Prentice-Hall.
1971 *An Introduction to American Archaeology,* Vol. II: *South America,* Englewood Cliffs, N.J.: Prentice-Hall.

Willey, G. R., and Sabloff, J. A.
1974 *A History of American Archaeology,* San Francisco: W. H. Freeman.

Wilson, Clifford
1972 *Crash Go the Chariots,* New York: Lancer Books.
1975 *The Chariots Still Crash,* New York: Signet Books.

Wilson, John A.
1951 *The Burden of Egypt,* Chicago: University of Chicago Press.
1955 "Egyptian Myths, Tales and Mortuary Texts," pp. 3-36, "Egyptian Historical Texts," pp. 227-64, and "Egyptian Oracles and Prophecies," pp. 441-49 in J. B. Pritchard, ed., *Ancient Near Eastern Texts,* 2nd ed., Princeton, N.J.: Princeton University Press.

Woolley, Leonard
1953 *A Forgotten Kingdom,* Baltimore: Penguin Books.
1965 *Excavations at Ur,* New York: Thomas Y. Crowell.

Wright, Herbert E., Jr.
1978 "Glacial Fluctuations, Sea-level Changes, and Catastrophic Floods," pp. 161-74 in E. Ramage, ed., *Atlantis: Fact or Fiction?* Bloomington, Ind.: Indiana University Press.

Yadin, Yigael
1975 *Hazor: The Rediscovery of a Great Citadel of the Bible,* New York: Random House.
1976 "Hazor," pp. 474-95 in M. Avi-Yonah, ed., *Encyclopedia of Archaeological Excavations in the Holy Land,* Vol. II, Englewood Cliffs, N.J.: Prentice-Hall.

Zink, David
1978 *The Stones of Atlantis,* Englewood Cliffs, N.J.: Prentice-Hall.

Index